MAKING SENSE OF ADULT LEARNING

Second Edition

Making Sense of Adult Learning

Second Edition

Dorothy MacKeracher

UNIVERSITY OF TORONTO PRESS
Toronto Buffalo London

Printed in Canada

Reprinted 2005, 2006, 2007, 2008, 2009, 2010

ISBN 0-8020-3778-X

∞

Printed on acid-free paper

National Library of Canada Cataloguing in Publication

MacKeracher, Dorothy
 Making sense of adult learning/Dorothy MacKeracher. – 2nd ed.

 Includes bibliographical references and index.
 ISBN 0-8020-3778-X

 1. Adult learning.   I. Title.

LC5225.L42M33 2004   374   C2004-903098-1

University of Toronto Press acknowledges the financial assistance
to its publishing program of the Canada Council for the Arts and
the Ontario Arts Council.

University of Toronto Press acknowledges the finiancial support
for its publishing activities of the Government of Canada through
the Book Publishing Industry Development Program (BPIDP).

Contents

Figures

Preface

This book has been written bearing in mind the needs of students who are preparing to become adult educators. It is not intended to be an authoritative commentary on, or theoretical statement about, the learning done by adult learners. Rather, I hope to provide those with a limited background in adult education with some basic ideas about how to work with adult learners in a variety of formal and informal settings.

This book grew out of a project begun in 1979 under the direction of Donald H. Brundage, then a faculty member of the Department of Adult Education, Ontario Institute for Studies in Education (OISE/UT), in Toronto. Don had obtained a small research grant from the Ontario Ministry of Education to do a literature search and write a report on adult learning principles. At that time I was a doctoral student in Adult Education and was hired as his research assistant. The project resulted in a report entitled *Adult Learning Principles and Their Application to Program Planning* (ALP Report).

The ALP Report was intended for teachers and planners who had been trained to work with children and adolescents and who might find themselves working with adult learners as a result of changes in the education system. In addition to sections on the characteristics of adult learners and the learning situation, the report also dealt with the retraining and professional development of such educators and with issues related to program planning. It was written to reduce the complexities of the issues involved to relatively easy-to-understand principles that could be applied in a wide variety of settings. The ministry published the 126-page report and set the purchase price at three dollars. Over a period of twenty years, the price gradually rose to six dollars. No figures are available to tell us how many K–13 educators actually purchased or used the report. However, we do know that it was purchased and used by many students in adult education programs across North America and by practising adult educators working in Canada, Asia, Australia, and the West Indies. The ministry stopped publishing the report in 1993.

In 1995 Thelma Barer-Stein, a colleague from my days as a student in OISE's Department of Adult Education, asked if I would consider revising the ALP Report. I discussed the matter with Don, and he encouraged me to go ahead with the project. He had retired in 1991 and was not interested in giving up his hard-earned leisure time. Earlier, when I left Toronto in 1986 to take a faculty position at the University of New Brunswick (UNB), Don and I had had plans to revise the ALP Report. We wrote letters back and forth but neither could find the time to actually do the work. We had two unresolved discussions about what should be included in the revised text: I wanted to include a section on a topic I was then calling 'social learning,' and Don wanted to include a section on 'transcendent learning.' Neither of us understood completely what the other was talking about. I now understand that I was sorting out issues related to relational or connected learning, a way of learning much discussed in feminist literature; and I understand Don's concern to be about transpersonal or spiritual learning, a focus of learning discussed mainly in religious, therapeutic, and counselling literature.

The first edition of this book offered a major revision and update of the ALP Report. I drew on course notes I had written over ten years for my graduate courses in adult learning. I included new material on gender and cultural differences in learning, spiritual learning, learning styles, and physical learning.

This second edition offers a reorganization of the chapters, a revision of several chapters, and a new chapter on contextual or situated learning. I was guided in the reorganization of the chapters by my students, who thought the chapters on learning cycles and learning styles should come earlier in the text, and in the revision by my own sense of what had been left out of the first edition. The new chapter on the contexts of adult learning came about because I was initially confused about the term 'situated learning.' This term was being touted by my colleagues in the UNB Faculty of Education as a 'new' concept. To me it sounded very much like 'old,' but very sound, adult education concepts.

I have been mindful of the advice I was given in writing the first edition, and have included more examples to illustrate the points I make and have described some of my own experiences as a learner and facilitator. I still cling stubbornly to my preferred assimilative learning style. I live and work in ways that strongly emphasize reflection and conceptualization. While I am conscious that occasionally I need to write using an accommodative learning style (based on action and concrete experience), I may never become really comfortable with it. I know how to use examples and why it is sometimes helpful to write in the first-person singular – goodness knows I remind my students of this writing style often enough – but I forget to do it because the examples seem self-evident to me and I view my own experiences as not particularly relevant to anyone else. If I have repeated my experiences or examples throughout the book, please forgive me.

Chapter 1 examines background issues and assumptions about adult learning that have guided my work over the last thirty years and my writing in this book. I have outlined nine assumptions about the learning-centred approach, the learning process, preferred strategies for learning, the nonnormative nature of learning, the role of brain and mind in learning, the situated or contextual nature of learning, the role of emotions in learning, learning how to learn, and philosophical approaches to learning. These assumptions are expanded in the remaining ten chapters of the book.

Chapter 2 examines some background characteristics of and assumptions about adult learners. All possible characteristics and assumptions could not be covered in one book, so I selected those I considered to be the most important: age-related changes, the role of past experience and prior learning, the role of time, the adult's well-established sense of self, and the nature of self-direction. At the end of the chapter, I have provided a model for thinking about how to match facilitator behaviours to learner characteristics.

Chapter 3 looks at three models that describe the learning cycle. The first is a very basic model derived from my own experience. The second model comes from the work of David Kolb (1984), who writes about experiential learning. Kolb's model is well known to most adult educators and is well covered in the literature and on the Internet. The third model comes from the work of Marilyn Taylor (1987), who writes about the inquiry sequence. Her model is not well known and is underutilized, but is always recognized by the adult learners in my courses as descriptive of their own learning experiences. I commend her model to the reader's attention.

Chapter 4 explores learning styles. It presents information about cognitive and learning styles and then examines in detail the learning styles that flow from Kolb's model of experiential learning. I find the Kolb model particularly useful because it provides information about how individuals can expand their learning strategies to encompass more styles, a virtue I do not find in other approaches to the concept of style.

Chapter 5 addresses issues related to the role of the brain and mind in learning. Another new-but-old concept in education is 'brain-based learning' or 'brain-compatible learning.' This concept adopts the position that since learning always involves the brain and mind, a wise educator will have some understanding about how the brain and mind work. I have tried to reduce the complexity of the topic to a few major ideas, but the chapter is long and may provide some readers with difficulties. This chapter also includes a topic I omitted in the first edition: the nature of multiple intelligences.

Chapter 6 examines the role of emotions and motives in learning. New research links emotions directly to the functioning of the highest levels of the brain. Writers in this field view emotions not simply as something that becomes attached to the learning process and to what is learned, or as a problem to be overcome, but as primary biological drivers that control how the brain and mind work. Those readers who are interested in this topic should pay some attention to writers in the field of evolutionary psychology such as Steven Pinker (1997) and in the field of evolutionary sociology such as Paul Lawrence and Nitin Nohria (2001). Their ideas are complex and informative and cannot be done justice in this limited text. This chapter includes another topic omitted from the first edition: the nature of emotional intelligence.

Chapter 7 takes a brief look at the nature of physical learning. I was advised to drop this chapter from this edition, but my students convinced me otherwise. They found the idea of physical learning both fascinating and useful. I have found it useful because in my second middle-adulthood phase of development I have had to learn many physical skills all over again – skills I took for granted in my first middle-adulthood. I talk briefly about the role of physical pain in learning, a topic much neglected in the field of adult education.

Chapter 8 addresses the issue of relationships in learning. This chapter focuses rather strongly on concerns expressed by adult women, but it is meant to convey the idea that individuals of both genders will need to be able to engage in relationships in order to be effective learners in the twenty-first century. And all adult educators will need to recognize the many roles of relationships in learning and how best to facilitate them.

Chapter 9 looks at spirit and soul in learning. When I wrote the first edition of this book, I could not find much on spirituality in learning. Today there are many books on the topic, although few directly address the issue of learning in our individual and collective journeys to find and develop our soul and spirit. In writing the first edition, I debated whether or not to include stories about my own spiritual journey, and finally wrote the chapter as a 'work in progress.' In many ways, the corresponding chapter in this edition is still a work in progress, but I now feel more confident that what I have written may be useful to others.

Chapter 10 is also a work in progress and addresses the many ways in which the terms 'situated,' 'context,' 'community,' 'culture,' and 'environment' are used in the adult education literature. This chapter expanded as I wrote it, and I finally had to cut out a few topics or I would have written another book. I was most impressed by the work I read on how our own environments tend to be invisible to us but are often clearly visible to others. This is true for both our cultural and knowledge environments and our physical and technological environments. We do not ask ourselves enough questions about these environments and how they affect our learning.

Chapter 11 was originally included in the first edition of this book. I questioned the need to keep it in the second edition, but again, my students and colleagues thought it was useful and encouraged me to retain it.

It is not necessary to read the chapters in order, although it would be wise to read Chapters 1 and 2 first because they establish the terminology and general perspectives used throughout the book. At the end of various chapters and sections within chapters, I have provided *learning and facilitating principles*. The format of these principles is not consistent throughout the book because different topics seemed to lend themselves to different types of principles. I would encourage you, the reader, to actively develop your own learning and facilitating principles. Mine tend to emerge from the context in which I do most of my work – in formal, university-level undergraduate and graduate programs. If my work was more predominantly in nonformal and not-for-credit programs I would have phrased the principles somewhat differently.

I would like to gratefully acknowledge the contributions made to this book by some wonderful friends and colleagues. My special thanks to Don Brundage for his support over the past fifteen years, and to Thelma Barer-Stein for persevering with me throughout the project. Over the past twenty years, I have been privileged to work with many remarkable students and colleagues at both OISE/UT and UNB. Many took the time to give me feedback about the first edition and to point out places where I needed to write more clearly and provide more examples. I have incorporated their ideas into this book wherever possible.

I want to extend my special thanks to my colleagues Diane Abbey-Livingston, Liz Burge, Ellen Carusetta, Patricia Cranton, Sonja Davie, Kathleen Howard, Neyda Long, Judy Roy, Pat Post, Marg Wall, and Janet Willis. They have encouraged me throughout by their many kindnesses in word and deed.

Finally, I want to thank my family, Mary, David, and Gordon, and the three new members of David's family, Mary, Anastasia, and Zoe. They have survived my days as a mother, a graduate student, and a geographically distant parent and grandparent. They helped me to grow in ways I never thought possible, and encouraged me every step of the way through their love and companionship and their wonderful sense of humour.

Dorothy MacKeracher
Fredericton, NB
November 2003

MAKING SENSE OF ADULT LEARNING
Second Edition

1 Assumptions about Learning

Before beginning a detailed consideration of the learning process, I would like to set out some of the underlying assumptions and ideologies that have informed me. In this chapter I will consider assumptions about learning; in Chapter 2, I will look at assumptions about adult learners. My descriptions are by no means exhaustive, and most will be elaborated in later chapters, in the terms most commonly found in the adult education literature, including disagreements about these assumptions.

My view of learning is very complex; my learning style allows me to see learning from many sides. I find it hard to present a comprehensive description and explanation of learning in a short definition and on a flat page. I would like to present the full spectrum of the learning process as a whole image in one compact, colourful, three-dimensional, pop-up model. But it can't be done – at least not within the confines of this book.

And I cannot answer all relevant questions on one page or in one chapter. By the end of any chapter, you may find that you have some important questions that remain unanswered. Bear with me. You may have to read to the end of the book before I get around to some of these questions.

In my course on adult learning, I ask students to create an analogy or metaphor to describe their view of learning. I tend to use two different metaphors: a jigsaw puzzle and a kaleidoscope. In both metaphors I use colour to represent different aspects of learning:

- Reds represent the pain and pleasure of the emotional aspects of learning.
- Oranges represent the intensity of the physical aspects of learning.
- Yellows represent the sparkle of the cognitive aspects of learning.
- Greens and blues represent the depth of the social aspects of learning.
- Indigos and deep purples represent the serenity of the spiritual aspects of learning.

Only when all the colours are brought together can I see the wonder of the interconnections that I understand as reflecting the learning process.

The Learning-Centred Approach

My understanding of learning is based on a learning-centred approach to learning-teaching interactions. The learning-centred approach focuses primarily on the learning process and the characteristics of the learner, and secondarily on teaching and the characteristics of those who help the learner to learn. Only when I focus my attention on the learning process and the learner do I understand more clearly what competent teaching, facilitating, training, planning, advising, and counselling processes would be like.

Other approaches to teaching or facilitating (I will use the terms interchangeably in this book), those that are *not* learning centred, might focus primarily on:

- the *content (knowledge or skills)* to be learned and how it is organized and presented (as part of a discipline);
- the *cognitive strategies and skills* to be used and how these can be strengthened through training;
- *appropriate learner behaviours* and how these can be elicited and modified through selected stimuli and reinforcement;
- the *technologies* to be used as an aid to learning and how they limit or enhance learning; or
- the facilitator and his or her facilitating activities.

In these approaches, learners would be perceived and assessed in terms of their competency to learn the content, how well they use cognitive strategies, whether they demonstrate appropriate behaviours, how they respond to the technologies, or how they participate in facilitating activities. That is, an approach that is *not* learning centred would view the learner as someone who responds to the facilitator, facilitating activities, resources, or technologies. Such responses can be assessed in comparison to 'correct' or 'appropriate' responses as defined by someone other than the learner.

The learning process and the learner are paramount in the learning-centred approach used in this book. The more we know about the basic processes of learning and the unique strategies used by individual learners to carry out learning activities, the better able we are to design appropriate activities and resources to facilitate that learning. In the learning-centred approach, the learning process is assumed to be of paramount importance, while facilitating is regarded as a responsive activity that adapts to the learner's activities and natural learning process.

Learners identify the content to be learned as the knowledge or skills they need for themselves, their work, or the world around them, or to solve problems. The resources selected are those most likely to enhance this learning. Any advice from the facilitator can be viewed, not as a prescription to be followed, but as a description of one direction among several alternatives.

I present the learning-centred approach not as the 'best' way to approach learning-facilitating interactions, but as the approach that I find works best and as one viable alternative that is particularly useful with adult learners. All approaches to learners and learning are useful in some contexts, with some learners, and for some content. Decisions about facilitating activities, content, resources, and technologies are the focus of the planning preceding or accompanying any learning or facilitating.

Schooling and education cannot be equated with learning as it is described in this book, for they are only the means for delivering the programs within which learning may occur. Learning is something done *by* the learner rather than something done *to* or *for* the learner. Learning proceeds independently of (and sometimes in spite of) education and schooling.

The assumptions about learning that inform this book include the following:

- Learning is a natural and dialectical process.
- The learning process is cyclical.
- Individual learners have preferred strategies for learning.
- Learning is non-normative.
- Learning is a function of the central nervous system.
- Learning takes place within a context.
- Strong emotions affect learning.
- Learning involves learning how to learn.
- What one values and believes to be true about learning is incorporated into one's philosophical orientation to learning and to learners, and determines how one is likely to facilitate learning.

Each of these assumptions is addressed briefly in this chapter and more extensively in subsequent chapters.

A brief word about the word 'facilitator': in the United States, this word has acquired a negative connotation because it is assumed to share its origins with the adjective 'facile,' a derogatory word meaning – according to my *Concise Oxford Dictionary* – 'easily achieved but of little value.' However, the same dictionary defines 'facilitate' as a verb meaning 'to make easy or less difficult or more easily achieved.' As Humpty Dumpty said to Alice, in *Through the Looking Glass*: 'When I use a word, it means just what I choose it to mean – neither more nor less.' I choose, therefore, to assign a positive meaning to the term 'facilitator' and use it throughout this text. Each reader should feel free to substitute his or her preferred term whenever and wherever 'facilitator' appears.

Learning Is a Natural Process

Learning has numerous definitions. Most writers in the field directly or indirectly describe learning as a naturally occurring process originating within the learner and growing out of the learner's need to interact with the environment. Alan Thomas (1991) ascribes two basic meanings to the word 'learning': 'possession' and 'process.' Learning as possession refers to learning objectives and outcomes as an 'intangible possession that people work to acquire' (p. 3); learning as process refers to the value of the process itself, as something people do rather than something they acquire.

Like breathing, learning is a normal function of living. And like breathing, learning can be hindered by inadequate activities and impaired resources or enhanced by appropriate activities and adequate resources. The activity of breathing stems from a need to reduce carbon dioxide and increase oxygen levels in the blood. Unexpected conditions may interfere with the act of breathing but not the need to breathe. The activity of learning stems from a need to make sense of experience, to reduce the unknown and uncertain aspects of life to a manageable level, and to act skilfully in ensuring one's survival and security. Unexpected conditions may interfere with the act of learning but not the need to learn.

Humans are meaning-making organisms. William Perry (1970) states that what an organism does is organize and what a human organism organizes is meaning. The most fundamental thing that we do with our life experiences is to organize them by making sense of them and giving them meaning (Kegan, 1982). The experiences humans must organize include both those we sense (feel) from the (internal) environment within our own bodies and those we sense (see, hear, smell, taste, touch) from the (external) environment around us. Learning activities help us to

- make sense of the chaos and confusion of raw, uninterpreted experience;
- reduce the unknown aspects of life to a manageable level;
- develop ways to predict how best to respond to and interact with both internal and external environments; and
- define our personal space in life and our personal view of the world in which we live.

In the field of evolutionary psychology, theorists have concluded that learning is an instinct that reliably develops in all humans without conscious effort and in the absence of formal instruction. Learning is described as being just as 'easy, effortless and "natural" to us as humans, as spinning a web is to a spider or dead-reckoning is to a desert ant' (Cosmides & Tooby, 1997, p. 11).

A Definition of Learning

Current theories on brain function suggest that the human brain is intensely aggressive and is designed to allow for learning throughout life (Caine & Caine, 1991; Hart, 1983). According to these theories, learning occurs as the brain extracts meaningful patterns from the confusion of daily internal and external experience. These patterns are then organized into meaning perspectives and personal constructs that make sense of and give meaning to experiences (Candy, 1987; Kelly, 1955; Mezirow, 1991) as well as programmed structures or strategies that control and guide further learning (Caine & Caine, 1991; Hart, 1983).

According to such theories, three conditions are required for learning (Cosmides & Tooby, 1997; Hart, 1983):

1 Enough raw data or experiences must be provided, with enough repetitions and variations on themes to allow differences in patterns to emerge.
2 Enough time and freedom from threat must be provided to allow the patterns to emerge naturally.
3 Sufficient prior meaning perspectives and strategies must exist in the learner's memory to handle new experiences productively.

If adult learners do not already possess these perspectives and strategies for handling new material, then the learning activities must provide opportunities to learn them (Feringer, 1978; Hart, 1983; Hebb, 1972; Thibodeau, 1979).

Learning, then, is a normal physiological and psychological activity that does not require external pressure or encouragement to begin and that proceeds out of inner drives fuelled by intrapersonal energy rather than out of external pressure fuelled by rewards and punishments. The basic problem confronting any facilitator is not how to motivate learning – since it happens both normally and naturally – but rather how to avoid setting up disincentives and obstacles that retard, block, or demotivate learning. Once such disincentives and obstacles are operating, however, the facilitator must take steps to neutralize or remove them, thereby allowing the learning process to return to its normal level of activity. If adults are not blocked in their learning activities, the facilitator can enhance learning by adding positive external conditions that encourage, influence, and reinforce learning (Hart, 1983; Wlodkowski & Ginsberg, 1995).

In this book, therefore, learning is defined as a process of making sense of life's experiences and giving meaning to whatever 'sense' is made; using these meanings in thinking, solving problems, and making choices and decisions; and acting in ways that are congruent with these choices and decisions as a means of obtaining feedback to confirm or disconfirm meanings and choices. Learning results in relatively permanent changes not only in meanings and behaviours but also in the ways one goes about making sense, making meaning and thinking, making choices, and acting.

Learning Is a Dialectical Process

I understand learning to be a dialectical process in that it involves interactive, constructive, and transformative dimensions (Basseches, 1984; Kegan, 1982; Riegel, 1973). A dialectical process is also referred to as a dialogical process (Taylor, Marienau, & Fiddler, 2000) because it involves a dialogue – whether carried out internally with oneself or externally with others – that explores alternative viewpoints in order to develop an integrated viewpoint synthesized from the best aspects of all alternatives.

The Interactive Dimension

Learning is *interactive* because we make meanings through exchanging information with our environment, most particularly with other persons.

1 We receive meanings in the form of information and ideas from others, whether in person or through developed resources.
2 We develop meanings from our own experiences.
3 We integrate the two sources of meaning into a constructed whole.

As learners, how much we are willing to adopt, unchallenged, the meanings provided by others is a measure of our *dependence*; how much we create meanings for ourselves without reference to others is a measure of our *independence*; and how much we develop shared meanings in interactions with others is a measure of our *interdependence*.

Because learning is interactive, our ability to communicate is an important feature of our ability to learn (Argyris, 1991; Rogers & Roethlisberger, 1991). Meaning is conveyed through our shared vocabulary (semantics), grammar (structure or syntax), and nonverbal expressions. Meaning also is conveyed through and influenced by the context in which the interactions occur and through the ways in which power and control are distributed among the persons who are interacting.

The Constructive Dimension

While we are not genetically programmed to respond to our world in a fixed way, as would a spider or a desert ant, we are programmed to construct (compose, make up) and make sense of our world by experiencing it directly through our senses, discerning patterns within those experiences, and assigning meaning to these patterns. Learning is *constructive* (constitutive, inventive) because it involves a process of endowing the world around us with social meaning. It is 'social' in the sense that we engage in this process with other humans. As humans, we not only endow our world with meaning, we have no choice but to do so (Caine & Caine, 1991; Hart, 1983; Kegan, 1982).

The sense we make of our world helps us both to describe and explain what has happened in the past and to predict what might happen in the future. We use our explanations and predictions to develop behaviours that will give us some control over what is happening now in order to obtain outcomes that are favourable to us. That is, we each construct our own 'theories' about how the world works based on our experiences, perceived patterns, and assigned meanings. A theory explains what has happened in the past, predicts what will happen in the future, and implies ways to control or respond to what is happening in the present. Every learner, in effect, is his or her own researcher and theorist about how the world works (Hunt, 1987; Kelly, 1955).

The meanings we assign to reality – and our personal theories about life and reality – provide us with a cognitive representation of the real world, a sort of personal mental map or model that is never an exact replication of the real world, but only an approximation of it. Further, each learner constructs a unique model. Our personal models or maps always include many omissions and distortions. Once we have developed our personal model of reality, we experience it as if it had an objective reality of its own. We then take this 'objectified reality' for granted, legitimizing it as 'the truth' and as a description of 'the real world.'

Since our objectified reality was created from the point of view of our personal experience, we each place our 'self' at the centre of our reality. To question what we take for granted may call into question our very existence; to have someone else question what we take for granted may feel like a personal rejection. When we deliberately re-examine meanings and taken-for-granted personal models of reality, we may feel uncomfortable and anxious. When our personal model of reality is called into question by someone else, we may feel distressed or disoriented.

Any new learning activity is affected by past experiences related to learning and how one regards one's self as a learner as well as by prior learning related to the knowledge, skills, and values to be learned. Past experiences and prior learning may be resources that enhance or barriers that hinder new learning.

To the extent that we share similar meanings for experiences, we also share similar models of reality and similar explanations about how to act as human beings. Gaining agreement about appropriate meanings is a basic problem for any social group. The meanings and the model of reality most often shared by members of any given social group are those created by the dominant members of that group. Without shared models, we would feel confused. With shared models, we tend to assume – unless we ask – that everyone else's model and meanings are the same as ours. Such assumptions frequently create conflict, confusion, and distress (Argyris, 1991).

The Transformative Dimension

Learning is *transformative* because it has the potential to lead to change. Personal meanings and one's personal model of reality can be changed during the constructive and interactive dimensions previously discussed. One may retreat from possible changes and return to what is already known. But learning normally results in new or modified meanings that are then used to reconstruct previously existing meanings.

The personal map of reality I use now is not an accumulation of everything I have learned over my lifetime, but rather a retrospective reconstruction that has brought previous meanings into congruence with my current meanings. For example, I once thought of myself as a 'bad mother.' While my past behaviour has not changed, I have transformed my understanding of that behaviour into a meaning that is more acceptable to my present self. I now perceive myself as a 'good mother' because I created numerous opportunities that challenged my children to develop and mature into competent adults.

Transformations occur through differentiation (separating, distinguishing) and integration (connecting, combining), resulting in increasing complexity and inclusiveness (Basseches, 1984). *Differentiation* can occur through identifying greater detail within selected aspects of the knowledge, skills or values being learned; or through becoming aware of the inadequacies of one's existing meanings or of the differences between one's own meanings and those espoused by others. *Integration* occurs when greater detail and different meanings are combined with previous detail or meanings, thereby modifying the latter.

Jack Mezirow (1991, 1995, 2000) describes three levels or types of learning transformations:

1 *Our meanings* (the content of our personal model of reality) can be transformed by modifying our knowledge, skills, or values.
2 *Our premises, assumptions, or habits of mind* (processes of learning, how we come to know what we know, and why we value what we value) can be

transformed by reflecting on and modifying the strategies, processes, and values underlying our meanings.

3 *Our meaning perspectives* (the general framework of meanings and cultural understandings underlying our entire model of reality) can be transformed by reflecting on, thinking critically about, and modifying the underlying assumptions, premises, or habits of mind.

In the process of these transformations, our personal model of reality is transformed in whole or in part and our associated perspectives, premises, strategies, and meanings are revised.

Meaning transformations occur regularly as new experience informs us of deletions and distortions in our model of reality. Premise transformations occur less regularly and require a conscious effort to think reflectively about what we know and how we know it. Perspective transformations occur even less regularly. Either they require a conscious effort to think critically about the assumptions underlying our premises or they occur spontaneously as revelations or 'ah-ha' experiences.

The Learning Process Is Cyclical

In day-to-day activities, the outcomes from one learning episode or experience both affect and are affected by the next learning episode or experience. In this way, the overall learning process can be understood as being cyclical and a lifelong process.

I envision the learning process as having five basic phases (see Figure 3.1, The Basic Learning Cycle, in Chapter 3) in which the learner

1 participates in experiences and activities that result in the intake of coded and uncoded information from internal and external sources as input to learning;
2 makes sense of experience by giving it meaning and value or affect, through using pattern-recognition and meaning-making cognitive and affective processes;
3 uses meanings and values in problem-solving and decision-making processes to make choices and develop plans for acting to achieve these choices;
4 implements action plans; and
5 receives feedback from the responses of others and from observing one's own actions.

This feedback becomes new information for the next learning cycle or precipitates new experiences and activities.

Many alternative activities and strategies are possible within each phase of the learning cycle. For example, in the first phase learners may prefer information that is

- visual as compared to auditory;
- derived from feelings that originate internally as compared to sensations originating externally;
- provided by nonhuman resources (e.g., books, manuals) as compared to human ones; or
- based on one's own interpretation of experience as compared to the interpretations of others.

The basic phases in the learning cycle can help the learner move ahead (through changes) in spiral fashion in desired directions. A learner can opt out of the process by retreating to the safety of existing knowledge, skills, or values, by stalling, or by forgoing the focus of one learning cycle and engaging in another. As learners, we can begin at any of the five phases involved and work through the sequence. I will return to the topic of learning cycles in Chapter 3.

As facilitators, we can use the model to select our starting activities and to guide subsequent activities. Our present understanding of the relationship between facilitating and learning, however, is very limited. Research on teaching and facilitating consistently shows that facilitator effects on learner achievement are unstable and that much facilitating behaviour is unrelated to learner outcomes (Candy, 1987; Pratt, 1979). The best predictor we have of this relationship is the B-P-E model proposed by Kurt Lewin (1936, as cited in Hunt & Sullivan, 1974): Behaviour is a function of the interaction between Person and Environment, or B $\rightarrow$ f (P, E) (p. 7). This relationship has been reiterated and extended by many authors (e.g., Bortner, 1974; Hunt, 1987; Hunt & Sullivan, 1974; Kidd, 1973; Knowles, 1990). The facilitator can be thought of as a very influential component of the environment through the provision of guidance, structure, information, feedback, reinforcement, and support. What we do know is that the process of learning should guide the process of facilitating rather than the other way around. I will return to the B-P-E model in Chapter 2.

Individuals Have Preferred Strategies for Learning

Each phase of the overall learning process involves a variety of

- possible strategies for attending, perceiving, remembering, thinking, planning, deciding, and acting processes;
- interactions with others playing responsive and directive roles; and
- contexts, situations, and learning environments.

The numbers of alternatives in each phase are myriad; and the possible com- binations among these alternatives challenge the mind.

Over a lifetime of learning, each individual develops preferred strategies and alternatives for each phase. For example, I prefer visual (written) infor- mation to auditory (spoken) information, ideas expressed on paper to those expressed on a computer screen, reflective strategies to experimental strate- gies, meanings that I have derived from my own experience to the meanings of others, learning alone or with one or two others to learning in a large group. I have come to value these alternatives so strongly that I am inclined to believe they are the best alternatives – for everyone.

My preferences constitute my learning style. Not only does my learning style direct my preferred approaches to most learning experiences, but it also biases my expectations about how others could (and should) learn. When I see other learners using alternatives, I sometimes wonder if they are actually learning or what they could possibly be learning.

In spite of all the possible alternative learning strategies and styles, the number of general learning styles and strategies is rather smaller than we might expect. I will discuss learning styles more extensively in Chapter 4.

Learning Is Non-normative

As a consequence of my personal model of reality and my preferred learning strategies, what I learn will usually be different from what you learn, even if we are participating in the same activity. What learners learn is rarely an exact copy of what the facilitator intended them to learn. Learners always modify what is presented through their own model of reality.

Facilitating activities may seek normative results; that is, the facilitator may seek to obtain learning results that are consistent and predictable for all learners and congruent with pre-established goals. Obtaining normative outcomes may be appropriate in preparing plumbers or electricians for the workplace. Such results, however, are rarely attained because the individ- ual's own internal resources will always modify what the facilitator seeks to obtain.

Learning Is a Function of the Central Nervous System

Learning is as much grounded in the physical structure and physiology of the brain as it is in the cognitive constructs and processes of the mind. The invariant physical organization of the brain creates certain constraints on the information-processing system of the human mind, just as the hardware places limits on the processing system of any computer system. The mallea- ble components of the human mind – such as the content and form of long- term memory and the strategies used in solving problems – can be modified through experience and learning, just as the software of a computer system can be modified (Charness & Bieman-Copland, 1992).

A healthy human brain has four learning features (Caine & Caine, 1991):

1 It can detect patterns (similarities and differences) within incoming information.
2 It has a prodigious ability to store information.
3 It can correct what it has learned through self-reflection.
4 It has an unlimited capacity to create new ideas.

The terms 'brain-based learning' and 'brain-compatible learning' are used to 'acknowledge the brain's rules for meaningful learning and [the facilitating that keeps] those rules in mind' (Caine & Caine, 1991, p. 3; Reardon, 1999). I will consider the brain and the mind in greater detail in Chapter 5.

Learning Takes Place within a Context

The primary concern of much formal education appears to involve transferring the knowledge, skills, and values of an academic discipline to the learner. The majority of adults, however, do not live in a world that is based on academic disciplines; rather, they live in contexts where they must apply what they have learned in practical situations. The terms 'situated learning' and 'context-based learning' have come to represent learning experiences occurring in real-world contexts (Brown, Collins, & Duguid, 1989; Hansman, 2001).

The concept of situated learning has been adopted to describe different approaches and types of adult learning. For example, the term can be used to:

• emphasize the need to immerse learners within the context or culture in which the knowledge being learned is also being applied. Learning a foreign language and preparing individuals for work in cross-cultural settings are examples of this emphasis (Jacobson, 1996).
• describe learning within a community in which newcomers learn from more experienced old-timers within the day-to-day work of the community. Apprenticeship, mentoring, or preceptorship programs are examples of this emphasis (Brandt, Farmer, & Buckmaster, 1993; Brown, Collins, & Duguid, 1989; Hansman, 1997; Lave & Wenger, 1991; Wilson, 1993).
• describe the possibility that individuals, organizations, or communities may develop knowledge based on the shared experiences of those who live and work within the organization or community (Argyris, 1991). Both organizational learning and community learning are typical of this use of the term (Drath, 2001; Poonwassie, 2001; Senge, 1990; Watkins & Marsick, 1993).
• emphasize the fact that the quality of the learning within any community is dependent on the quality of the relationships among the members of the

community. These relationships are affected by such factors as age, race, gender, class, ethnicity, sexual orientation, and physical/sensory ability of participants; and by equity and equality in the sharing of power and resources among participants (Caffarella & Merriam, 2000). Critical research in women's studies, literacy, community development, and cultural studies, and the practices that flow from such research, illustrate this emphasis (Clark, 1999; Flannery, 1994; Kilgore, 2001; Quigley, 1997; Sheared, 1994; Shore, 1997).

- inform alternative approaches to prior learning assessment through granting visibility to 'outsider' knowledge that both differs from and is comparable to academic knowledge (Michelson, 1996; Wong, 2001).
- describe the ability of some learners to learn more easily in social relationships than alone (Baxter Magolda, 1992; Belenky, Bond, & Weinstock, 1997; Belenky, Clinchy, Goldberger, & Tarule, 1986). Feminist pedagogy is grounded in this use of the term (MacKeracher, 1993; Morrish & Buchanan, 2001).

I will return to most of these uses of the term 'situated learning' in later chapters.

Strong Emotions Affect Learning

Learning is much affected by emotions from three sources: those we bring to the learning process, those that are generated during the learning process, and those we feel when we receive feedback about whether we have succeeded or failed in our learning endeavours. At low to moderate levels, emotions can enhance or motivate learning; at high levels, emotions – both positive and negative – can hinder learning. Adults who are experiencing either acute distress or euphoria are equally unlikely to be participating in learning activities.

Roby Kidd (1973) tells us that adults have more emotional associations with the material to be learned than do children. We sometimes mistakenly assume that adults do not have emotional responses to learning because their methods for controlling their emotions are often both elaborate and effective. I will return to the role of emotions in learning in Chapter 6.

Learning Involves Learning How to Learn

The concept of 'learning to learn' is endorsed and promoted by educators at all levels of the educational system. Whether we know it or not, when we learn we are also learning how to learn. Like learning, learning to learn can be thought of as both a goal or outcome and a process (Candy, 1990).

As a goal, learning to learn challenges individual learners to develop the skills and knowledge for learning more effectively in various contexts and settings. As a process, learning to learn consists of two groups of interrelated processes and activities (Smith, 1990).

1 The *intrapersonal set* includes such skills as critical thinking, self-reflection, and self-control.
2 The *interpersonal set* includes such skills as engaging in dialogue with others and reporting on the interactive dimension of learning in the ongoing dialectical process.

Philip Candy (1990) describes learning to learn as involving higher order cognitive skills that rest on increased self-reflection (self-awareness and self-control). These higher order cognitive skills include problem solving, critical thinking, and planning for learning purposes. Such skills must also be accompanied by appropriate attitudes. Critical thinking, for example, 'does not consist merely of raising questions or of indiscriminate skepticism' but also comprises attitudes and behaviours that, taken together, can be labelled 'the critical spirit or critical attitude' (Candy, 1990, p. 45). The critical approach to learning involves calling into question established knowledge and the assumptions that inform it (Brookfield, 1987).

Self-reflection also includes skills and special attitudes calling on individuals to accurately describe not only their own physical and social activities, but also their mental activities and emotional responses in learning situations. The individual, therefore, must adopt a self-critical attitude as part of learning to learn. Both critical and self-critical attitudes have potentially positive and negative outcomes. They are a necessary precursor of change; yet they sometimes create distress that can slow or even stop the learning process.

Of the three levels of transformational learning described by Jack Mezirow (1991, 1995), transforming both premises and meaning perspectives contributes to learning to learn.

• Transforming premises requires a critical assessment of the learning processes through which we create meaning in order to determine dysfunctional processes. Meanings or concepts can be changed without radically altering the model of reality within which they are integrated, but a change in our ways of learning can transform that model.
• Transforming meaning perspectives involves consciousness raising, self-reflection, critical thinking, and awareness of the constraints within which one's personal model of reality was developed and is operating.

Through such activities, the individual becomes aware of distorted, incomplete, or repressed information and interpretations that underlie the entire model. Perspective transformation involves both a critical reappraisal of the supporting assumptions and the development of new assumptions as well as a transformed model of reality.

Learning to learn is described in the literature under a variety of terms: 'second-order change' (Watzlawick, Weakland, & Fisch, 1974); 'reflection-on-action' (Argyris & Schön, 1974; Schön, 1987); 'double loop learning' (Argyris, 1991); 'meta-formal schemata' (Basseches, 1984); 'metacognition' (Novak & Gowin, 1984); 'metalearning' (Maudsley, 1979); 'deutero-learning' (Bateson, 1972); and 'paradigm shift' (Barker, 1993; Inglis, 1994; Koestler, 1964).

It is clear from the literature that not all adults have developed the skills necessary for learning to learn in conscious and deliberate ways (Candy, 1987; Collett, 1990). Those who have such skills appear to be more productive learners than those who do not. It is also clear that the most effective learning requires not only critical thinking, self-reflection, and self-direction but also input from external sources and objective observers. Without input from others, the individual learner can become stalled in self-perpetuating errors and false assumptions (Candy, 1987).

Philosophical Approaches to Learning

What we believe and value about the learning endeavour constitutes our philosophical approach to learning. Draper (2001) states that our philosophy 'encompasses the principles, values, and attitudes that structure our beliefs and guide our behaviors' (p. 153). While we rarely articulate our philosophy or give it a label, we can probably articulate beliefs and values in response to a series of questions on learning. These questions include:

- Who is learning what?
- From whom?
- By what approaches?
- For what purpose?
- Under what circumstances?
- With what consequences?

Alan Thomas (1991) adds one more question to this sequence – At whose expense? – a question that brings beliefs and values about learning into the political realm, which topic is well beyond the scope of this text.

A number of writers have analysed the possible answers to these various questions and have identified a bewildering number of philosophical orientations. Some writers analyse the responses to all the questions; others focus on only one question. For example:

- Cyril Houle (1961) postulates three motives for participating in formal learning activities: goal oriented, learning oriented, and activity oriented.
- James Draper (2001), Lorraine Zinn (1990, 1999) and Susan Scott (1998)

describe five philosophical approaches to adult education: behaviourism, liberalism, progressivism, humanism, and radicalism.
- Dan Pratt (1999; Pratt & Collins, 2001) identifies five perspectives on teaching: transmission, apprenticeship, developmental, nurturing, and social reform.
- John Elias and Sharan Merriam (1995) describe four competing philosophies in literacy education: politicizing, vocationalizing, socializing, and academizing.
- Jack Mezirow (2000) reports on three domains of learning – instrumental, communicative, and emancipatory – and describes four types of learning – elaborating existing frames of reference, learning new frames of reference, transforming points of view, and transforming habits of mind.
- Allan Quigley (1997) identifies four approaches to literacy education: vocational, liberal, humanist, and liberatory.
- Roger Hiemstra (1988) describes seven philosophical systems: idealism, realism, progressivism, liberalism, behaviourism, humanism, and radicalism.
- Harold Beder (1991) identifies three philosophical orientations: liberal-progressive, counter critique, and personal growth.
- Adrian Blunt (2001) reduces many of the ideas about perspectives on educational policies and practices to two paradigms: the technical-rational and the participatory-liberatory.

To simplify the discussion here, I will begin by considering how the questions on learning listed above might be answered.

Who Is Learning What?

Answers to the question 'Who is learning?' are many and varied. We can view our learners in terms of characteristics specific to the learning process, such as learning style, cognitive style, types of abilities, and motives for learning; or general characteristics such as gender, race, age, ethnicity, sexual orientation, language, class, religion, and abilities. Categorizing learners can result in stereotyping, so choose your categories carefully, keep them flexible, and keep your mind open to the possibility that you may need to change your mind.

Answers to the question 'What is being learned?' are also many and varied. The content can focus on knowledge, skills, values, or beliefs and can be defined by the learner(s), by experts, or by the discipline. In general, adult educators believe that learners learn more effectively when what is being learned has relevance to their lives, and when the content is as learner defined as possible. The knowledge, skills, and values to be learned can be created by the learner on the basis of personal (subjective) experience; can be socially approved and received by the learner from expert sources; or can be based on the integration of subjective and received knowledge, skills, and values.

Learning from Whom?

The person(s) in charge of the learning process can be the learner or others such as facilitators, program planners, textbook authors, resource creators, or computer programmers. Different persons can be in charge during different phases of the learning process: planning, managing the implementation of the plan, developing the learning resources, and evaluating the results. Attitudes about who should be in charge during different phases of the learning process contribute considerably to one's philosophical orientation. In the field of adult education, particularly in North America, a general belief exists that the more the learner can be involved in the various phases of the learning process and the more they are in charge, the more they are likely to learn. Cultures that are less likely to value individual effort and self-reliance and more likely to value group effort and harmony are also more likely to believe that the learner is better served by acquiescing to experts or co-operating with others in deciding how to learn (Ziegahn, 2001).

Learning by What Approaches?

Two basic approaches to learning are available: self-directed or autonomous learning and other-connected or relational learning. Mezirow (2000) states that adult programs should be designed 'to help adults realize their potential for becoming more liberated, socially responsible, and autonomous learners' (p. 30).

In the past, general beliefs in adult education supported the view that the preferred means for adult learning was autonomous in nature, while learning that was relational was frequently relegated to the role of providing interpersonal support and to advancing learning in co-operative and collaborative or social action contexts. Our understanding of the nature and role of relational learning is gradually transforming these beliefs through the work of feminist (Belenky, Bond, & Weinstock, 1997), Native (Cajete, 1994), and cross-cultural educators (Mama, 2002; Noble, 2000). I will discuss autonomous and relational learning more extensively in Chapter 8.

Both basic approaches to learning can be further modified by the use of technologies ('devices' to assist in the process), ranging from the low-tech of the talking circle or chalk talks to the hi-tech of computer-managed instruction or web-board interfaces.

Learning for What Purpose?

Darkenwald and Merriam (1982) have summarized numerous learning statements into five essential purposes that enable the learner to

1 cultivate intellect through developing thinking and problem-solving skills, critical and reflective skills, and learning-to-learn skills;
2 develop in ways that are personally satisfying and self-actualizing;
3 acquire the knowledge, skills, and attitudes necessary for adapting to or coping with the conditions that affect their lives, thereby improving their personal and social contexts;
4 contribute to social transformation through working with others; and
5 work in group settings and make organizations more effective.

These five statements of purpose are closely aligned with several of the philosophical orientations outlined earlier.

Learning under What Circumstances?

Many writers in the field of adult education believe that adults learn voluntarily, that they cannot be coerced to learn. Thomas (1991) argues that learning is the result of an act of will and that, while adults can be induced by threat of dire economic or legal consequences to learn specific skills and values, 'any teacher knows that no outside force can actually compel someone to learn anything' (p. 14). There are two circumstances, however, under which adults can be considered nonvoluntary learners. The first occurs when an adult, upon legal conviction, is sentenced by a judge to attend a rehabilitative learning program such as those that focus on driver re-education, anger management, or substance abuse. The second occurs when an adult encounters a life situation that radically transforms his or her life. These situations include unemployment or divorce, a major illness or accident, or the death of an intimate. In response to these situations, the individual may begin as a nonvoluntary learner, but as time passes and the situation changes, he or she may become a voluntary learner.

Learning with What Consequences?

Adrian Blunt (2001) outlines two major consequences of adult learning programs, based on two different paradigms. The 'technical-rational paradigm' results in essential knowledge, skill, and values acquisition by members of society, particularly by members of the labour force, and the achievement of sound social and economic development through creating and maintaining productive members of that society. The 'participatory-liberatory paradigm' results in the essential social development of individuals and the development and maintenance of democratic institutions, as well as the achievement of social equity and justice in a society that is both diverse and inclusive.

Naming Your Philosophical Orientation

Not all the ways of thinking about adult learning can fit into a single philosophical orientation; many spread across several orientations. With that in mind, I used the four basic orientations proposed by Quigley (1997) and the two paradigms outlined by Blunt (2001) to sort my answers to the six questions based on my own experience. Figure 1.1, Philosophical Orientations towards Adult Learning, outlines the results of this process. You can see that trying to slot ideas into neat categories and boxes doesn't quite work. There is too much possibility of overlap along almost every row in this figure.

   What does it all mean in practical terms? If, for example, you sit on a community committee responsible for the development of a literacy program and you have the feeling that the committee members are talking at cross-purposes to each other, you might find it useful to have the members discuss their philosophies about learning and teaching. Members espousing the technical-rational paradigm would not be thinking about literacy programming in the same terms as those espousing the participatory-liberatory paradigm. Even within the technical-rational paradigm, those from a vocational orientation might be talking about a literacy program that is quite different from the one being proposed by those from the liberal orientation. Such a discussion might not yield consensus, but at least you would know the basis for your differences of opinion.

LEARNING AND FACILITATING PRINCIPLES

Based on the assumptions about learning described in this chapter, we can make a few assumptions about what constitutes good facilitating strategies.

- They will mirror the natural cycle of learning.
- They will present sufficient information and a variety of learning experiences to allow learners to identify patterns of meaning.
- They will provide sufficient time and freedom from threat to allow learners to identify their own meanings and to integrate these with previously existing meanings.

- They will provide opportunities for learners to understand the meanings used by others and to work collaboratively to develop shared meanings.
- They will acknowledge and build on the learner's past experiences and prior learning.
- They will encourage interaction among learners and between learners and facilitator.
- They will provide a variety of activities that will accommodate, as much as possible, the learning styles of individual learners.

Figure 1.1
Philosophical Orientations towards Adult Learning

	Technical-Rational Paradigm		Participatory-Liberatory Paradigm	
	Vocational Orientation	Liberal Orientation	Humanist Orientation	Liberatory Orientation
Education is mainly for ...	Occupational preparation and re-training	Acquiring social and cultural knowledge, socialization	Personal growth, self-actualization	Critical thinking, political awareness
Content is defined largely by ...	Occupation and experts	Culture, society, discipline, and experts	Learner	Learners and facilitator
Learning process directed largely by ...	Facilitator and resource creators	Facilitator	Learner	Learners working with facilitator
Main approaches to learning are ...	Autonomous, expert-directed	Autonomous, self-directed	Relational, self-selected	Relational, collaborative, co-operative
Knowledge is mainly ...	Received	Received	Subjective	Integrated
Purpose of learning is mainly ...	Developing skills and knowledge for coping and adapting	Cultivating intellect	Personal development	Social transformation and organizational effectiveness
Consequences of learning include ...	Knowledge, skills and value acquisition for vocational competence and economic productivity	Knowledge, skills and value acquisition for social participation	Personal and social development and maintenance of social and democratic institutions	Achievement of social equity and justice; inclusion and diversity

2 Assumptions about Adult Learners

Ideal adult learners are described in the adult education literature as autonomous individuals (Selman, 2001) capable of identifying their own learning needs and planning, carrying out, and assessing their own learning activities (Sork, 2000). The impetus for this view derives from the work of Malcolm Knowles (1970, 1980), Allen Tough (1971, 1979), and Jack Mezirow (1991, 2000).

When Knowles introduced North American adult educators to the term 'andragogy' in 1970, he described adult learners as being self-directed, as having a reservoir of experience that becomes a resource for learning, as being motivated to learn in response to the tasks of their social roles, as being concerned about the immediate application of knowledge, and accordingly as preferring to participate in problem-centred learning activities. Knowles intended to present a clear distinction between adult learning and child learning. His statements, however, were read as overgeneralizations that did not hold true for all adult learners or all learning contexts. In 1980, therefore, he revised his assumptions as follows (pp. 43–4):

- Adult learners move from dependency towards increasing self-directedness as a normal aspect of maturation.
- Adults accumulate an increasing reservoir of experience that becomes an increasingly rich resource for learning.
- Adults are motivated to learn in order to cope more satisfyingly with real-life tasks or problems.
- Adults are concerned about developing increased competence to achieve their full potential in life and about the immediate application of knowledge and skills.
- Adults prefer to participate in performance-centred learning activities.

This set of assumptions was also controversial. The change from 'self-directed' to 'increasing self-directedness' and from 'problem-centred' to 'performance-centred' did not satisfy those who saw the Knowles' distinctions between child and adult learning as being based on assumptions that would not hold up under close scrutiny. However, Knowles clearly succeeded in encouraging adult educators to be more critically reflective about their assumptions about adult learners and adult learning.

Tough (1971) was more concerned about distinguishing between formal education and informal learning. His research addressed the question: How do adults learn naturally – when they are not being taught? His concept of self-directed learning projects became the basis for extensive research. Tough's conclusions (1979) were that most adults engage in an average of eight major learning projects each year and that only 10 per cent of these projects were associated with educational institutions. The majority of projects could be defined as self-directed.

By 1980, the concept of self-directedness was firmly established in the adult education literature. More recently, Mezirow introduced the concept of perspective transformation (Mezirow & Marsick, 1978) and expanded this concept into the theoretical concept of transformative learning (Mezirow, 1991, 2000). His description of transformative learning, however, continues to present the adult learner as autonomous, although other writers (Belenky & Stanton, 2000; Kasl & Elias, 2000; Yorks & Marsick, 2000) are now challenging this description.

By 2000, critical theorists, writing about the members of marginal groups in society – women (Belenky, Bond, & Weinstock, 1997; Belenky et al., 1986; Gilligan, 1982; Horsman, 1999; Lyons, 1988), racial and cultural minorities (Flannery, 1994; hooks, 1994; Poonwassie, 2001; Shore, 1997), and learners with learning and physical disabilities (Hamilton, 1995; Orenstein, 2001; Sutcliffe, 1990) – also challenged the ideal of the autonomous learner. These writers promoted the assumption that some adult learning can more accurately be described as 'relational' than as autonomous, as being based not on self-directedness but on connecting to others in the learning process; and as 'situational,' as changing in response to the context in which the learning is occurring (Brown, Collins, & Duguid, 1989; Hayes, 2000).

In this chapter, therefore, I want to consider assumptions about adult learners that underlie both sides of these concepts. I would warn the reader that describing both sides at the same time is difficult because writers in the field often use different words to describe a single concept. Sometimes these words convey more value to one side than to the other. For example, those who believe in the greater importance of self-directedness tend to describe two opposing learning styles as 'field independence' and 'field dependance,' with greater virtue attached to the former style. Those who believe in the greater importance of relatedness have suggested these opposing learning styles should be called 'context insensitive' and 'context sensitive,' with greater virtue attached to the latter style.

As in Chapter 1, I have organized my thoughts about adult learners in terms of the assumptions that form the basis for this book. My assumptions are not unlike those proposed by Knowles (1980).

- Adults can and do learn throughout their lifetime.
- Adults are not mature children, nor are children immature adults.
- Adults change over time.
- Adults accumulate experiences and prior learning over their lifetime; the older they grow, the more past experiences and prior learning they bring to bear on current learning.
- The role of time in the life of an adult has important implications for the learning process.
- Adults bring to the learning process an established sense of self and an inclination to protect this self from perceived threats that might arise in learning interactions.
- Both self-directedness and relatedness to others contribute to how adults prefer to learn.

Adults Can and Do Learn

The work of Allen Tough (1971) clearly shows that adults engage in a wide variety of learning activities in response to their daily needs and problems. They may not define these activities as 'learning' since there may be no apparent connection between the activities and formal schooling or the educational system; but the activities are clearly recognizable as learning activities. Adults experience a sense of well-being when they do learn and when their environment supports and encourages learning.

Recent work in fields related to adult education indicates that adults of all levels of intelligence, all ages, and all stages of development up to the moment of death are capable of learning. These implications are to be found in the works of developmental psychologists such as Borysenko (1996), Chickering and Reisser (1993), Fiske and Chiriboga (1990), Levinson (1986, 1996), Basseches (1984), and Kegan (1982, 1994); of educational gerontologists such as Birren and Bengtson (1988), Birren et al. (1996), Fisher and Wolfe (1998), and Peterson (1983); of thanatologists such as Imara (1975) and Kübler-Ross (1970); and of special needs educators who work with learning challenged adults, such as Hamilton (1995), Orenstein (2001), Simpson (1979), Sutcliffe (1990), Vanier (1970), and Williams (1992).

Adults Are Not Mature Children, Nor Are Children Immature Adults

The literature in the field of adult education describes a basic difference of opinion about the nature and characteristics of adults as learners in comparison with those of children. Some writers (e.g., Cranton, 2000a; Hart, 1983;

Houle, 1972) maintain that learning is learning and is the same at every age. Others (e.g., Knowles, 1970, 1990; McKenzie, 1977) maintain that adult learning and child learning are both qualitatively and quantitatively different. Still others avoid the issue by discussing the wide variations found among adult learners (e.g., Flannery, 1993; Squires, 1993).

My reading and experience persuade me that the cognitive and physiological processes involved in learning may indeed be similar in adults and children, since they are based on processes that do not change markedly over time. However, the social, emotional, developmental, and situational variables that affect learning are different for adults and children. Baltes, Reese, and Lipsitt (1980) provide a conceptual model that helps put the many variables affecting learning into perspective. They state that lifelong learning and development are influenced by three major groups of factors.

1 *Biological and environmental factors*, such as physical growth and age-related change, and traditional *age-related experiences*, such as socialization and education, are very influential in learning and development during childhood and adolescence, decline during adulthood, and begin to rise again during the later years, beginning with retirement.
2 *Historical factors* are associated with the events and contexts of each passing era and have specific effects on the learning and development of individuals within each generation, age cohort, and social group. For example, those who were eighteen years old in the 1930s would be profoundly affected by the onset of World War II while those who were eighteen years old in the 1990s would be equally affected by the increasing incidence of AIDS; but the effect on each group would differ. Historical factors are viewed as being most influential during adolescence and young adulthood but as declining in influence in later years (Baltes, Reese, & Lipsitt, 1980).
3 *Life events* are specific for each person. Examples might include having a parent die when one is a child; developing cancer as a young adult; or deciding to return to college in middle age. Life events are cumulative, and their influence on learning and development rises steadily from childhood to old age.

The joint impact of these three groups of factors, mediated through the knowledge and strategies of the developing individual, accounts for differences in learning characteristics between childhood and adulthood. If we add to these the cultural and situational factors, they also account for differences in learning characteristics between younger and older adults, between men and women, and between cultural groups. I will return to some of these issues in later chapters.

The major differences between learning in childhood and adulthood are

Figure 2.1
Differences between Adults and Children as Learners

Adults	Children
• Have extensive pragmatic life experiences that tend to structure and limit new learning. Learning focuses largely on transforming or extending the meanings, values, skills, and strategies acquired in previous experience.	• Have fewer pragmatic life experiences. Learning focuses largely on forming and accumulating basic meanings, values, skills, and strategies.
• Experience major pressures for change from factors related to family, work and community roles and expectations; and from personal needs for continuing productivity, self-definition, responsibility, and connection to others.	• Experience major pressures for change from factors related to physical growth and socialization, and preparation for future family, work and community roles.
• Have learning needs related to current life situations and future expectations.	• Have learning needs related to developing meanings and strategies for understanding current and future experiences.
• Have the capacity for using generalized, abstract thought.	• Are more likely to use specific, concrete thought.
• Are likely to be able to verbally express their own needs and describe their own learning strategies, allowing them to negotiate and collaborate in planning their own learning programs.	• Are likely to non-verbally express their own needs and learning strategies, encouraging 'expert' observers and interpreters to plan learning programs for them.
• Are assigned a responsible status in society and are expected to be productive.	• Are assigned a non-responsible status in society and are expected to play and learn.

summarized in Figure 2.1, Differences between Adults and Children as Learners. These differences are sometimes aspects of a continuous and ongoing characteristic, as in the accumulation of experience; and are sometimes aspects of a discontinuous characteristic, as in the shift from concrete to abstract thought. The summary helps us to understand people's behaviour and is not meant to reflect universal, absolute differences. The summary is drawn from the work of Brundage and MacKeracher (1980), Hiemstra and Sisco (1990), Kidd (1973), Knowles (1990), and McKenzie (1977).

Adults Change over Time

Some of the changes that occur in adulthood can be attributed to learning, but other changes must be attributed to such processes as aging and developing.

Age-Related Changes

Age-related changes that actually affect learning are very few, and these few are related to physiological changes. Physiological factors relate to physical well-being, sensory acuity, and effectiveness of physiological and physical responses in learning activities, including stress responses (discussed in Chapter 6 under emotions and motives in learning); physiologically based learning preferences (discussed in Chapter 4 under styles in learning); and brain functions (discussed in Chapter 5 under brain and mind in learning).

Adults reach full physical maturity by their early twenties. Until their late forties they normally experience no major physical changes other than those induced by accident, illness, stress, childbirth, or lifestyle. From the late forties on, they may gradually become aware of two general physical changes: in sensory acuity and in the speed of physical responses.

SENSORY CHANGES
With increasing age, the acuity of the sensory receptors for vision and hearing declines very slowly. Usually these declines can be corrected and may be so imperceptible that the individual remains unaware of change. Such declines affect learning by reducing the quantity and quality of the information input to the learning process, specifically by reducing the accuracy and amount of sensory information taken in. Adults who experience declines in sensory acuity typically develop coping behaviours to deal with such changes. Some deliberately place themselves in relation to others so their hearing losses are minimized or gather information in other ways, such as lip-reading. Others cope by using information from past experience to replace unseen or unheard material (Birren & Schaie, 1977; Hiemstra & Sisco, 1990; Kidd, 1973; Novak, 1993).

The implications of sensory changes for learning are few, particularly when the learning environment provides a wide range of repetitive information in both visual and auditory modes. In environments where a range of information is not available, learners may begin to replace absent information in unproductive ways. Occasionally, conditions within the learning environment may inadvertently augment sensory losses.

The major age-related auditory change is loss of high-frequency sounds (hissing consonants such as *th*, *sh*, *ch*, *f*), a condition that renders normal speech garbled and muffled. To help learners with this problem, speak clearly and distinctly and try to pitch your voice as low as possible. Every room has a distinct auditory environment that needs to be checked. Technological devices such as florescent lights and visual projectors produce a humming sound that diminishes audible sound even further. And hard, reflective surfaces may create an echo that has the same effect (Lai, 1990).

The major age-related vision changes are an increase in the focal length of the eye (making reading more difficult), a mild decline in ability to discriminate between some colour combinations (brown, yellow, and orange fade), and an increase in the time required to adjust vision to changes in light intensity. Other changes include loss of vision around the edges of the visual field (tunnel vision and loss of night vision) and at the centre of the visual field (macular degeneration and loss of colour vision).

While visual problems affect older adults more frequently than younger adults, a wise facilitator develops good visual materials for learners of all ages. Some specific hints for developing better visual aids are contained in the work of Albright and Graf (1992), Davis (1993), Malmstadt and VonBargen (1991), and Naeyaert (1990):

- For print documents, use a font size of no less than twelve characters per inch. Large print is not necessary for most learners, but small print should be avoided for all learners.
- A serif font is better in print documents (serifs are the little strokes at the extremities of the main strokes of a letter). Times Roman is the most common serif font. The serifs are lost in successive photo reproductions, gradually making the print very difficult to read. Reproduce print material from an original copy whenever possible.
- A sans serif font (i.e., without serifs) with all lines the same width is better for projected documents. For learners with some visual problems, serif letters bleed into each other in projected material. Ariel and Helvetica are the most common sans serif fonts. In print material, such fonts are useful to distinguish headings.
- Avoid using fancy or discursive fonts (e.g., italics) on projected documents.
- Visual material using colours should provide a high contrast between letters/figures and background. On paper, black or dark blue print on an off-white or dull yellow (i.e., matte finish) background is best. On projections, white or pale yellow on dark green, blue, or purple is best. Avoid cluttering the background with distracting designs or photographs.
- In all visual material, avoid using red on green or green on red, contrasts that are invisible to colour-blind learners.
- When using projectors (overheads, slides, films, VCR, computerized data projector), adjust room lights and window coverings to improve the quality of the projection, reduce glare, and allow learners enough time to adjust to changes in light intensity.

Hearing losses result in communication problems that have a profound effect on learning in group settings. Communicating with hearing-impaired learners can sometimes tax the ability of those who hear normally, often leading them to talk louder and slower and eventually to sound as if they were speaking to a small child. Vision losses do not have the same devastating effect on social interactions. We need to keep in mind that visually impaired persons are not necessarily hearing impaired and that their visual impairment does not render them learning impaired.

SPEED OF PHYSICAL RESPONSES

The second age-related change is a general reduction in the speed of response of the central nervous system. This change should have no effect on learning, except in extreme cases, provided learners are allowed to pace their own learning. All adults are adversely affected by time constraints, older adults more so than younger adults (Arenberg, 1994; Hiemstra & Sisco, 1990).

Some older learners may experience difficulty responding effectively in novel or emergency situations. This change is the result of both a mild decline in the rate at which nervous impulses are transmitted – a change that should not itself be problematic – and a general energy decline caused by combinations of poor health, poor nutrition, and poor physical fitness.

Individually, a lessening in the speed of response or reduction in overall energy should not be a problem. When the learning or responding must be done under pressure of time, the decline in speed of response can be further aggravated as a result of chronic pain, disease, fatigue, and emotional or physical distress. All these factors aggravate the overall effects of physical change.

While sensory acuity and speed of response may decline in older learners, there is no corresponding age-related decline in their ability to make meaning, or in the effectiveness of their learning responses (Arenberg, 1994; Birren & Schaie, 1977; Hiemstra & Sisco, 1990). Older adults generally require more time to learn material, although experience, good health and fitness, and good learning strategies will compensate for all but the most marked declines in sensory and physical capacities.

Developmental Changes

Some of the changes that occur in adulthood must be understood as being an outcome of the process of development. The adult education and psychology literature is awash with concepts, models, and theories about adult development. Many of these tell us very little about how adults learn and what characteristics affect the learning process. A reading of this literature does offer a few generalizations that could be helpful to facilitators of adult learning. A review of the literature is beyond the scope of this book. However, one or two models offer some practical information.

Zick Rubin (1981) tells us that adult development is characterized by both stability and change. Deeply ingrained patterns of behaviour remain constant throughout life unless something fairly dramatic happens to change them; at the same time, an individual's feelings and behaviours related to autonomy and inclusion keep changing throughout life unless they get stuck. Learning experiences create pressures for change and help individuals bring these pressures under their own control.

Robert Kegan (1982, 1994) describes both internal and external pressures for change as alternating between a need for more inclusion and connection and a need for more autonomy and separateness. When an individual moves too far towards meeting inclusion needs, pressure builds to meet autonomy needs; when the individual moves too far towards meeting autonomy needs, pressure begins to build to meet inclusion needs. In Kegan's model, the individual is always in a process of change and development.

Kurt Riegel (1973) presents a dialectical model of adult development in which change proceeds as a result of changes within and interactions among four dimensions of human life.

1 *Inner-biological* – drives and needs arise from shifts in the internal balance of biological systems, such as the shift in sex hormones that might occur during pregnancy or menopause.
2 *Individual-psychological* – drives and needs arise from shifts in the cognitive and emotional systems, such as shifts in emotional states (through distress), in how one defines self (through individuation), and in one's model of reality (through learning).
3 *Cultural-social* – demands or pressures for change arise from social or cultural interactions, such as entering into new social roles (motherhood, job promotion), alterations in family constellations (the empty nest, the sandwich generation), and changes in economic conditions (bankruptcy, winning the lottery).
4 *Outer-physical* – demands of pressures for change arise from the physical environment in which one lives, such as catastrophes (floods, fire) or natural changes (seasons).

Riegel's model indicates that these four dimensions interact with each other, sometimes balancing and reinforcing each other but sometimes conflicting. An adult experiences a crisis when the pressures from two or more of these dimensions come into conflict. The role of the facilitator is to help learners identify sources of change and to respond to these in timely and effective ways. For example, in pregnancy and early motherhood, the demands of the inner-biological and cultural-social dimensions may support each other but come into conflict with a woman's needs in the individual-psychological dimension.

LEARNING AND FACILITATING PRINCIPLES

Adults learn best when they are in good health, are well rested, and are not in distress.

The facilitator can be helpful to adult learners by being aware of the physical well-being of individual learners.

Adults learn best when their vision and hearing are in the best condition possible and when the learning environment can assist learners to compensate for any loss of sensory acuity.

The facilitator can adapt both the environment and learning resources to take vision and hearing problems into account.

Adult learning is not normally affected by changes in physical characteristics except in the cases of profound age-related changes and of rehabilitative learning, such as might follow severe illness or accident.

Any age-related physical changes in learning are difficult to detect; for example, auditory acuity may decline almost imperceptibly over a long period of time, and the adult may be unaware of his or her own hearing difficulties.

Adults do not learn productively under time constraints. They learn best when they can set their own pace for learning and when time pressures are kept to a minimum. For older adults, time pressures become increasingly counterproductive.

Facilitators should plan activities with flexible time limits and provide alternatives for learners who need more time to learn something.

Adults Accumulate Past Experiences and Prior Learning

Adults accumulate experience and prior learning over their lifetime; the older they become, the more experience and prior learning they bring to bear on current learning. The meanings developed from past experiences are part of the individual's personal model of reality. This model includes both meanings and values (constructs or concepts) that help to make sense of past experience, impute sense to current experience, and predict future experience. Life experiences are also used to develop skills and strategies (processes or procedures) for reflecting on, reconstructing, and organizing the past; acting, reacting, and interacting in the present; and anticipating the future. Each person's model of reality is dynamic rather than static, and is open to constant revision, expansion, and transformation as the result of further experience and learning.

Changing the Meaning of Experience

Our personal model of reality never incorporates all our experiences, but rather rests on selected experiences or generalizations about experiences. Many details of an experience remain obscured in the background while we select out some details to form a 'figure.' In gestalt psychology, a 'figure' is the central pattern of our recalled and generalized experiences. In comparison to the background or 'ground,' the figure is that part of the experience that is more vivid or has more affect or emotional attachments, is more complete in detail, has shape and is more thing-like, and is nearer to us in time, space, or relevance.

The part of experience not selected for the figure fades into the ground that accompanies the figure. The manner in which details are selected for inclusion in a figure contributes to the distortions or deletions within our personal model of reality.

The relationships between figure and ground are not fixed or immutable. When different individuals reflect on the same experience, some perceive structures (persons, events, or ideas) as figures; some perceive processes (learning, thinking, remembering) as figures; and some perceive both processes and structures as figures. However we make sense of experience, we need to expend energy if we wish to overcome the human tendency to conserve existing relationships rather than modifying old ones or developing new possibilities.

When helping students learn about figure-ground relationships – and coincidentally engage in critical reflection – I ask them to select a learning event or project from their past experience.

- Then I ask them to recall details from the figure through a series of questions: Who was involved? What happened? When and where did it happen? What was learned?
- Next, I ask them to recall details from the ground through a different series of questions: Who was not involved? What did not happen? When and where did it not happen? What was not learned? I encourage them to provide nonsensical, even irrational, answers to these questions.
- Then I ask them to move some of the details from the ground into the figure and to think through the consequences of this shift. For example, if you move a person who was not involved into the figure, what would happen to your understanding of the experience?

The resulting shift often allows students to understand their experience from a different point of view and to transform the meanings they use to make sense of it.

The Place of Experience in Learning

Some aspects of past experience have an important effect on learning. First, our personal model of reality is generally understood as consisting of several tightly interwoven components. Some of these components include our

- self-system including how we understand ourselves as actors or our self-concept, and the values we assign to ourselves or our self-esteem;
- professional or occupational knowledge (meanings, values, skills, and strategies);
- practical knowledge about daily living;
- cultural knowledge about how things work in our society; and
- our personal narrative or story that tells us who we are and records our biography.

We each invest a vast amount of emotional energy in the development of our personal model of reality, and we place ourselves at the core of the model, since we perceive reality from the centre of our own existence. When we enter into learning activities, we tend to use at least part of our energy to protect and defend our model and our self from potentially disconfirming experiences. If we lack self-confidence and feel as if some part of our model has been rejected or discounted by others, we may feel rejected or discounted as a person and become distressed.

Adults have more experience than children in the pragmatic realities of life, and have developed many ways of perceiving and understanding that experience. The adult's personal model of reality simultaneously defines, creates, and restricts perceptions and understanding of new experiences. In response to today's information explosion and accelerating change, an individual's model requires constant updating and revision at an ever-increasing rate. Toffler (1970) proposed the term 'half-life' to describe how quickly an adult's professional knowledge and skills need to be updated. For some professionals, such as computer programmers and information specialists, the half-life is uncomfortably short, perhaps six months or less; for other professionals, such as educators, the half-life is much longer. In the first group, the major learning need is keeping up with change; in the second group, the major learning need is preventing stagnation.

The Place of Past Experience in Learning

Past experience is an essential component in learning, both as a base for new learning and as an unavoidable potential obstacle. Past experiences structure the ways that an adult will approach new experiences, determine which information will be selected for further attention and how it will be interpreted, and determine which knowledge (meanings and values) and skills (strategies, tactics, and styles) will be employed in the learning process.

If these are found to be unsuitable, the learner will first search back through all previous experience for suitable knowledge and skills to apply indirectly. If nothing can be found, then the learner is faced with a dual challenge: first, to acknowledge the inadequacy of the knowledge or skills they already hold (thereby questioning their self-concept as a competent person); and second, to trust themselves to enter into learning that will result in an as-yet-unknown transformation of that self-concept. The first part of this challenge represents in some sense a failure of the existing self-concept, and the second represents risk of new failure.

There is a paradox for the adult. While the self-concept must undergo partial change in the process, that same self-concept must be relied on to manage the change. The learner may respond to such situations by becoming confused or angry, withdrawing to a more comfortable environment, or avoiding learning experiences altogether. More productively, the learner could adopt a questioning and reflective stance leading to a more profound understanding of self.

Past experiences always enter into adult learning unless the learning experience or content is wholly new to the learner. Adult learning focuses primarily on modifying, transforming, and reintegrating knowledge and skills, rather than on forming and accumulating them, as in childhood.

We tend to assume that the learning processes involved in transformations are different from those involved in formations. Very little can be found in the literature distinguishing between the two. Mezirow (1991, 2000), E.W. Taylor (2000), Clark (1993), Hart (1983), and Freire (1973) indicate that transformations require

- greater input of energy (the body invests considerable energy in maintaining established patterns, a conservative tendency that must first be overcome if these patterns are to be transformed);
- more time than formations;
- examination and critical reflection of established knowledge and skills at the level of direct attention before being altered;
- testing new behaviours in 'safe' situations as a means for reducing potential threat to the self; and

• awareness of details in both figure and ground and willingness to perceive relationships between the two.

Transformations are based on raising figure-ground relationships to attention and then reorganizing them on a new basis by bringing material in the
ground into the figure or moving material in the figure to the ground. This
process also contributes to an increasing awareness of distorted and
repressed realities and to correcting them (Clark, 1993; Denis & Richter,
1987; Weiler, 1988).

Using Past Experience in Learning

When we base learning principles on the notion that adults' past experiences form the basis of all learning, we may also be presupposing that adult
learners have already acquired all the knowledge and skills necessary for
current learning. Such assumptions are not tested often enough and may
prove erroneous.

For example, work by Piaget (as described in Hunt & Sullivan, 1974, pp.
131–8) indicates that, as a result of cognitive development, adult learners
will have already attained generalized and abstract strategies for thinking
(formal operational thinking). However, research shows that the average
adult is more likely to use concrete and specific strategies for thinking
(concrete operational thinking) (Arlin, 1986; Labouvie-Vief, 1992; Thibodeau, 1979). These results do not indicate whether the concrete stage of
thinking represents nonattainment of the abstract and generalized stage or
is a retreat from the formal stage of thinking in response to the conditions
of daily life.

If we proceed with learning activities assuming that all adult participants
have all the necessary knowledge and skills and we later discover some are
missing essential components, we are likely to perceive such learners as
incompetent, ignorant, stupid, stubborn, unmotivated, or even deviant
(Brim & Wheeler, 1966). Such perceptions would be rapidly communicated
to learners through our nonverbal behaviour, creating further distress for
them.

While past experience is an essential component in adult learning, using it
in relation to current learning presents a problem. Many adults cannot perceive connections between past experiences and current problems. Only
some parts of past experience may be relevant to the present context. The
facilitator may need to assist the learner to identify potentially relevant past
experiences and to actively seek connections with the current situation. I
find that when learners are asked to provide examples to illustrate certain
topics, they often tell stories that appear, on the surface, to have no connection to current learning. I usually ask them to clarify their example and

explicitly identify the connection. Some learners tell such stories without consciously being aware of these connections.

LEARNING AND FACILITATING PRINCIPLES

Past experience of adult learners must be acknowledged as an active component in learning and accepted as a valid representation of their experience. Past experience can be both an enhancement to new learning and an unavoidable obstacle.

Learning is facilitated when the learner's past experience is used by both learner and facilitator as a resource for learning in some activities.

Past experience accumulates with time; therefore its potential for helping or hindering the learning process increases with age.

Adults learn more productively when the learning content bears some perceived relationship to past experience, or when past experience can be applied directly to new situations.

Learning is facilitated when time and opportunities are provided to reflect on past experience, to find connections between past experience and new knowledge and skills, and to integrate these.

Past experience presents the adult learner with a paradox. In the learning experience, the knowledge (meanings and values) and skills (strategies, tactics, and styles) based on past experience and forming part of the present self-concept are being changed. These changes, in turn, may disconfirm or threaten the self-concept. At the same time, the self-concept must be a trusted agent in managing the learning process.

Learning is facilitated in learning environments that are free from threat and that provide support for personal change.

Adult learning focuses largely on transforming knowledge and skills derived from past experience. This process requires more energy and more time than learning based on formation of new knowledge. It also requires that past experience be brought into awareness, and that new behaviours be tested in safe and trusted environments.

Learning activities need to include opportunities for testing

> *new behaviours in relative safety, developing mutually trust-ing relationships, encouraging descriptive feedback, and reduc-ing fear of failure.*

All adults do not necessarily possess all the knowledge and skills required for new learning activities. Acquisition of the missing com-ponents must be regarded as an essential part of all learning activi-ties.

> *Learning is facilitated when learners' existing knowledge and skills are assessed to identify their strengths and weaknesses, and to determine if components essential to the learning con-text are missing.*

Adult learners may need considerable assistance in verbalizing and clarifying their current problems, identifying how learning activities could help in solving these problems, and specifying these activities in terms of learning objectives and directions.

> *Learning is facilitated when the learning activities provide opportunities to talk about and share experiences.*

Time Plays a Role in Adult Learning

The time perspective of some adult learners differs from that of children. A child tends to perceive time as including a present and an infinite future. As individuals move beyond young adulthood, they begin to perceive time as including an ever-increasing past, a fleeting and pressured present, and a finite future (Marshall, 1980; Neugarten & Datan, 1973). Children and young adults tend to measure time as 'time since birth'; adults past forty may begin to measure time as 'time until death' (Neugarten & Datan, 1973). This shift from an increasing span of time to a decreasing one has consequences for learning.

The ever-increasing past provides an ever-increasing model of reality that can both help and hinder learning. The larger and more enriched the model becomes, the greater its potential for helping or hindering. When existing knowledge conflicts sharply with what is to be learned, learners will need additional time to re-evaluate what they already know and to modify it slowly before reintegrating it back into their existing knowledge. Since life experiences accumulate over time, older learners may experience more con-flict than younger learners. Conflicts that cannot be resolved will be inte-grated into existing knowledge only very slowly, if at all. Knowledge for which the learner has no experiential base may be acquired without conflict but may not be easily understood or immediately applied.

The fleeting present involves many conflicting concerns, needs, drives, and problems. These conflicts become essential content to the learning process. Solutions to current problems, while often readily apparent to an observer, must come from within, be consistent with the individual's model of reality, and be implemented from the individual's own resources.

Solutions that are suggested by others and that do not 'fit' into an individual's model of reality are generally rejected. The pressures on an adult to resolve conflicts and solve problems quickly make the discovery of personally meaningful solutions more difficult to accomplish. The perceived finite future for middle-aged and older adults tends to create the illusion of a need to hurry, to change and learn quickly, and to get on with life. This illusion also grows out of our traditional (and erroneous) beliefs that learning and education are once-in-a-lifetime activities that will provide for all future contingencies, and learning is an activity distinct and separate from living and working (Kidd, 1973; McClusky, 1970; Thomas, 1991).

LEARNING AND FACILITATING PRINCIPLES

Adults tend to experience a need to learn quickly and get on with living. They are often reluctant to engage in learning activities or content that does not appear to have immediate and pragmatic application within their life.

> *Learning is facilitated when learners can assess their own learning needs and select their own learning goals and directions for change. If this is not possible, then learners should have a complete understanding of the objectives established by others, should be able to accept these, and should be willing to commit themselves to the selected direction for change.*

Adults Have an Established Sense of Self

Adults bring to the learning process an established sense of self and an inclination to protect this self from perceived threats that might arise in learning interactions. The ability of human beings to form abstract ideas allows them to think about themselves and how they appear to others. Our sense of self evolves out of our experience with objects and other persons and the kinds of interactions we have with them. In other words, we construct our 'self' out of our experience with the object world. The self is 'an internalized image, a composite representation, constructed by a selective and imagina-tive "remembering" of past encounters with significant [others in our world]' (Engler, 1986, p. 22).

We experience our self as having continuity and sameness across time and contexts, as being consistent in our interactions with others, and as being recognized by others on the basis of this continuity and consistency. Even when we develop and change in terms of our knowledge and behaviour or in our understanding of ourselves, we still experience our adult self as hav-ing an inner core that maintains some continuity with the self we knew in childhood and adolescence.

The self is a core construct of our personal model of reality. It comprises meanings from various elements of experience:

- physical elements contribute to the body-image;
- cognitive elements to the self-concept;
- emotional or affective elements to the self-esteem;
- social elements to the social self; and
- spiritual elements to the higher or ideal self.

Roby Kidd (1973) tells us that all new learning experiences are given meaning in terms of some relationship to the self, or 'are ignored because there is not a perceived relationship, or are denied organization or given a distorted meaning because the experience seems inconsistent with the struc-ture of the self [and threatens it]' (p. 130).

A child's self-concept is in the process of being formed, and so each new learning experience may vary the structure but not threaten it with fragmen-tation or disconfirmation. The adult's self-concept is already well-formed, and new learning experiences have the potential for fragmenting it or par-tially disconfirming it. Adults defend the 'self' against the threats inherent in learning activities until they perceive that the worst will not happen and that change in their self-concept can lead to positive results.

A search of the literature on adult learning and the self-concept provides the following ideas about the function of the self-concept and self-esteem in the learning activities of adults.

- The fate of the self is *the* central issue in healthy personality development and learning (Engler, 1986; Erikson, 1968; Kegan, 1982, 1994).
- Adults who value their own experience as a rich resource for further learning or whose experience is valued by others are better learners (Combs, 1974; Thibodeau, 1979).
- Adults are more concerned with whether they are changing in the direc-tion of their own idealized self-concept than with whether they are meet-ing objectives established by others (Huberman, 1974; Lam, 1976). Some

adult learners hold an idealized concept of themselves requiring that they act as independent learners and set their own goals for learning. If a facilitator insists that such individuals learn in relation to pre-established goals, they may see this requirement as threatening to their self-concept.

- Adults learn best when they are involved in developing learning objectives for themselves congruent with their current self-concept and ideal self (Tough, 1979). Many adult learners are quite willing to accept some learning goals that have been pre-established by the facilitator; but it helps to offer them the opportunity to set some goals for themselves.
- Adults with higher self-esteem and a more positive self-concept are more ready to accept change. There is a positive correlation between flexibility as a personal characteristic and self-esteem (Klopf, Bowman, & Joy, 1969).
- The self is affected by each new role taken on by the learner. Role learning provides the basis for most adult learning needs (Brim & Ryff, 1980; Kidd, 1973; Knowles, 1990).
- The most essential component of the self in relation to learning is self-seen-as-learner (McClusky, 1970). If adults think that learning and the adventure of change are as much a part of their lives as their work and family roles, they will be much more likely to enter into learning with positive and flexible attitudes. If adults think that learning is only for children or is associated with a nonresponsible status in society, they may not participate willingly in learning activities. The self-seen-as-learner role also appears to be an essential component in learning how to learn (Candy, 1990; Smith 1990).
- Role learning is carried out not through formal, logical, or sequential processes but through interpersonal interactions, modelling, and experimenting (Goslin, 1969). The role of learner can be learned most productively when adults observe and interact with others using such role behaviour in normal daily activities and where they have a safe environment in which to test it out (Brown, Collins, & Duguid (1989).
- Distress, disorientation, and personal crisis may follow an individual's perception that their self-concept has been disconfirmed or discounted by others or that their self-concept has lost meaning (Hanna, 1987; Mezirow & Marsick, 1978; M. Taylor, 1987).

Development of the Self

An unresolved issue related to 'the self' lies in our conception of how the self develops. We have already seen that the self emerges as a function of our interactions with others. Traditional developmental theories tend to see all personal development in terms of self-development, as a process of differentiating one's 'self' from a matrix of 'others' (Hunt, 1971). Levinson (1978), for example, talks about 'becoming one's own man.'

Jean Baker Miller (1991) questions why development should be seen as a series of transitions that lead to 'essential separations from others' resulting in 'an inner sense of separated individuation' (p. 1). Miller states that the ideal of a self-concept based on separation from others does not fit the life experiences of most women and questions whether such a process accurately reflects the life experiences of men. Ideas about individuation and separation, as derived from traditional human development models described by such authors as Jung (1964), Erikson, Erikson, and Kivnick (1986), Loevinger (1976), and Levinson (1976, 1996), dominate our collective view of the preconditions of mental health. These ideas are powerful because they have become prescriptions for what should happen and for what 'normal' development should be like. Those whose life experiences do not fit this traditional model may feel that their self-concept is inadequate and that their personal development has not been normal, and by extension that they are inadequate 'selves' and 'not-normal' as persons.

Ruthellen Josselson (1992) comments that relationship as a goal of developmental processes is not found in traditional developmental theories. She goes on to state that where 'the phenomena of interpersonal connection in human life are acknowledged at all, they serve merely as a backdrop for the more apparent dramas of [the autonomous] self' (p. 1).

Miller (1991) and Josselson (1992) propose an alternative conception of human development, one that encompasses the life experiences of both men and women. In their model of human development, the self is still conceived as developing in and through interactions with others, but the emphasis is placed on the qualities, not of one's separation from others, but of one's connections to others. Such development is promoted in interactions between the developing child and his or her caregivers, particularly in relation to the child's emotions. Miller goes on to say that the child responds to the emotions of others and the self-concept emerges not as 'a static and lone self being ministered to by another ... , but much more of a self inseparable from a dynamic interaction' (J.B. Miller, 1991, p. 14).

Miller argues that this process of development is present in children of both sexes, but gender-biased, culturally induced processes of socialization take over at a very early age. Most girls are encouraged to develop a self-concept based on attending to and responding to others and on thinking and learning interdependently. Most boys are encouraged to develop a self-concept based on standing alone, thinking and learning independently, and acting autonomously.

Kegan (1982, 1994) adopts a similar view of human development, but sees the lifelong process of development as moving through successive phases that alternate between an emphasis on the self-as-exclusive and autonomous and the self-as-inclusive and relational. Lyons (1988) assessed the self-concepts of both men and women. She reported that while many men and women use a combination of both relational and autonomous concepts to describe themselves, more men that women rely primarily on a perception of themselves as separate from others, and more women than men rely primarily on a perception of themselves as connected to others.

These differences in how we conceptualize self-development raise questions about adults' participation in learning activities. Persons defining themselves in mainly autonomous or separate terms may participate differently in learning activities than those defining themselves in mainly relational or connected terms. Baxter Magolda (1992) reports that although college men and women do not differ much in what they learn, they do differ in their preferences for how they carry out learning activities. Men more often than women learn more effectively in settings involving autonomy, mastery of the material, individual achievement, working with others to challenge one's own thinking, and focusing primarily on self-directed learning even when engaged in collaborative contexts. Women more often than men learn more effectively in settings involving relationships, connecting learning to one's own life experiences, understanding the experiences of others, and focusing on a collective or collaborative perspective even in individualized learning contexts. I will return to these differences in Chapter 8.

An individual's description of the self tends to be idiosyncratic. Adult learners share relatively few labels for their self-concepts. The literature, however, relies on descriptive labels derived from adult learning and personality theory. For example, few adult learners would describe themselves as a 'self-directed learner,' yet many use the behaviours associated with this label. They would be more likely to describe themselves as 'someone who figures things out for myself' – hardly a label that can be used for research purposes.

LEARNING AND FACILITATING PRINCIPLES

Adults enter learning activities with an organized and integrated set of descriptions and feelings about themselves that influence the learning process. The description is the self-concept; the feelings are the self-esteem.

> *Learning is facilitated when the self-concept and self-esteem of each learner are valued as they are presented by the learner.*

Adults with positive self-concept and high self-esteem are more responsive to learning and less threatened by learning environments. Adults with negative self-concept and low self-esteem are less likely to enter learning activities willingly and may feel threatened by such environments.

Adults are more concerned about changing in the direction of their own ideal self than about meeting standards and objectives set by others.

> *Facilitators working with adults need to know how they conceptualize adult learners as well as how adult learners conceptualize themselves. Where the two conceptualizations are incongruent, the facilitator should pay more attention to the learners' descriptions of themselves.*

Adults learn best in environments that provide support and safety for testing new behaviours.

Adults learn best in environments that provide opportunities both for developing interpersonal relationships with the facilitator and other learners, and for demonstrating their mastery and understanding of the content to be learned.

> *Facilitators need to be able to assist learners wishing to master the content and learn independently, as well as those preferring to discuss issues with others as a means for understanding their own experience and that of others. Both types of activities should be an integral part of all learning experiences.*

Self-Direction

Both self-directedness and relatedness to others contribute to learning. The idea of self-direction, as a characteristic of adult learners and as an approach to learning, is probably the most discussed and debated issue in adult education (Caffarella, 1993; Merriam, 2001). Because I cannot possibly cover the numerous variations on the theme of self-direction, I present only the highlights. For a more detailed and comprehensive discussion, I recommend Philip Candy's 1991 book *Self-Direction for Lifelong Learning*.

The term 'self-direction' is problematic because few writers, researchers, and educators take the time to provide a clear, functional definition. Candy (1991) points out that 'self-directed,' when applied to learning, can be either a goal of or a process used within learning activities; and when applied to the learner can be either a general personal characteristic (not related to learning) or a characteristic with specific meaning for the learning process.

Self-Direction as a Personal Characteristic

Since we are concerned in this section with the characteristics of learners, we will begin by considering how the term 'self-directed' is used to describe people in general. On the basis of a detailed review of the literature, Candy (1991, p. 125) states that a self-directed or autonomous person is able to invoke a coherent set of beliefs, values, and attitudes that views the self as autonomous and that serves as a basis for

- conceiving goals and plans;
- exercising freedom of choice;
- using rational and critical reflection;
- using will power to follow through;
- assessing plans and choices; and
- exercising self-restraint and self-discipline.

Candy goes on to describe self-direction as characterized by the will and capacity to carry through to completion any actions without having to depend on others for support or encouragement. This idea implies that autonomous persons are self-contained and do not need to respond to others. In fact, the person who is impervious to the opinions of others or uncaring about the effects self-directed choices have on others is as undesirable as one who relies too heavily on the approval of others. Self-direction is also characterized by doubt, which leads to reviewing and reconsidering the premises and logic underlying knowledge, plans, and choices to detect error.

Most adults do not escape the socializing influences of others in determining their set of beliefs, values, and attitudes. The characteristics that describe a self-directed person, therefore, represent an ideal set that few are able to invoke in all contexts. Self-direction should be understood as behaviour resulting as much from the interaction between the individual actor and the characteristics of other persons, groups, or institutions as from a personal trait (Pratt, 1988).

Self-direction can be understood in three ways:

1 as an innate disposition, trait, or characteristic one is born with;
2 as an acquired quality developing naturally with increasing age; and/or
3 as a learned characteristic.

Considering self-direction as an innate characteristic, we can talk about individuals who have a natural predisposition to doubt and to go their own way. If self-directedness is innate, then facilitators will have very little effect in helping individuals develop it. If self-directedness evolves as a natural aspect of human development, then facilitating activities should have little effect on encouraging such development. In both cases, therefore, the best a facilitator can do is to provide opportunities for self-directed persons to do their own thing.

However, if self-directedness is a learned characteristic, then it is amenable to the educative process. Presumably we could develop facilitating activities to encourage and support the development of self-directed characteristics. It is a mistake, however, to believe that simply providing certain freedoms in the instructional setting will inevitably lead to the exercise of the learners' personal autonomy. As with all behaviours, the exercise of self-direction is affected as much by personal characteristics of the individual as by characteristics of the environment.

Self-Direction as a Specific Characteristic of Adult Learners

Self-direction as a specific characteristic of adult learners adds some new dimensions to the discussion. When Candy (1991) reviewed the literature on the skills and competencies required for self-direction in learning, he described the ideal self-directed learner as someone capable of exercising control over the tasks to be mastered in the learning process, and of working independently, by

- being methodical and disciplined, logical and analytical;
- being reflective and self-aware;
- demonstrating curiosity, openness, and flexibility;
- being interdependent and interpersonally competent, as well as independent and self-sufficient;
- being persistent and responsible, as well as venturesome and creative;
- showing confidence and having a positive self-concept; and
- having knowledge about, and skill in, learning generally (i.e., knowing how to learn), especially skill in planning and assessing learning.

This list certainly describes an ideal learner, someone who may exist only in the hearts and minds of adult educators. Lists of this type have been criticized for at least four reasons.

First, the list represents the characteristics that are expected of able-bodied, white, middle-to-upper-class males in Euro-American societies (Walker, 1984). Lists of competencies are rarely developed on the basis of the learners being female, members of racial and cultural minorities, persons with different abilities, or members of the working class or the poor (Caffarella, 1993; Flannery, 1994; Shore, 1997). A few of the many questions that could be asked about this list are:

- What does being methodical and self-disciplined have to do with being self-directed as a learner?
- Could a self-directed learner be analogical and holistic rather than logical and analytical?

- Is it possible that self-direction in learning is a consequence of success in learning, rather than a required, pre-existing competency?
- Is learning how to learn the same for those who have sensory or physical disabilities as it is for persons who are able-bodied?
- Does the word 'responsible' mean the same to men and women?

Second, the manner in which these competencies are used, and to what end, differs greatly depending on the philosophical orientation one adopts as an educator. This list seems to fit best with the humanist orientation described in Chapter 1. Those who espouse the vocational orientation might not wish to encourage curiosity, openness, flexibility, venturesomeness, or creativity; nor would they be likely to encourage learners to plan and assess their own learning. Those who espouse the liberatory orientation are unlikely to encourage independence, since it is through interdependence that learners increase their awareness of the conditions that constrain them and through interdependence that groups can plan and implement social change.

Third, adult educators often fail to take into account situational differences (Pratt, 1988). Individuals may be very self-directed in learning activities related to their own work but very dependent in learning activities related to knowledge or skills lying outside their expertise. Among the learner characteristics that will affect how individuals behave are not only their self-directedness but also their level of expertise and general familiarity with the knowledge and skills to be learned (Candy, 1991).

Fourth, the self-directed competencies on the list are not easily measurable or assessable. Attempts have been made to develop a means for assessing individuals in terms of self-directedness. The two most frequently used are the Self-Directed Learning Readiness Scale (SDLRS) (Guglielmino, 1977) and Oddi's Continuing Learning Inventory (OCLI) (Oddi, 1986). Both tests have been used in research studies, and both have a strong following among adult educators. A major concern about the tests is that their supporters claim them to be context free and culturally unbiased (Candy, 1991). However, both tests appear to measure self-directedness in school- and book-oriented contexts, and as a result, may be inappropriate for assessing learners in informal contexts. A learner may be self-directed in one context but paralysed in another. Learners from a non-Euro-American culture may have no experience with the idea that they have a choice in what or how things are learned.

A related problem is that it is unclear what a low score means, particularly on the SDLRS. The SDLRS assesses the degree to which individuals perceive themselves as possessing eight competencies usually associated with self-directed learning. Bonham (1991) reports that a low SDLRS score means an antipathy to all modes of learning rather than a preference to have others direct learning activities. This implies that a high score on the SDLRS may indicate a positive attitude towards learning in general, rather than a positive attitude towards learning described as self-directed.

The Development of Self-Directedness in Learning

Finally, we should consider how self-directedness in learning develops. We do know that simply placing adult learners in a context with few constraints and telling them to be self-directed is an inadequate (some would even say unethical and incompetent) way to facilitate the development of self-directedness. Within the literature on self-directed learners, there is some speculation about how self-direction as a characteristic develops. Two underlying assumptions of such research are that an individual can have more or less of the characteristic (i.e., self-direction is quantifiable) and that an individual acquires more of the necessary components of the characteristic over time (Knowles, 1990). Delahaye, Limerick, and Hearn (1994) – as well as Grow (1991), Smith (1989), Pratt (1988), and Kasworm (1983) – view self-direction as situation specific and describe changes in self-directedness using a modified version of situational leadership concepts (Hersey & Blanchard, 1982). The general tenor of their ideas is that adults change in their need for direction, support, and structure over any learning episode. Most begin with a high need for structure and direction and a low need for support. Over time the need for support increases quickly, then decreases towards the end of the learning activities, while the need for direction and structure decreases gradually over time.

While self-direction is rarely described as a role, many writers imply that all adults value the 'role of self-directed learner.' This belief has become part of the mythology of adult education and, as a myth, blinds us to the fact that some adults cannot, will not, or do not perform as self-directed learners. Believing in such a myth may also prevent critical examination of its inherent assumptions. If we assume that all persons reach adulthood valuing the role of self-directed learner, then the development of the necessary knowledge, skills, and motives to perform the role ought to be relatively easy to accomplish through specially designed activities. Grow (1991), for example, describes four stages in the development of self-directed learners: the individual moves from using dependent behaviours to being interested in becoming self-directed, then to being involved in being self-directed, and finally to becoming fully self-directed as a learner. In the process the learner develops competencies in gathering data, organizing and retrieving information, thinking critically, setting goals, and assessing progress. The development process can be nurtured through facilitating methods that call for the use of these competencies in collaborative learning, discovery learning, contract-based learning, individualized instruction, learner-controlled instruction, problem-based learning, and independent study.

LEARNING AND FACILITATING PRINCIPLES

Self-direction as a personality characteristic or trait involves such activities as conceiving goals and plans; exercising freedom of choice; using critical reflection; using will power to follow through; assessing plans, choices, and outcomes; exercising self-discipline; and carrying out these activities without having to depend on others for encouragement and reassurance.

Self-direction in learning is facilitated when opportunities are provided in which learners can use these activities.

Self-directed plans, choices, and assessments are strongly affected by the socializing influences of other persons.

Self-direction may be an innate disposition but it can also be learned.

Self-direction in learning is facilitated when the learner is assisted to learn how to learn.

The exercise of self-direction is situation specific; it can be constrained or enhanced by the learner's environment.

Self-direction in learning is facilitated when the environment is free from any constraints that might impede self-directedness.

As a specific characteristic of learners, self-direction requires skills and behaviours for engaging in learning, cognitive capabilities and competencies, and appropriate affect/value orientations about the nature of the inquiry process and beliefs about how knowledge is generated.

The development of self-direction in learning is facilitated when the learning program includes opportunities for direct instruction in the competencies required, and for involvement in activities calling for the use of these competencies.

Matching Learner Characteristics to Facilitating Behaviours

In an extensive review of the theoretical models that match learner and facilitator characteristics, Hunt and Sullivan (1974) state that 'the person occupies the central role in any psychological theory, and educational planning should begin with the [learner] rather than with teaching methods' (p. 31). They advocate the use of the B-P-E model, first proposed by Lewin (1936), to develop theoretical matches. In the learning-facilitating context, the *P* stands for 'Person' (the learner) and can include any characteristic of a learner that affects learning. The *B* stands for 'Behaviour' and can include any outcome (the knowledge, meanings, values, skills, attitudes that are learned; how the learner responds to the learning process; and so on) that occurs during or after the learning-facilitating interaction. The *E* stands for 'Environment' and can include any factor within the learning situation or context that might affect learning, including, for example, facilitator behaviours, quality of the physical environment, nature of the learning resources, and technologies. The B-P-E model is written as: $B \rightarrow f(P, E)$ and is read as: Behaviour is a function of the interaction between the Person and the Environment. This is not a mathematical formula that can be tested through research; nor is it a theory. The model postulates a relationship among three major components of learning-facilitating interactions. It does not specify that the characteristics of a learner or a facilitator *cause* certain behaviours, only that there is an as-yet-undetermined relationship among Person, Behaviour, and Environment.

Hunt and Sullivan (1974) distinguish between two kinds of individual differences that can be matched by facilitator behaviours:

1 contemporaneous characteristics or traits that are relatively stable over time and/or consistent across situations; and
2 developmental characteristics that change over time and/or in response to the perceived environment.

We need to think flexibly about characteristics in terms of this distinction. For example, if on the basis of initial responses in a learning context, we describe an adult learner as using dependent behaviours, we may come to think of that behaviour as a fixed trait. We might then treat such learners as dependent persons and not see that their behaviours change as their anxiety goes down or as they gain a sense of personal control in the learning context. If we continue to treat such learners as dependent, they may come to resent such treatment, or perceive themselves as constrained from developing independent behaviours because our facilitating denies them the opportunity to do so. For example, we might give them help with an answer if they look puzzled or complete a sentence if they get stuck on a word, instead of giving them time to work it out for themselves.

A major difficulty in conceptualizing adult learner characteristics is that the concepts have a tendency to become fixed labels. Evidence of the learner's behaviour contradicting such labels may be discounted or denied, a serious disservice to adults. Not much information is available regarding how characteristics change over time in response to developmental changes in the learner or to changes in the environment. We need to know more about the environmental characteristics or facilitator behaviours that are most likely to help the individual develop increasing independence or inter-dependence.

The B-P-E model can be used to consider how the characteristics of learners interact with the characteristics of learning environments. The outcomes of such interactions could yield a series of facilitating principles.

Developing a Matching Model

To develop a matching model, the concepts used to describe Person, Behaviour, and Environment must bear some relationship to each other. Candy (1987) describes research in which learners wanting more direction and those wanting more permissiveness were randomly assigned to facilitators who provided either a more structured environment or more freedom. Figure 2.2, Assessment of Facilitators in a Matching Model, outlines this match, indicating the outcomes or behaviours in terms of how the learners assessed the facilitators.

The B-P-E model predicted that a positive match would occur between the want-more-direction learners and the structure-providing facilitator and between the want-more-permissiveness learners and the freedom-providing facilitator. Mismatches would occur between the want-more-direction learners and the freedom-providing facilitator and between the want-more-permissiveness learners and the structure-providing facilitator. In Candy's research, the learners' assessment of the facilitators supported the matching model. The most dissatisfied learners were those who wanted more direction but were mismatched with the freedom-providing facilitator (Candy, 1987).

Such results indicate that adult learners are not homogeneous and vary widely on any given characteristic. Most learning groups include individuals representing different aspects of any given characteristic. The normal facilitating behaviours of any facilitator will match some but rarely all adult learners in a group setting. Facilitators can approach this problem by learning a variety of facilitating behaviours that will match different characteristics. These can be used differentially with individual learners or to add variety when working with groups of learners. A facilitator who tries to match all the behaviours of all the learners in a learning group at the same time is bound to fail or burn out in the attempt.

The idea of matching facilitating characteristics to learner characteristics becomes more complicated when considering developmental characteristics. Hunt and Sullivan (1974) discuss different matches one might develop

Figure 2.2
Assessment of Facilitators in a Matching Model

P = Person Characteristics	E = Environmental Characteristics	
	Facilitator Provides Structure	Facilitator Provides Freedom (i.e., little or no structure)
	Matched	Mismatched
Learner Wants More Direction	Facilitator assessed in positive terms	Facilitators assessed as 'never lectured, poorly prepared, couldn't answer questions in straightforward manner'
	Mismatched	Matched
Learner Wants More Permissiveness	Facilitators assessed as 'lectured too much, discouraged viewpoints other than own'	Facilitator assessed in positive terms

Source: Adapted from: P.C. Candy (1987).

when considering the developmental characteristic of cognitive complexity. A 'comfort' match would provide facilitating behaviours at a level of cognitive complexity exactly matching the learner's current level of cognitive complexity; a 'developmental' match would provide facilitating behaviours at a level of cognitive complexity slightly higher than the learner's current level; and mismatches would occur if the facilitating behaviours were either below or much higher in complexity than the learner's current level. For example, learners who think in conceptual categories that have only a minimal connection to other categories (dualistic thinking) need a well-structured environment with clear rules as a comfort match and an environment with more flexible rules and less structure for a developmental match. Such a model bears similarities to the situational leadership model proposed by Hersey and Blanchard (1982).

Take time to consider the learner characteristics described in this book in terms of how each might be understood as a range of learner behaviours. Consider whether the characteristic is developmental in nature or a fixed trait, and what facilitating behaviours would match or mismatch the variations within the characteristic. You may want to develop a list of facilitator behaviours and skills to learn in becoming a more effective adult educator.

3 Cycles in Learning

Basic Learning Cycle

There are many ways to describe the overall learning process. I have combined the ideas of several writers – including Boud, Keough, and Walker
(1985), Jarvis (1987), Kolb (1984), and M. Taylor (1987) – with my own experience to develop Figure 3.1, The Basic Learning Cycle. This figure describes
learning as a cyclical process in which five basic phases are repeated in suc-
cession. The knowledge, skills, and values learned in one cycle are recycled
and revised through subsequent cycles. In these five phases, the learner

- participates in experiences and activities resulting in the intake of coded
  and uncoded information from internal and external sources as input to
  learning;
- makes sense of experience by giving it meaning and value, or affect,
  through using pattern-recognition and meaning-making cognitive and
  affective processes;
- uses meanings and values in problem-solving and decision-making processes to make choices and develop plans for acting to achieve those
  choices;
- implements action plans; and
- receives feedback from the responses of others and from observing one's
  own behaviour.

Feedback becomes new information in the next cycle of learning or precipitates new experiences and activities.

I have attempted to make the figure self-explanatory, but some additional
comments may help. The numbers used for the following points refer to the
numbers found on Figure 3.1.

Figure 3.1
The Basic Learning Cycle

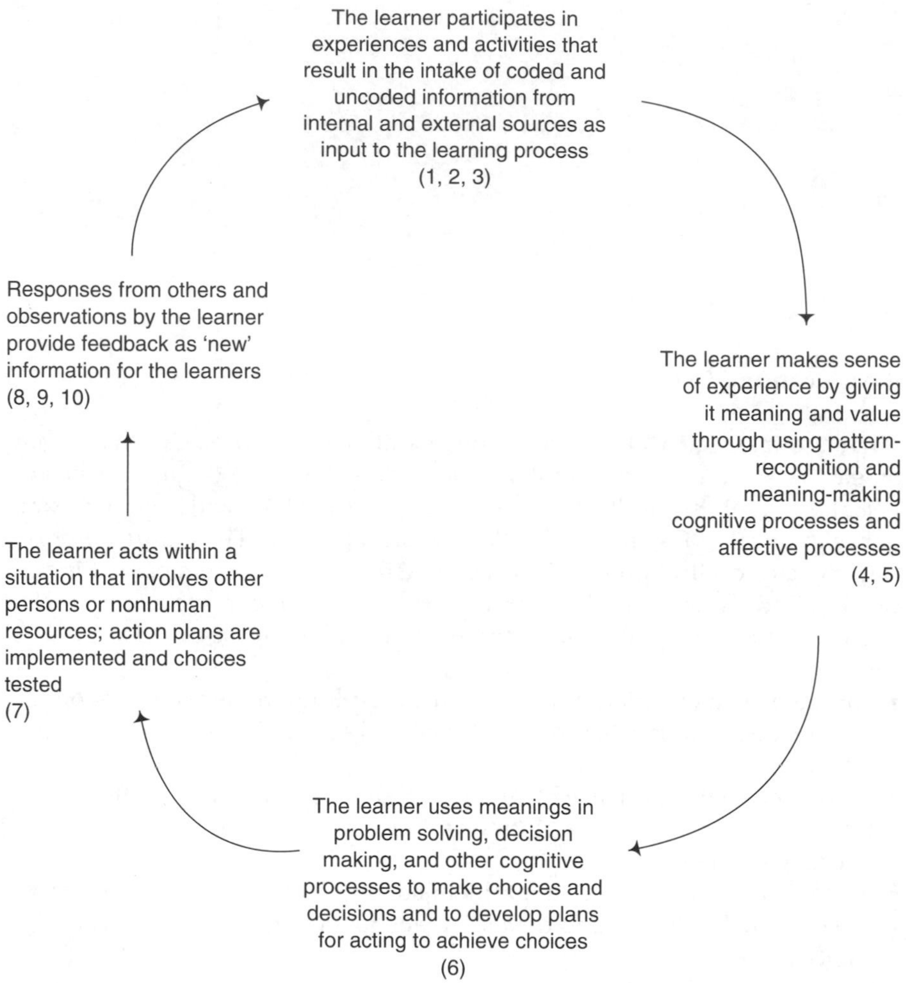

The learner participates in
experiences and activities that
result in the intake of coded and
uncoded information from
internal and external sources as
input to the learning process
(1, 2, 3)

Responses from others and
observations by the learner
provide feedback as 'new'
information for the learners
(8, 9, 10)

The learner makes sense
of experience by giving
it meaning and value
through using pattern-
recognition and
meaning-making
cognitive processes and
affective processes
(4, 5)

The learner acts within a
situation that involves other
persons or nonhuman
resources; action plans are
implemented and choices
tested
(7)

The learner uses meanings in
problem solving, decision
making, and other cognitive
processes to make choices and
decisions and to develop plans
for acting to achieve choices
(6)

1 Learning always occurs within a specific context that contributes, both
  directly and indirectly, to whatever is learned. The context is difficult to
  represent in a figure; think of this book as the context for this figure, a context affected by the assumptions presented in Chapters 1 and 2. Learning
  in context is sometimes referred to as 'situated learning' (Brown, Collins,
  & Duguid, 1989).
2 The richness and accuracy of the information taken in through experiences and activities will be limited by the information available within the
  learning context, the acuity of learners' sensory receptors, learners' focus

of attention, and their prior expectations about the information, experiences, and activities. In turn, these factors are affected by such variables as age-related changes, physical health, cognitive style, previous experience and existing knowledge, skills, and values.

3 The intake of information is controlled by the learner. What the learner takes into the brain as information is rarely an exact replica of the information presented in learning materials. Each learner modifies incoming information according to already existing meanings and ideas in the learner's model of reality. For example, learners with math phobia perceive any problem presented in mathematical terms as impossible to solve – before they have tried to solve it – even if it is a problem they are quite capable of solving in everyday contexts.

4 The meanings and values used to make sense of incoming information or new experiences are drawn from the meanings and values currently existing within the learner's model of reality. If no meanings or values are found in memory that can be applied to the incoming information, then the learner will need to create new ones or modify existing ones. Learning, therefore, is much affected by memory and by the personal model of reality held there.

5 Cognitive processes occur at varying levels and states of consciousness (Boucouvalas, 1993). Levels of consciousness are defined by brain-wave frequencies and indicate the extent to which a person's attention is focused internally or externally. Levels range from high frequencies associated with agitation and distress (the *gamma* level) to low frequencies associated with deep sleep or coma (the *theta* and *delta* levels). Most learning occurs at the *beta* level, or full consciousness and direct, externally focused attention; but much learning also occurs at the *alpha* level, or muted consciousness and indirect, internally focused attention.

From an observer's perspective, learning goes on inside the individual and can be inferred from changes in observable behaviour such as verbal responses or changes in skilled responses. From a learner's perspective, learning at the beta level is indicated through self-awareness and self-observation. For example, when I am learning to use a new computer program, I am fully alert and attending to what is going on around me. I know I am learning through being aware of what is going on inside my mind.

Learning that occurs at the alpha level is initially out-of-consciousness, but I can infer that I am learning from changes in my behaviour, and I can bring this learning to awareness through introspection. For example, I have been trying to re-learn how to walk downstairs following knee replacement surgery. During eight weeks of intense physiotherapy, I couldn't get my knees to do what they were supposed to do. The harder I tried, the more painful my knees became. In the meantime, I became a regular participant in an aquacize program. The instructor reminded me quietly each session to not use my knees too strenuously. And after eight months of gentle exercise, I discovered my knees had learned – all by themselves seemingly – to walk downstairs without causing pain.

6 Learning proceeds more effectively if the learners can verbally describe their internal learning processes. Externalizing cognitive processes usually carried out internally helps bring such processes to a level of awareness that encourages learners to correct their own learning. This procedure, known as 'cognitive apprenticeship' (Collins, Brown, & Newman, 1989), involves, first, an expert doing an activity (problem solving) and verbally externalizing the expert cognitive processes he or she is using; then learners trying a similar activity while externalizing the novice processes they are using, and following these attempts with a discussion of the differences between the expert and the novice processes. This alternation of expert and novice activities is repeated until the learners begin to recognize their own errors and to correct their cognitive processes before acting on them.

7 A decision to act may result in behaviour as fleeting as a shift in the focus of the eyes or as complex as a decision to change one's occupation. Fleeting and simple decisions occur too rapidly to rise to awareness. Complex decisions are more likely to be made at levels of consciousness involving awareness and direct attention, although influenced by lower levels, and may take longer to make as well as to implement.

8 Useful feedback tells learners about the results of their activities in comparison to expected outcomes. Feedback is a function of information and is subject to the same distortions as the original information. It can be more effective when it is provided from an external source, such as a trusted other. Information from feedback provides the learner with a sense of success or failure.

9 Feedback becomes reinforcement for the learning particularly if learners value their own performance or value the feedback they receive from others. Reinforcement, in turn, can provide the learner with a feeling of having been rewarded (if the feedback is what the learner expected or is willing to accept) or of having been punished (if the feedback is not what the learner expected or is willing to accept).

10 Immediate feedback may be viewed by the learner as part of the learning cycle, but delayed feedback may be perceived as not being associated with the learning cycle. When feedback and reinforcement are immediate, their value to the learner is enhanced.

Kolb's Learning Cycle

David Kolb (1984) proposed a cycle to describe how we learn from experi-

Figure 3.2
Kolb's Experiential Learning Cycle

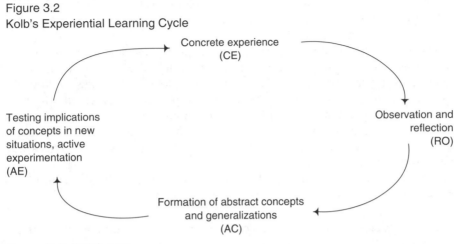

Source: Kolb (1984), p. 21.

ence (see Figure 3.2, Kolb's Experiential Learning Cycle). The cycle is similar
to the one shown in Figure 3.1 but is based on four phases rather than five.
The cycle begins when the learner is involved in a specific experience (*Concrete Experience* or *CE*). The learner reflects on this experience from different
points of view and gives it meaning (*Reflective Observation*, or *RO*). The
learner then integrates the meanings from this experience with those from
other personal experiences to develop explanations that become part of the
personal model of reality, or combines the meanings with explanations and
theories proposed by others; and draws conclusions (*Abstract Conceptualization*, or *AC*). These conclusions are used to guide decision making and planning of related actions that are then implemented (*Active Experimentation*, or
AE), leading to new concrete experiences.

Concrete experiences occur in our daily activities in the family, workplace,
and community. They can also be activities deliberately structured to illustrate a particular issue or to ensure that learners have a specific type of experience to draw on in subsequent activities. In addition, they can provide
opportunities for learners to recall and share a personal experience that has
occurred to them outside of the learning environment. A concrete experience is most effective when followed by an activity in which the learners
reflect on that experience.

Reflective activities should help learners deconstruct their experience by
differentiating various components of the experience and developing meanings for each. For example, in my courses on teaching, I arrange for learners
to experience different methods – case studies, role plays, simulations,
debates, metaphors, and so on. After each, we discuss the experiences in

relation to their personal learning and teaching styles, as well as the perceived effectiveness of each method, its strengths and weaknesses, and its possible use in other contexts.

The meanings learners assign to their experiences can be related to, or integrated with, existing meanings in their model of reality to expand their overall understanding of the experience and to develop new or revised meanings. These meanings can range from highly specific, contextually limited ideas to highly abstract, widely generalizable concepts. Kolb (1984) tells us that the emergence of ideas and concepts cannot be considered to be the outcome of the learning process until they are tested in new experiences and new contexts.

Active experimentation, therefore, involves actively testing out ideas or putting plans into action. Such activities might include:

- sharing ideas so that others can comment on them through oral or written feedback;
- actively testing a concept through hypothesizing and research;
- implementing a plan of action to see how it works;
- trying something new or really different that has an element of risk to it;
- transferring ideas found useful in one setting or context to new settings or contexts.

Testing or experimenting activities are carried out most easily in 'safe' environments in which mistakes are not a reason to feel embarrassed or unsuccessful.

The consequences of any active experiment or testing become 'feedback' that provides new information and can begin a new cycle of learning. Feedback can be provided only after the learner has acted overtly. When feedback is immediate, the learner is better able to connect consequences to actions. When feedback is delayed, the learner may not be able to make clear connections between the consequences and the actions. The farther apart the action and the consequences are in time, the less likely it is that the feedback will contribute to satisfaction and success or to correcting ideas or actions.

The most private (internal) part of the learning cycle occurs between RO and AC (lower right-hand segment). During this part, the facilitator is effectively shut out from what the learners are thinking unless they are encouraged to think out loud. The facilitator can be most helpful if the learner can verbalize what is occurring internally. The most public (external) part of the learning cycle occurs between AE and CE (upper left-hand segment). During this part, the facilitator can see what the learner is doing and can provide immediate feedback.

Variations on Kolb's Learning Cycle

Kolb (1984) describes the learning cycle as proceeding in one direction only. Some learners do not make full use of all four of the learning phases. Abbey, Hunt, and Weiser (1985, p. 485) describe those who are able to make effective use of all learning phases as balanced. They also describe four types of 'unbalanced' learners:

1 Those who use abstract conceptualization ineffectively, or bypass it entirely by moving directly from reflective observation to active experimentation, are called 'northerners' (because they bypass the 'south pole' of the model). They may have trouble conceptualizing or making meaning from their experiences, and their reflections tend to remain unconsolidated. Such learners sometimes worry about 'carving ideas into stones.' A facilitator needs to help them develop generalized ideas about their experiences that could be tested or applied in new situations.
2 Those who use active experimentation ineffectively, or bypass it entirely by moving directly from abstract conceptualization to concrete experience, are called 'easterners.' They have trouble putting plans into action and spend much time buried in thought. Such learners sometimes worry about acting too quickly. A facilitator needs to help them rejuvenate their ideas through experimentation or revise them through feedback.
3 Those who use concrete experience ineffectively, or bypass it entirely by moving directly from active experimentation to reflective observation, are called 'southerners.' They may reflect on the mechanics of their actions without benefit of emotional feedback, resulting in mechanical and sterile revisions of knowledge. Such learners do not want to deal with the potential disconfirmation of concrete experiences. A facilitator needs to help them recognize their feelings and integrate these feelings with their thinking.
4 Those who use reflective observation ineffectively, or bypass it entirely by moving directly from concrete experience to abstract conceptualization, are called 'westerners.' They are likely to develop unclear conceptual frameworks because their ideas remain unarticulated through reflection. Such learners tend to be intolerant of inaction. A facilitator needs to help them pause in the learning process long enough to reflect on their experiences.

Abbey, Hunt, and Weiser (1985) also describe learners who make full use of only two of the four learning phases. They describe these learners as 'stuck' and as persons who are likely to enter counselling or psychotherapy sessions. Such learners may move back and forth between two phases so quickly that their learning appears to violate the unidirectional nature of the cycle. However, such truncated learning can also be understood as moving in the direction predicted by the model but as bringing the learner too quickly through two skipped or abbreviated phases. The authors also speculate that a few maladaptive learners may be stuck in one phase of learning.

More Variations on Kolb's Learning Cycle

Over the years since I first encountered Kolb's model, I have found myself doodling with it in an attempt to understand the learning that occurs in different contexts. For the sake of brevity, I will discuss only two of these variations.

In my first variation, I considered how the experiential model could be used to describe and understand the learning cycle that occurs in traditional classrooms. I began with my own experience and used the model to describe how I respond to lectures or assigned readings.

You can see from Figure 3.3, Kolb's Model Modified – Version 1, that the cycle I developed is similar to Kolb's model in the Concrete Experience, Reflective Observation, and Abstract Conceptualization phases. Lectures and

Figure 3.3
Kolb's Model Modified: Version 1

Concrete Experience (CE)
Listening to a lecture
Reading paper/text

Reflective Observation (RO)
Thinking about the ideas described in the lecture/text, whether I agree with them, where they fit with other ideas, discussing the ideas with others

Abstract Conceptualization (AC)
On my own, inventing new ways to understand the ideas, doodling with any models, developing new or modified meanings, concepts, and ideas, finding new words for modified meanings

Active Experimentation
Thinking about sharing my half-baked ideas with others at class sessions and about asking questions to clarify my understanding about possible feedback

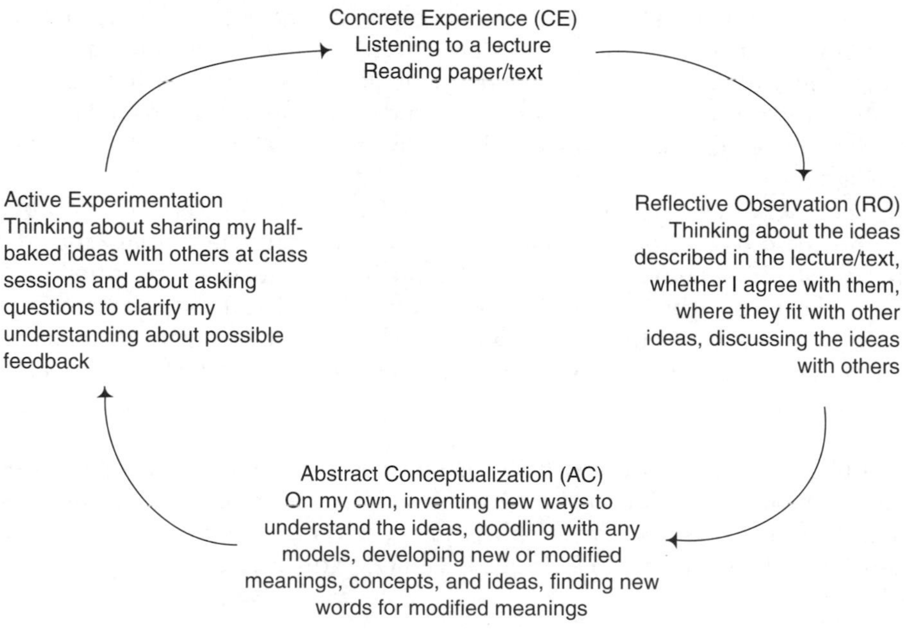

readings do not lend themselves immediately to active experimentation; and my learning style, like that of the easterners in Abbey, Hunt, and Weiser's (1985) article, includes a preference for short-circuiting the Active Experimentation phase. I spend too much time thinking about how others might respond to my half-baked ideas and not enough time trying them out through sharing them. Thinking about doing something is neither active nor experimental. As a result, I rarely receive corrective feedback about my ideas.

When I worked up the courage to share this variation with others, some agreed with it, but most pointed out that I had placed a lecture, viewed by many as an abstract conceptual activity, under the heading of Concrete Experience. They also pointed out that I had included other learners in activities in which they would not have included them. I had several reactions to this feedback.

Perhaps the first phrase could be described as 'Experience' (rather than 'Concrete Experience') and viewed as varying from concrete to abstract. In an 'abstract experience,' a learner might be receiving knowledge from others through a lecture or reading. The RO phase in the cycle could then be understood as combining the received knowledge with subjective knowledge (my personal model of reality). The AC phase could involve using this combined knowledge to either develop new knowledge or modify existing knowledge that would then be shared in the AE phase. I thought this version of Kolb's model might be useful in describing the received, subjective, and constructed ways of knowing proposed by Belenky et al. (1986). Received knowing describes knowledge we receive from others – experts, authorities, parents. Such knowledge is often used without being corrected through personal experience. Subjective knowing describes knowledge we create based on our own experiences and often use without correcting it through comparing it to the knowledge espoused by others. Constructed knowing describes knowledge that involves the integration of received and subjective knowledge. We will encounter these 'ways of knowing' again in Chapter 8.

In trying to define an experience as concrete or abstract, however, I found very little agreement among my colleagues. I came to the conclusion that an experience is 'concrete' for me when I already know something about the content and feel comfortable in the context, but 'abstract' when I know little about the content and feel uncomfortable in the context. In other words, as my distress level goes up, my perception of the experience becomes more abstract. I think this is because I can distance myself from my emotions in an abstract experience but cannot in a concrete experience; and the presence of strong emotions makes the experience more concrete.

The feedback about how I included others reminded me that Kolb's model does not address the issue of where and how others are included in the learning cycle. This concern was raised by Lanie Melamed and Irene Devine (1988) in a report on women's reactions to Kolb's model, but my way

Figure 3.4
Kolb's Model Modified: Version 2

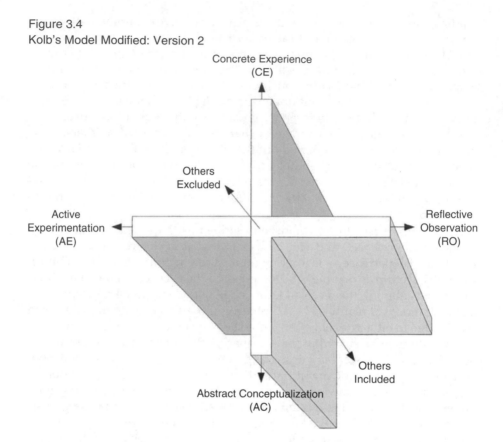

of including others did not correspond to the concerns raised by these writers. I concluded that an interpersonal dimension could become a third dimension in Kolb's model. More than ever, I wanted to create a pop-up model of the learning cycle, but have had to settle for the 'three-dimensional' drawing in Figure 3.4, Kolb's Model Modified – Version 2.

I deliberately include others only in the Reflective Observation phase. In the other phases I accept the presence of others but would prefer to work alone. These personal preferences do not correspond to those of other learners. I have concluded, therefore, that *individual learners have personal preferences for social interaction that vary for each phase of the learning cycle* and that these preferences differ among adult learners. In Figure 3.4, you have to imagine that the learning cycle is still cyclical but undulates up and down in relation to interpersonal preferences.

You can see that my doodling takes my thinking about the learning cycle off in a variety of directions. I would encourage you to doodle your own way to a fuller understanding of Kolb's model.

LEARNING AND FACILITATING PRINCIPLES

Learning is a cyclical process, a sequence of activities. Under normal circumstances, the activities proceed in one direction. The learning process may involve periodic oscillating between adjacent phases – returning to the concrete experience during reflection, returning to readings or reflections while developing abstract ideas, returning to ideas while planning and executing tests of ideas, returning to actions through feedback. However, defying the general direction of the activities tends to reduce the productivity of experiential learning.

> *An effective facilitator plans activities that support each phase of the learning cycle and uses these activities in the same order as suggested by the learning cycle.*

Feedback becomes input to a new cycle of learning. It contributes to feelings of satisfaction and success when it closely follows actions.

> *Avoid arranging the facilitating activities so that active experimentation activities come at the end of a learning session when there is no time for feedback or debriefing. Always complete any active experimentation activities with plenty of time to give feedback to the learners – cut the AE activity short if necessary.*
>
> *Avoid sending learners away from a learning session feeling anxious or threatened or angry, particularly if the feedback is likely to be negative. Between one session and the next, either the learners will forget what happened and any subsequent feedback will be useless, or their negative feelings will escalate, bringing conflict and dissatisfied learners to the beginning of the next session.*

Facilitators also go through a learning cycle in learning how to respond to learners. The facilitator's learning cycle is fuelled by feedback from the learners.

> *Give yourself time to reflect on how you are responding to learners. Don't judge your responses until you have had time to reflect on them and develop alternative plans for the future.*

Taylor's Learning Cycle

Another four-phase model of the learning process has been proposed by Marilyn Taylor (1979, 1987) and is shown in Figure 3.5, Taylor's Model of the Learning Cycle: Critical Points in the Inquiry Sequence. Taylor's model focuses on the learning cycle when it is self-directed (i.e., self-managed) and involves a personal concern. While Taylor does not claim that the model is generalizable to all adult populations, the experience of many adult educators suggests that the model is useful, particularly in programs that use a humanistic approach to teaching and learning. Her model encompasses four phases of learning and four transitions (1987, 183–91).

The Disorientation Phase

Taylor's learning cycle begins with a *disconfirming event* or destabilizing experience. This transition may occur because the individual encounters change and experiences its consequences as involving a major discrepancy between expectations and reality. Some learners deliberately seek out change, but more often changes occur that are not anticipated. For example, a young mother may go out to work full-time, thus bringing change into her life and that of her family. While she is adapting to these changes, her children may become difficult to handle because they don't want their mother away from home. The first set of changes that have been deliberately sought may not result in a disconfirming experience, but the second set might. Other possibilities include:

- other persons may change or develop in ways that demand a response from the learner;
- new technologies may be introduced into the workplace;
- new ideas may surface in the popular media;
- physiological changes (from aging, stress, illness, or accident) may occur that demand an adaptive response.

If the change is experienced as disconfirming, that is, one that disconfirms one's self-system or personal model of reality, then the individual is thrown into a *disorientation phase* in which confusion, anxiety, and tension increase and the learner experiences a crisis of self-confidence. At this time, the individual may withdraw from others because of feelings of inadequacy or because others are blamed for being the cause of the confusion. In formal learning programs, the person most frequently blamed is the facilitator for not providing enough direction, not being clear about instructions, or not being helpful. By withdrawing from others, the learner may disengage from

Figure 3.5
Taylor's Model of the Learning Cycle: Critical Points in the Inquiry Sequence

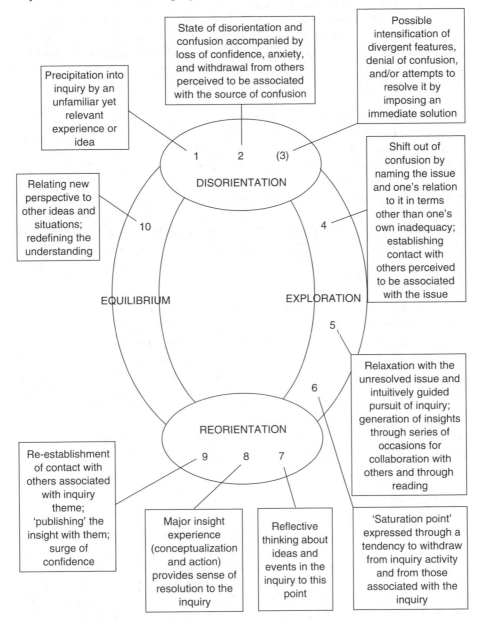

Source: Adapted from Taylor (1979, 1987).

the relationships most likely to offer the support necessary to make sense of the disconfirming event.

The transition out of the disorientation phase occurs when the learner is able to *name the central issue* problem, or source of confusion by entering into interactions with others. In Taylor's opinion, those who cannot do this may become locked into a period of expanded and intensified confusion in which they seek a quick, prescriptive solution that frequently leads to more confusion. For example:

- some learners try to become more organized on the assumption that their problem has to do with lack of control;
- some learners ask others to name their problem and prescribe solutions;
- others deny that they have a problem and suppress the disconfirming information as if it had never happened; and
- some may simply opt out of the learning cycle.

Gavin and Taylor (1990) describe these learners as engaging in a decremental cycle of learning; I will discuss this cycle at the end of this section.

The Exploration Phase

Those who can name the central issue and make contact with others enter the *exploration phase*, in which the individual becomes engaged in searching for information or ideas that could assist in resolving the identified problem.

The search leads to intensive and extensive inquiry activities in which new information and ideas are gathered from other individuals or from resources such as books or films, and new ways of doing things are tested. These activities usually involve interactions with others. In this phase the individual is working to identify relevant information and find alternative solutions rather than imposing a quick and prescriptive solution. When individuals have gathered enough information, they usually *withdraw to think things over.*

The Reorientation Phase

Following the reflective transition, the individual enters a *reorientation phase*, in which he or she comes up with a major synthesis that integrates ideas and experience to provide a new understanding of the issue that caused the disconfirming event. The learner consciously acknowledges that learning is a process in which he or she is the agent. This process can be facilitated by others, but the learner is where the learning happens and the learner's own views and judgments are centrally involved.

The transition out of the reorientation phase and into the equilibrium phase is marked by *sharing the major insight* with others. At this transition, the learner does not need the self-affirmation that closes the disorientation phase but does need affirmation of the intelligibility and practicality of the new perspective or insight.

The Equilibrium Phase

The *equilibrium phase* is characterized by consolidating and elaborating, refining and applying the new perspective. This phase involves a much reduced emotional intensity. The new perspective may be shared with individuals in other contexts or tested out as new behaviour in new settings. These activities will eventually lead to new disconfirming experiences.

Decremental Cycle of Learning

Gavin and Taylor (1990; Gavin, 1992) describe a *decremental cycle of learning* engaged in by learners who enter a protracted disorientation phase and deny they have a problem or blame others for their current situation. This cycle also encompasses four phases, the first being disorientation.

These learners then enter a second or *construction phase* with their feelings of blame intact, intent on 'building a case' for their perception of the situation:

- They close off open information gathering in favour of biased inquiries designed to support their point of view.
- They engage in relationships in which others are used to confirm predetermined opinions.
- Satisfaction in other areas of life may be imported to mask underlying negative and depressive feelings.

The construction phase replaces the exploration phase of the more positive learning cycle. Movement out of the construction phase is a private affair leading to a third or *consolidation phase* in which the learner closes off all exploratory options and returns to existing ideas and behaviours. The fourth phase, *decremental equilibrium*, does not involve a comfortable and positive stability, but is unsettled. The learner may experience a new disorientation phase without a new disconfirming event and with very little warning.

General Comments on Taylor's Model

Taylor makes no statement about the amount of time required to move through the entire cycle. The model probably occurs over several days, weeks, or even months if the problem is complex and the inquiry difficult.

Kolb's model can be thought of as contributing short cycles that drive the longer cycle proposed by Taylor.

Taylor's model includes the period of confusion, anxiety, and tension often associated with learning as an integral aspect of the first phase of the learning cycle. In including this period in the learning cycle, Taylor makes confusion and anxiety a 'normal,' even expected, part of learning.

The model proposed by Kolb (1984) does not include this highly emotional phase, and some learners could believe that confusion or anxiety should not occur during the learning process or that they must get over their emotional responses before 'real learning' can take place. Taylor also includes a phase in the cycle that describes the integration of what has been learned into one's personal model of reality and self-system and the transfer of this learning into different contexts. Kolb seems to be describing learning that takes place in one context only; transfer would be seen as an entirely new cycle of learning.

When I introduce students to Taylor's model, I get two types of responses. The most frequent response is:

> Why didn't you tell us this would happen? I thought I was the only one who was confused and anxious. I thought I was crazy or stupid.

I sometimes introduce Taylor's model in a course when I sense that many learners have become confused and are convinced they are not smart enough to be in the class. By introducing the model, I provide them with an easy way to re-enter into dialogue with others and share their concerns.

The second response is:

> Don't try to predict what I'll do next!

Fortunately, this response does not occur too often. I suspect that learners who respond this way are very self-directed and confident and can't imagine that they will ever become confused or anxious as learners.

Recognizing which learners are in which phase of the learning cycle is not easy. As facilitators, we need to pay attention to what learners are trying to tell us through their words and their body language. Some of my observations include:

- A glazed look in the eyes and very general, inarticulate, or repetitive questions, particularly about course assignments and activities, indicate a learner who is in the disorientation phase. Have the learners tell you, as the facilitator, what they understand about their assignments and activities, rather than telling them the information over (and over) again.
- Complaints about instructions for completing course assignments and activities suggest learners are in the disorientation phase.

- A learner who repeatedly asks the facilitator what books/journals to read or how to do an assignment is likely in the disorientation phase. Learners in the exploration phase can generally find their own books and journals after an initial suggestion, and tend to get on with doing their assignments and activities without much assistance from the facilitator.
- A learner who wants to share a great idea, book, or article is likely in the exploration phase.
- A learner who expresses a desire to share a personal idea but is reluctant to do so is likely in the reorientation phase and just needs some encouragement. A good facilitator can recognize an idea that is original for the learner and can prevent other learners from jumping on the idea with both feet.
- Learners who want to share what they have learned are in the reorientation phase.

LEARNING AND FACILITATING PRINCIPLES

Learning that is related to personal concerns proceeds more effectively when learners define the problem, establish goals, and conduct the inquiry process for themselves, providing their personal meaning to experiences.

> *If learning relates to personal concerns, encourage the learners to set their own learning agenda, and provide opportunities for them to discuss their confusion and anxiety and to share their meanings and insights.*

The learning cycle includes periods of high emotionality, particularly at the start.

> *Assure learners that an emotional phase is a normal part of learning and provide opportunities for them to talk about their feelings, whether positive or negative.*

Gavin and Taylor (1990) describe several facilitating strategies that support Taylor's model of learning:

> - *The disorientation phase calls for supportive relationships and opportunities to talk through the 'problem,' for encouraging learners to talk about their negative feelings, and for avoiding attempts to cheer them up.*
>
> - *To help a learner name the problem, the facilitator needs to serve as an affirming other by accepting the learner's*

description of the problem and by avoiding a premature leap into problem solving.

- *In the exploration phase, facilitators can provide information and learning resources and encourage the development of learning partnerships.*

- *In the reflective transition, facilitators should be available to serve as attentive, empathetic, and reflective listeners.*

- *In the reorientation phase and the transition that follows it, facilitators can be most helpful by providing opportunities to share insights and their possible application, and by assisting in the development of ways and means for applying these insights in the learner's workplace, family, or community.*

4 Styles in Learning

Learning style is sometimes defined as the characteristic cognitive, affective, social, and physiological behaviours that serve as relatively stable indicators of how learners perceive, interact with, and respond to the learning environment. The terms 'learning style' and 'cognitive style' are often used interchangeably although they are not exactly the same. Learning style is seen as broader and more inclusive than cognitive style (Keefe, 1987).

- The concept of learning style tends to be used by educators because it is more practical in applied terms than cognitive style.
- The concept of cognitive style tends to be used more by psychologists because each style is usually a more clearly defined and easily measurable personal trait compared to a learning style.
- The concept of learning style tends to include interpersonal components that are missing from the concept of cognitive style.
- Consistent individual differences in the ways of *organizing* experiences into meanings, values, skills, and strategies are called cognitive styles. Consistent individual differences in the ways of *changing* meanings, values, skills, and strategies are called learning styles.

I will consider the concept of cognitive style before moving on to the concept of learning style.

Cognitive Style

The brain represents the physical side of mental functioning; the mind represents the cognitive side. Wilder Penfield, a noted neurosurgeon, once said that he never saw a thought when he did brain surgery but he still believed in the concepts of thought and thinking. We experience the collective electrical and chemical activity of the brain as cognitive processes. We know about cognitive processes because we are capable of being aware of, and thinking about, our own thinking. The concepts we have developed to describe cognitive processes are many. In this chapter, we will consider cognitive style as a general concept; in Chapter 5 we will examine in greater detail the cognitive processes that underlie these styles.

Cognitive Style and Cognitive Ability

Cognitive style is different from cognitive ability. The differences between them are important and can be explained in at least four distinct ways.

1. Cognitive *ability* refers to the content (what you know) of cognition; cognitive *style* refers to the manner or mode (how you know) used to process information. Two individuals may be equal in ability to solve problems but go about the solving process in quite different ways and come up with different solutions (Messick, 1976).
2. Cognitive *ability* can be equated with traditional concepts of intelligence and reflects the level of one's maximum performance in completing cognitive tasks; cognitive *style* reflects one's preferred strategies (generalized habits) for completing cognitive tasks. Cognitive style has very little to do with intelligence, although traditional means for measuring intelligence tend to favour those who use the analytical cognitive style (A. Miller, 1991).
3. Cognitive *ability* is understood as referring to specific cognitive tasks; cognitive *style* is understood as referring to behavioural traits that are akin to personality traits. Cognitive ability enables specific types of mental performances on such cognitive tasks as verbal comprehension and spatial manipulation. Cognitive style refers to consistent individual differences in strategies used to process information, strategies that are seen as somewhat like other personality traits and that function as 'general organizing and controlling mechanisms' (A. Miller, 1991, p. 31).

   Cognitive style is thought of as a higher-order (more general) organizing principle that can recruit lower-order (more specific) cognitive abilities and strategies. In at least some individuals, styles may be embedded in personality in such a way that learners may not be able to change their prevailing cognitive style even though they wish to do so (Harvey, Hunt, & Schroder, 1961; A. Miller, 1991).
4. Cognitive *ability* is understood as being unipolar, cognitive *style* as bipolar. Cognitive ability is usually conceived as a singular dimension (unipolar) of cognitive behaviour. An individual's ability ranges from high to low on each dimension. An individual learner cannot be assessed as being *both* high and low on any given dimension. For example, an individual may be high or low in verbal ability, but not both.

Most cognitive styles are understood as ranging across paired behaviours (bipolar) with opposing poles being perceived as occupying opposite ends of a behavioural continuum. The more a learner uses one of the paired behaviours, the less he or she uses of the other. Individual assessments place a learner at some point along the continuum. The individual can be described as being high on one cognitive style – such as narrow scanning – and low on its opposing style – such as broad scanning; both descriptions would be correct (A. Miller, 1991).

Writers who promote the use of paired cognitive styles invariably state that both poles of the continuum are equally valuable, each having adaptive qualities in different contexts. The idea that cognitive styles are value-free is hard to sustain when the description of one style clearly indicates that it is more virtuous than and thus preferable to the other. Sternberg (1997) suggests that when one of the paired cognitive behaviours is clearly more valued and useful than the other, the behaviour being described is more likely a cognitive ability.

An example of this value problem is provided by the paired cognitive behaviours referred to as the *field dependence/field independence* (FDI) style (Witkin & Goodenough, 1977). In field independence, the individual can clearly distinguish a figure from the ground or perceptual field in which it is embedded, and multiple figures can be perceived as separate and distinct from each other. Learners who use the field-independent style often have trouble perceiving the ground and finding connections among the different parts of the total field. As a field-independent person, I rarely see deer or moose when I am driving across country; I concentrate too hard on the road, thus limiting my perceptual field to the 'figure' of the road in front of the car.

In field dependence, the learner sees the overall organization of the perceptual field as fused and the figure(s) as almost impossible to distinguish from the ground and from each other. Learners who use the field-dependent style often have trouble distinguishing figure from ground or focusing on one part of the field to the exclusion of other parts. My field-dependent colleagues, whether they are the driver or the passenger, see deer and moose in profuse numbers along the same highways. I would rather think that my car emits a deer/moose repellent, which is why I never see them, than think that I am missing some very important information that might affect my safety record.

When field dependence–independence was originally described by Witkin and Goodenough (1977), the independence pole was imbued with all the virtue and those who were field dependent were described as if they were 'dependent' (not self-directed) persons (A. Miller, 1991). Research indicates that more men than women use field independence and more women than men use field dependence. Margit Eichler (1988), a noted feminist scholar, suggests that this pair of cognitive styles should be renamed 'context blindness' and 'context awareness.' The tests used to measure FDI are timed and call for correct answers rather than preferences. For this reason, Robert Sternberg (1997) states that FDI is more likely an ability than a style.

Analytic and Holistic Cognitive Styles

Specific cognitive processes – such as narrowing attention or recalling a name – are often categorized into three general overarching processes: perceiving, remembering, and thinking. Within each of these overarching processes, specific and paired cognitive strategies are viewed as contributing to two basic cognitive styles; an analytic style and a holistic style (Entwistle, 1981; A. Miller, 1991). These two styles and the paired strategies are summarized in Figure 4.1, Analytic and Holistic Cognitive Styles. Some writers view each of the paired behaviours as cognitive styles in their own right.

The analytic cognitive style allows an individual to perceive an experience in terms of detailed, distinguishable features; store information in memory in terms of differentiated, narrow categories and verbal codes; search memory through convergent strategies; and use sequential strategies in thinking

Figure 4.1
Analytic and Holistic Cognitive Styles

	Analytic Style	Holistic Style
Perception		
• Pattern Recognition	Feature analysis	Prototype matching
• Attention	Limited/intensive scanning	Diffuse/extensive scanning
	Field independence (discrete)	Field dependence (global)
Memory		
• Representation	Verbal-analytical memory codes	Visual-analogical memory codes
• Organization	Narrow categories (differentiated)	Broad categories (overlapping)
	Semantic memory	Episodic memory
• Retrieval	Convergent search strategies	Divergent search strategies
Thinking	Paradigmatic thinking	Narrative thinking
• Classifying	Sequential, serial, systematic	Simultaneous, global, redundant
• Reasoning	Logical reasoning	Analogical reasoning
	• uses literal analogies	• uses poetic analogies
	• avoids metaphors	• uses idiosyncratic metaphors
• Inferring	Actuarial judgment	Intuitive judgment
	• based on hypotheses	• based on collected attributes

Sources: A. Miller (1991), Entwistle (1981).

and reasoning. It allows the individual to study each part of an experience as a 'discrete entity in isolation from all other parts and their surrounding context' (A. Miller, 1991, p. 32). Being able to distinguish differences within and among experiences plays an important role in such tasks as finding flaws in complex systems or identifying behaviours that could be corrected through feedback. Taken to the extreme, the analytic style can result in the individual becoming paralysed by minutiae and losing touch with a broader reality. The analytic style is described by various writers as articulated, differentiated, rigorous, constrained, convergent, critical, and ordering.

The holistic cognitive style seeks to keep an experience whole by perceiving connections within the experience and similarities with other experiences; stores information in memory in terms of broad and overlapping categories and visual codes; searches memory through divergent strategies; and uses simultaneous or global strategies in thinking and reasoning. The holistic style allows the individual to remain aware of the whole experience and is fundamental to creative processes. Taken to the extreme, the holistic style can result in the individual's losing sight of essential detail.

Authors who write on the subject do not agree on whether cognitive styles can be modified through learning and whether they are affected more by genetic inheritance, early socialization, or environmental influences (Jonassen & Grabowski, 1993). Most adult learners may be capable of using the cognitive processes that subserve both the analytical and the holistic styles, but individuals tend to prefer one style over the other. If our preferred style does not work, we reluctantly may try the other.

Alan Miller (1991) and Noel Entwistle (1981) view the analytic and holistic cognitive styles as basic aspects of cognition that, in more mature cognition, are used together to contribute to a higher-order capacity in which 'previously differentiated parts are combined with intuitively sensed wholes to form complex patterns, thereby fashioning order out of chaos' (A. Miller, 1991, p. 33). Miller calls this combined capacity the synthetic/integrated style and views it as the epitome of rational and creative thought; Entwistle refers to the same style as being that of a 'reasonable adventurer' (p. 67). He goes on to describe individuals who fit none of these three styles as immature learners who tend to be passive, dependent, and reproductive in their learning.

Learning Styles

Learning ability generally refers to the content of thought or to what we learned; learning style refers to how we have learned it (Messick, 1976), or generally describes how we prefer to learn. Most adults are capable of using the strategies that underlie several different styles but prefer to rely on the strategies they know best. The term 'learning style' tends to include both the cognitive styles already described as well as affective, social, and physiological styles of responding to learning tasks or learning environments.

Combining a number of learning strategies to identify a few overarching learning styles is somewhat more difficult than combining a range of cognitive strategies. Each learning style seems to describe different qualities of person, behaviour, or environment. Figure 4.2, Adults' Learning Styles, sets out the variety of strategies that are thought to contribute to adults' learning styles. Note that the cognitive styles we have already considered are found in the uppermost row of the figure.

Affective styles encompass those behaviours that have to do with attention, emotion, and valuing. Attention components of affective style relate to how the learner is most likely to attend to their experiences and what will affect that attention. Optimal attention lies somewhere between boredom and excitement.

Raymond Wlodkowski (1997) describes motivation as the natural capacity to direct energy in the pursuit of a goal. Motivational components relate to expectancy and importance. Expectancy is the relative certainty (optimism/pessimism) that desired outcomes will follow certain actions (risk taking/cautiousness). Importance relates to the extent to which the learner desires certain types of activities (competitive/co-operative) and outcomes (achievement/affiliation). I will return to other aspects of affective styles in Chapter 6.

Physiological styles are biologically based modes for responding to learning activities that are grounded in personal health and fitness, age-related factors, biological rhythms, and accustomed reactions to characteristics of the physical environment. Sex-related responses to learning are sometimes included under physiological styles. However, the position to be presented in Chapter 8 will be that sex-related responses are more appropriately considered as being gender-related interpersonal or social styles of learning.

One model that does attempt to view learning styles from a global perspective was developed by Lynn Curry (1983; Atkins et al., 2001), who uses a three-layered onion metaphor to classify the behaviours affecting an individual's learning style.

The outer layer reflects *instructional preferences* and is composed of behaviours that are more observable, less stable, and more easily influenced by external conditions than the middle and inner layers of the model. Instructional preferences are affected by environmental conditions, current emotional issues, sociability, and the context of learning. Dunn and Dunn (1977, 1978) have proposed a method for assessing the instructional preferences that contribute to learning styles. Their test assesses individuals on environmental, emotional, sociological, physiological, and psychological factors within the instructional environment.

Figure 4.2
Adults' Learning Styles

	Cognitive styles related to receiving information	Cognitive styles related to forming and retaining information
Cognitive Styles	Perceptual modality preferences • visual, auditory, kinesthetic, gustatory	Conceptual tempo • impulsivity vs. reflectivity
	Field dependence vs. field independence • broad vs. narrow	Conceptualizing styles • holistic vs. analytic
	Tolerance for incongruous or uncertain experiences	Breadth of categorizing • broad vs. narrow
	Processing styles • global/simultaneous vs. discrete/sequential	Cognitive complexity vs. cognitive simplicity
		Levelling/over-generalizing vs. Sharpening/over-discriminating
	Affective styles related to attention in learning	Affective styles related to motives for learning
Affective Styles	Exploratory • high vs. low	Local of control • intrinsic v. extrinsic
	Persistence/perseverance • high vs. low	Achievement vs. affiliation
	Level of anxiety • high vs. low	Risk-taking vs. cautiousness
		Competitive vs. co-operative
	Tolerance for frustration • high v. low	Self-as-learner • optimism vs. pessimism
	Learning behaviours related to physical or physiological factors	
Physiological Styles	Time-of-day (circadian) rhythms Need for mobility Responses to variations in light, sound, temperature Age-related changes Sex-related behaviour Health-related behaviour	
	Learning behaviours related to social or relational factors	
Interpersonal Styles	Relational vs. autonomous learning Connected vs. separate procedural knowing	

Source: Adapted from Keefe (1987) .

The middle layer reflects *information-processing styles* and is composed of behaviours that, in comparison to the outer layer, are less directly observable and somewhat more stable, although modifiable through learning new strategies. A variety of learning styles are included in this group, and are measured by self-diagnostic instruments such as:

- Grasha-Reichmann Student Learning Style Scale (GRSLSS) (Grasha, 1993), which measures three paired styles: social (competitive/collaborative), emotional (avoidant/participatory), and need for structure (dependent/independent);
- Gregorc's Style Delineator (Gregorc, 1982), which measures and combines two paired learning strategies for perception (concrete/abstract) and organization (sequential/random);
- Kolb's Learning Style Inventory (Kolb, 1985), which measures and combines two paired behaviours for perceiving information (concrete experience/abstract conceptualization) and processing information (reflective observation/active experimentation);
- McCarthy's Hemispheric Mode Indicator and the 4MAT System (McCarthy, 1985, 1986), which combines the two paired behaviours identified by Kolb (1985) with cerebral lateralization (described in Chapter 5);
- Suessmuth's Learning Style Inventory (Suessmuth, 1985), which measures preferences for types of information (visual, auditory, kinesthetic), types of learning (language, numerical, experiential), and types of reporting (written, oral).

The innermost layer reflects *cognitive personality styles* affecting an individual's approach to adapting and assimilating information. Cognitive personality styles are viewed as relatively permanent traits and are less amenable to change through learning. The field dependence–independence style (Witkin & Goodenough, 1977) described previously is an example of a cognitive personality style. It can be measured using the Group Embedded Figures Test (GEFT) (Oltman, Raskin, & Witkin, 1970). Other styles in this group are based on Carl Jung's theory of psychological types and, like the GEFT, are measured using paper-and-pencil instruments that call for a trained interpreter. This group of instruments sort individuals on the basis of four paired characteristics: introversion-extraversion, thinking-feeling, intuiting-sensing, and judging-perceiving. Three such instruments are:

- Myers-Briggs Type Indicator (Myers, 1985);
- Keirsey Termperament Sorter (Keirsey & Bates, 1984); and
- Person Empowerment Type Check (Cranton, 1998, 2000b).

General Ideas about Learning Styles

Each adult has personally preferred strategies for processing information and for learning. These strategies determine how the learner goes about learning tasks but not how well the learner learns.

Preferred strategies can be clustered into learning styles. Various authors hold different perceptions about what learning strategies are essential. Often there is little overlap between the models. For example, Gregorc (1982) classifies learning behaviours in terms of preferences for concrete/abstract perceptions and sequential/random ordering of information. Grasha (1993) classifies learning behaviours in terms of competitive/collaborative interactions with colleagues, avoidant/participant enthusiasm, and dependent/independent need for structure and support.

Each group of adult learners, therefore, will be heterogeneous in nature, and every individual within the group will be a complex mixture of style and ability. Adult learning facilitators should *not* assume that a group of adults of the same gender and age with similar social, economic, occupational, and educational characteristics will share common learning styles or abilities (Cawley, Miller, & Milligan, 1976; Cranton, 1998; Curry, 1983; Even, 1978; Jonassen & Grabowski, 1993; Messick, 1976).

The literature does not predict how individual adults develop their learning styles. It does have something to say about the fact that different yet meaningful patterns are created from the same experiences by learners with different learning styles.

For example, field-independent learners prefer task-focused activities that allow them to be independent and impersonal and to maintain an acceptable distance between emotions and ideas. They differentiate figures that lead to discrete concepts having little overlap with other concepts. These differentiated figures and concepts can be detached from the context in which they are developed, and therefore can be perceived as generalizable and transferrable to other contexts.

Field-dependent learners, on the other hand, prefer highly interactive activities that allow them to be interdependent and interpersonal, and to emphasize the connections between emotions and ideas. They develop relatively undifferentiated figures that lead to broad, often overlapping, concepts. These undifferentiated figures and concepts can rarely be detached from the context in which they were developed, and therefore are perceived as context specific and not easily transferrable to other contexts (Huff, Snider, & Stephenson, 1986; Jonassen & Grabowski, 1993; Messick, 1976; A. Miller, 1991; Witkin & Goodenough, 1977).

In general, field-independent learners demonstrate greater competency in analytical cognitive functioning, while field-dependent learners demonstrate greater competency in global interpersonal functioning. If learners of both styles participate in the same learning activity, each will perceive the experience differently and develop different interpretations based on individual perceptions. For example, during a first class, field-independent learners may clearly hear information about course assignments but may not understand that they are expected to learn from fellow students, while field-dependent learners may figure out which fellow students to interact with and learn from, but may not clearly hear much information about specific assignments.

One way to help adults learn how to learn more effectively is to direct their attention to their own characteristic ways of perceiving and point out those aspects of experience they are overlooking. A means for accomplishing this task would be to have learners discuss their perceptions of course requirements and expectations in small groups and then report back on the shared perceptions of the group – if there are any.

Effective facilitators need to be aware of their own learning style, how this style affects their preferred facilitating strategies for helping individual learners, and how learners with similar or different learning styles are affected by these facilitating strategies. When field-independent facilitators are assisting field-dependent learners to make sense of their own experiences, the facilitators need to be aware that they and the learners could be using different styles, and further that each style could be addressing different sources of information.

Learning Styles Are Value-Neutral

Cognitive styles and learning styles are theoretically value-neutral. There is no 'one best way to learn'; adults with differing styles manage to learn quite productively. Each style is adaptive in some situations and for some learning tasks, but not adaptive in others. Individual facilitators and institutions, however, may favour one style over another (Even, 1978). Sometimes the less favoured style is perceived by the facilitator or institution as a 'disability,' and the learners who use such styles may become labelled as slow or disabled learners.

An example might help illustrate the problem. Suessmuth (1985) has developed a learning style inventory that assesses a learner's preference for reporting learning through written or oral styles. In most formal educational institutions, the preferred style for reporting is writing, so that a facilitator can have concrete evidence on which to base an assessment should anyone ever question it. Learners registered in formal classes who prefer the oral reporting style are frequently out of luck. If they have difficulty reporting their learning in written form, they are sometimes perceived – and sometimes perceive themselves – as 'learning disabled.' I advise such learners to speak their 'paper' into a tape recorder and then transcribe the tape. New technologies make it possible for learners to speak their paper into a computer equipped with voice-recognition software and to obtain a complete typescript ready for editing.

Suessmuth identifies three general types of personal learning style preferences:

1 *Language learners* prefer to hear (auditory) language or see (visual) language. They are best at remembering information in word forms.
2 *Numerical learners* prefer to hear (auditory) or see (visual) numbers. They are best at remembering and using information in numerical forms.
3 *Auditory-visual-kinesthetic (AVK) learners* prefer to learn through personal experiencing and need sensory stimuli. They need to manipulate material and be totally involved; they may become distracted if not entirely involved.

In an educational system that views language as the most important medium for learning, numerical and AVK learners will be at a disadvantage. AVK learners, in particular, are likely to be perceived as unmotivated or learning disabled when asked to do learning tasks involving words. We can choose to define such differences as 'disabilities' when those differences deviate from the expectations of the educational institution, or we can choose to celebrate learning styles as differences that demonstrate the range of unique ways in which adults learn.

Adults tend to self-select learning situations and learning-facilitating relationships that enhance their own learning style. They appear to be very proficient at knowing intuitively which facilitators and which learning situations are not for them.

Learning Style and Self-Direction

In the field of adult education, very little research has addressed the relationship between self-direction and independence in learning, and specific cognitive and learning styles. It seems reasonable to assume, for example, that adults who use the field-independence style will more likely be self-directed and independent learners than those who use the field-dependence style. If this is true, then a major principle of adult education – supporting self-directedness and independence – may be ignoring the needs of field-dependent learners. And if theories suggesting that these traits or styles are relatively immune to change are also true, then, as facilitators, we may experience considerable difficulty in helping all adults to become self-directed. Further, the literature suggests that self-directed learners are best supported by warm, caring, friendly, and nonjudgmental facilitators – characteristics more often found in field-dependent adults. Some writers, therefore, may be recommending a mismatch between facilitating and learning styles that still other writers predict will lead to dissatisfaction. More research needs to be done in this area (Even, 1978).

Other theorists in learning style research (M. Taylor, 1987; Kolb, 1984) indicate that while adults tend to begin learning experiences with their preferred style, they also use other styles throughout the learning process, although less often and perhaps less productively (Abbey, Hunt, & Weiser, 1985).

LEARNING AND FACILITATING PRINCIPLES

Adult learners have individual learning and cognitive styles and mental abilities.

> *Facilitators can assist adult learners to learn how to learn by helping them become aware of their own learning styles and then how to develop the strategies that typify the styles in which they are weak.*

A group of adult learners will be heterogeneous in terms of learning and cognitive styles and mental abilities.

> *The facilitator should not try to match the styles of all the individual learners in a learning group. A better plan is to help them become aware of their own learning styles and to develop skills in those styles they tend to avoid. Facilitators should develop a variety of activities that offer all learners some opportunities to use their preferred learning styles.*

When a mismatch occurs between the learning/cognitive style of the learner and that of the facilitator, the result will likely be mutually unsatisfactory.

> *Facilitators must be willing and able to respond to each style and must be aware of their own styles and how these affect the processes they use to assist learners.*

Cognitive styles and learning styles are value-neutral. There is no 'one best way to learn.' Each cognitive/learning style is adaptive in some situations and not adaptive in others.

> *In discussing learning styles with learners, facilitators should discuss the strengths and weaknesses of all styles. They should avoid the constant use of their own learning style as the starting point for facilitating activities, and definitely avoid any implication that a specific learning style is not adequate.*

Adults tend to be proficient at self-selecting those learning situations and learning-facilitating interactions that best enhance their own learning/cognitive styles.

Adult learners prefer to start with the learning activities they are most comfortable with and to avoid those they see as difficult or that they like the least.

> *Facilitators tend to start facilitating with the activities that typify their own learning style. The starting activity determines the overall nature of the learning program.*

Cognitive/learning styles are not related to intelligence, mental ability, or actual performance.

Kolb's Model of Learning Styles

Because there is so much literature on the topic of learning styles, I focused on general issues in the previous section and will limit the discussion of specific learning styles to the model proposed by Kolb (1984). We can reconsider Kolb's cyclical model of learning (presented in Chapter 3) by drawing lines that connect Active Experimentation to Reflective Observation (horizontal axis) and Concrete Experience to Abstract Conceptualization (vertical axis). In Figure 4.3, Kolb's Learning Styles, we now have two dimensions, each representing two opposing but related behaviours.

1 The abstract-concrete dimension deals with taking in experience and understanding it, either through reliance on conceptual interpretation and symbolic representation (abstract conceptualization), or through reliance on the tangible felt and sensed qualities of immediate experience (concrete experience).
2 The active-reflective dimension deals with transforming what has been taken in and understood through either internal reflection (reflective observation) or active external manipulation (active experimentation).

Learning, and therefore knowing, requires both a means for taking in and understanding experience through representing that experience in the mind as concepts or felt sensations, and a means for transforming the resulting representations. 'Simple perception is not sufficient for learning; something must be done with it' (Kolb, 1984, p. 42). Kolb points out that, while both poles of each dimension are necessary for complete mature learning, all learners are not equally skilled in using all four types of activities.

Figure 4.3
Kolb's Learning Styles

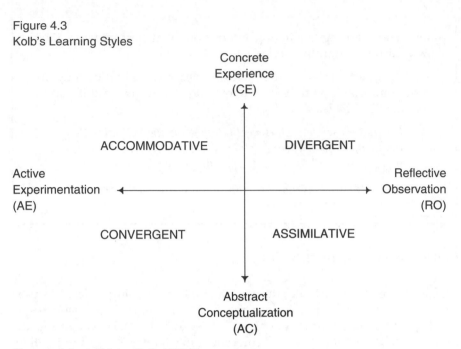

Source: Adapted from Kolb (1984).

When the opposing behaviours are connected, the model is divided into four quadrants that represent four different learning styles. Each of the four learning styles – divergent, assimilative, convergent, accommodative – represents strengths in one aspect of each of the above two dimensions of learning. Kolb's (1985) Learning Style Inventory allows individuals to assess their own learning style. I urge you to obtain a copy of Kolb's inventory and assess your learning style using his well-validated instrument. Since his test cannot be reproduced here, we will use a less formal process.

First, consider the behavioural descriptions that typify the opposing means for grasping and understanding experience, the concrete-abstract dimension (vertical axis in Figure 4.3).

Concrete Experience (CE) emphasizes the use of information derived from personal experiences. Learners skilled in using concrete experience rely on feelings and sensations rather than thoughts, are concerned about the uniqueness of each new experience, and avoid comparing new experiences with previous ones.

Abstract Conceptualization (AC) emphasizes the use of logic, ideas, and concepts. Learners skilled in abstract conceptualization rely on thoughts rather than feelings or sensations, compare new experiences to old ones to discover similarities and differences, and develop abstract concepts to describe ideas about these comparisons.

Consider your preferred approach to learning in terms of these opposing means for understanding experiences, and place an X on the vertical axis in Figure 4.3 to indicate where you perceive yourself as a learner on this dimension. If you prefer information derived from personal experiences, place your X close to the CE end of the axis. If you prefer ideas and concepts, place your X close to the AC end. If you prefer images and metaphors, place your X closer to the centre depending on whether your images and metaphors are more concrete or more abstract (your choice).

Next, consider the behavioural descriptions that typify the opposing means for transforming your understanding of experiences, the active-reflective dimension (horizontal axis on Figure 4.3).

Reflective Observation (RO) involves understanding the meaning of experiences and situations by observing and describing them. Learners skilled in using reflective observation transform knowledge through reflective thinking. They do this by understanding why things happen rather than how they work, observing others before trying things out, and developing several different meanings for an experience.

Active Experimentation (AC) involves actively influencing people and changing situations. Learners skilled in using active experimentation transform knowledge through practical applications. They do this by understanding what works rather than why, trying things out first, and learning through trial and error.

Consider your preferred approach to learning in terms of these opposing means for transforming knowledge, and place an X on the horizontal axis in Figure 4.3 to indicate where you perceive yourself as a learner on this dimension. If you have a strong preference for contemplating experience, place your X close to the RO end of the axis. If you have a strong preference for getting on with doing something, place your X close to the AE end. If you do both but tend to think first before acting, place your X near the centre on the RO side. If you do both but tend to act first and think about it later, place your X near the centre on the AE side.

Your learning style is now identified as the quadrant bordered by the two arms of the vertical and horizontal axes on which you have placed your Xs. Compare the descriptions of the four styles with your awareness about how you learn. Do you think you ended up in the most appropriate quadrant?

If your Xs are on the CE and RO ends of the axes, you may be divergent as a learner. The greatest strength in this style lies in imaginative ability and awareness of meaning and values, viewing concrete experiences from many different perspectives, and organizing many relationships into meaningful wholes. The weakness of this style is that, taken to extremes, learners can become paralysed by perceiving too many alternatives, unable to choose among them.

If your Xs are on the AC and RO ends of the axes, you may be assimilative as a learner. The greatest strength in this style lies in the ability to put together many different ideas to form concepts, models, or theories that are logically sound, and in combining disparate ideas into an integrated whole. The weakness of this style is that, taken to extremes, learners may build 'castles in the air' without an understanding of the experiences upon which they are built and/or without considering their practical application.

If your Xs are on the AC and AE ends of the axes, you may be convergent as a learner. The greatest strength in this style lies in problem solving, decision making, and the practical application of ideas. The weakness of this style is that, taken to extremes, learners may end up solving the wrong problem because they did not consider all the alternatives and because they did not want to waste time chewing things over.

If your Xs are on the CE and AE ends of the axes, you may be accommodative as a learner. The greatest strength in this style lies in doing things, in carrying out plans and tasks, and in taking risks by getting involved in new experiences. The weakness of this style is that, taken to extremes, learners may solve problems in an intuitive trial-and-error manner without understanding why they have made certain choices, or they may engage in meaningless activity and make trivial improvements in how things get done.

You may find that, while you have a preferred style, you also use some aspects of one or both learning styles adjacent to your preferred style. You can see from these descriptions that each learning style has strengths and weaknesses. The useful part of Kolb's model is that you do not have to feel pigeon-holed; you can become a more well-rounded, all-purpose learner by improving the skills associated with the learning styles you least prefer. For most learners, this will be the style diagonally opposite your strongest preference. Kolb (1984) tells us that divergent learners usually need to improve their deciding skills (decision making, goal setting); assimilative learners, their acting skills (seeking and exploring opportunities, risk taking); convergent learners, their valuing skills (listening with an open mind, imagining the implications of situations); and accommodative learners, their thinking skills (organizing information, developing concepts based on personal experience).

When my course on adult learning is considering the effect of learning style, I ask the learners to first assign themselves to their preferred learning style group. Then each group is asked to develop answers to the following questions:

- What do you do first when you start to learn something new?
- What can others do that gets in the way of your learning?
- What can others do that helps your learning?
- If you were going to teach a course session on (architectural history of the city, the nutritional value of fast food, how to read a geological map, the theory of gravity), how would you proceed?

As each group reports back, I ask them to identify any conflicts among the groups. Many of the ideas included in the learning and facilitating principles below have come from the resulting discussions.

LEARNING AND FACILITATING PRINCIPLES

Adult learners generally prefer to start their learning with activities that typify their learning style. For example:

- Divergent learners like to begin by talking things over with other learners in order to 'get the big picture.'
- Assimilative learners like to begin by finding a book and reading about the topic in order to understand where they might go next.
- Convergent learners like to begin by defining the learning task and setting some clear goals.
- Accommodative learners like to begin by doing something – they don't want to think things over, or plan things; they just want to get on with it.

Each learning style sets up obstacles and frustrations for learners who prefer other styles. However, mature learning groups function best when different individuals can take leadership for different aspects of the learning cycle.

Facilitators tend to start with the activities that represent their preferred learning style on the assumption that this is the 'best way to learn' and the best way to 'get things off on the right foot.' The activity chosen as a starting point will affect the design of the remainder of the process.

While no facilitator can please every learner, attempts should be made to include a variety of activities in each teaching-learning session and to begin sessions at different points in the overall cycle.

- Assimilative learners like to start facilitating activities with readings or lecture-style presentations of concepts, theories, or models. Facilitators who prefer the assimilative style tend to prepare for facilitating sessions by focusing on the logical order for presenting information. They may not provide enough concrete examples to illustrate their abstract points. They rarely begin by asking learners to participate in an experience.
- Convergent learners like to start facilitating activities by defining the learning task, outlining the learning objectives, and then letting learners get on with things for themselves. Facilitators who prefer the convergent style tend to prepare for facilitating sessions by setting out goals, objectives, and expectations for a learning program. They rarely begin by having learners identify alternative tasks or objectives.
- Accommodative learners like to start facilitating activities by getting learners to do something, often a structured experience in which all learners can participate. Facilitators who prefer the accommodative style tend to prepare for facilitating sessions by selecting examples, activities, and experiences that illustrate what they want the learners to learn. They rarely begin by giving a lecture.
- Divergent learners like to start facilitating activities by sharing experiences or brainstorming in order to generate ideas. Facilitators who prefer the divergent style tend to prepare for facilitating sessions by setting up a metaphor or an activity to be used to bring in a variety of different ideas, or by establishing questions or issues around which brainstorming activities can be conducted. They rarely begin by setting goals or defining the learning task.

Who provides the input, who directs the activity, where the learning process starts, and where it is expected to go are determined by separate decisions. Learners, facilitators, or both acting collaboratively can take responsibility for these activities or decisions.

Feedback can occur only when the learner uses overt behaviour, which occurs only between active experimentation and concrete experience. Learners who prefer reflective observation may have trouble getting enough feedback to guide their future learning if they avoid overt actions that can be assessed by others. Facilitators who prefer reflective observation may not provide enough activities where learners can test out ideas and get feedback.

Learners who avoid reflective learning tend to repeat the same mistakes over and over again. Such learners can be encouraged to take time to pause and reflect on what has happened through the provision of reflective activities such as small group discussions and journal writing. Only through reflective activities can mistakes be identified and plans developed to avoid repeating the same mistakes. Cognitive apprenticeship, an idea to be discussed in Chapter 7, is one technique for encouraging reflection (West, Farmer, & Wolff, 1991).

Learners who avoid active experiments also avoid having their ideas or actions exposed to the scrutiny of others. In order to correct or modify their ideas and actions, such learners need to be encouraged to share their ideas-in-progress and to test out their ideas through planned action. Action research (Quigley & Kuhne, 1997) and the classroom assessment projects described by Angelo and Cross (1993) provide ideas for how to plan such actions.

Learners who avoid developing abstract ideas are often afraid that their ideas will be 'carved in stone.' They like ideas that are flexible. Often such learners are also afraid that their ideas will be discounted or ignored. They need assistance in proposing tentative or 'half-baked' ideas just for the fun of it through such activities as brainstorming and making lists. Von Oech's books (1983, 1986) offer other suggestions.

Learners who avoid concrete experiences are often afraid to emerge from the protection of the super-rational 'ivory tower.' They don't like the chaotic, disorganized aspects of reality, preferring to impose order on reality in terms of their concepts and theories. They need assistance to 'get their feet wet' just for the fun of it. The books in the series *Handbook of Structured Experiences* (Pfeiffer & Jones, various dates) offer lots of suggestions for such activities.

Learning Style and the Learning Environment

Another interesting aspect of the Kolb model is that it can be used to predict the facilitating style and learning activities most supportive of the four learning phases and four learning styles. Fry (1978; Fry & Kolb, 1979) reports that *concrete experience is best supported by an affectively complex environment*. In such environments, the primary purpose is to participate in an actual experience, using the experiences to generate insights and feelings, and receiving feedback related to personal needs and goals. In affectively complex environments, the facilitator is most helpful when serving as a role model and relating to learners on a personal basis, as a colleague rather than an authority. Facilitating techniques that seem to support concrete experience include group projects, demonstrations, visualizations, field trips, case studies and critical incident reports, and structured or laboratory method activities that are then discussed. The affectively complex environment supports both accommodative and divergent learning styles.

Reflective observation is best supported by a perceptually complex environment (Fry, 1978; Fry & Kolb, 1979). In such an environment, the primary purpose is to understand something, identify relationships among ideas, collect relevant information, and engage in research activities. A perceptually complex environment provides access to many different types of information in a variety of perceptual modes (books, films, arts and crafts), from both personal and impersonal (expert) sources, and provides many opportunities to discuss ideas with colleagues. In this environment, the facilitator is most helpful when serving as a mediator, discussion leader, or process facilitator and when providing feedback about the processes being used. Facilitating techniques that seem to support reflective observation include discussion groups, buzz groups, journal writing, interviewing, creativity activities, puzzles, quiet meetings or talking circles, inquiry projects, brainstorming, and consciousness raising. The perceptually complex environment supports both divergent and assimilative learning styles.

Abstract conceptualization is best supported by a symbolically complex environment (Fry, 1978; Fry & Kolb, 1979). Here the primary purpose is to use knowledge to solve problems or identify solutions and answers. Information is provided in symbolic form through books, research data, diagrams, and so on. In this environment, the facilitator is most helpful when acting as the 'content expert,' the representative of the body of knowledge being learned, and by providing feedback about the aptness of proposed solutions or the logic of proposed concepts, theories, and models. Facilitating techniques that seem to support abstract conceptualization include lectures, reading papers, individual projects, problem-solving activities, forums and panels, debates, seminars, model building, and proposal writing. The symbolically complex environment supports both assimilative and convergent learning styles.

Active experimentation is best supported by a behaviourally complex environment (Fry, 1978; Fry & Kolb, 1979). Here the emphasis is on providing opportunities to apply knowledge or skills in practical situations. The information brought to the situation has been abstracted by the learner from previous experiences and is compared with information that can be extracted from the immediate situation. In this environment, the facilitator can be most helpful by serving as a coach or adviser and providing feedback about how the learner's behaviours are affecting the overall situation or the task to be completed. Facilitating techniques that seem to support active experimentation include hands-on activities, games, simulations, field placements or internships, mentoring, drill and practice, role playing, action research, and learning contracts. The behaviourally complex environment supports both convergent and accommodative learning styles.

Variations on Kolb's Model

Kolb's model has been used by other writers to both simplify and expand on his central ideas. McCarthy (1985) combines each of Kolb's learning styles with left and right hemisphere functions to generate eight styles of learning. She also reports on the likes and dislikes of each learning style with regard to facilitating techniques and assessment procedures. Huff, Snider, and Stephenson (1986) report McCarthy's ideas as follows:

- *Divergent learners* like group work, group grading, pass/fail grading, self-evaluation, unobtrusive observation, participation grading, and time to reflect. They dislike a lack of opportunities to talk things over with others, timed tests, computer-assisted instruction, debates, and 'just do it.'
- *Assimilative learners* like comments on papers and tests, written tests and essays, multiple choice tests, and collecting data. They dislike role playing, pass/fail grading, subjective tests, and group grades. They also dislike being asked to express their opinions before they have had time to think things over carefully by themselves.
- *Convergent learners* like field trips and labs, hands-on activities, mobility, and skill-oriented evaluation. They dislike memorizing, written assignments, group work and group grading, peer evaluations that involve 'feelings,' being given the answers by others, and discussions that appear to be off-topic.
- *Accommodative learners* like interdisciplinary approaches, lots of examples of the topic being considered, open-ended questions and activities, flexible assignments, and self-discovery projects. They dislike assignments without options, repetition and drills, reflecting, and inactivity.

5 Brain and Mind in Learning

To understand learning fully, we need to consider cognitive aspects of learning and explore the relationship between brain and mind. When we speak of the brain, we are speaking of the physical structure and the physiology of the human nervous system. When we speak of the mind, we are speaking about the collective cognitive processes and constructs that we use for learning, perceiving, remembering, thinking, deciding, solving problems, and so on.

Here are some of the things we know about the relationship between body, brain, mind, and learning:

- Prolonged practice of a physical task in the imagination through visualization can lead to significant physiological change. For example, simulated leg exercise leads to increased heart and respiration rates (Blakemore & Frith, 2000).
- Facial expressions have a strong effect on mental states. If you frown, you'll begin to feel depressed; if you smile, you'll begin to feel better. Adults learn better in a positive mental state. So encourage adult learners to smile.
- Both sensory overstimulation (information overload) and understimulation (boredom) can produce physical stress responses that interfere with learning. Adults who are getting too much or too little information for their current learning task may not be learning (Hart, 1975).
- Laughter produces a synchronous response in the two cerebral hemispheres, making learning more vivid and adding affect to whatever is being learned, thereby making it easier to remember. Laughter in the right place makes learning more fun and much easier (Wischnewski, 1983).
- Learning and a lively environment help reduce the possibility of cognitive decline in old age and greatly improve mental functioning at all ages. Generally, lack of environmental stimulation reduces intelligent behav-

iour. A nerve cell requires optimal stimulation if it is to develop connecting links (dendrites) to other nerve cells; the more links, the more efficient thinking becomes. Sensory deprivation results in below-normal stimuli to nerve cells. Such cells may develop 'stubby dendrites' and lose their links to other dendrites and their contribution to thought processes (Blakemore & Frith, 2000).

- Physical activity, when used alternately with mental activity, enhances learning by providing the brain with time out to process ideas and experiences. When you get tired from your learning activities, take a break with a physical change: go for a brisk walk, do yoga exercises, scrub the floor, go dancing, or do the gardening to give your thought processes time to work things out without interference from the sergeant major in your mind who is constantly at you to work harder.
- People can alter their emotional state by forming specific mental images. Positive images lead to positive emotions; negative images to negative emotions (Blakemore & Frith, 2000).

I will begin the discussion about the brain and mind in learning by considering how the nervous system functions and then move on to consider the mind, cognition, intelligence, and cognitive development.

The Nervous System

The nervous system (brain, spinal cord, and peripheral nerves) consists of an estimated one trillion nerve cells or neurons, the vast majority of which are clustered in the brain. Each neuron is a powerful and complex, microscopic, information-processing and -transmitting system. Each consists of a central body, an elongated extension or axon, and many small branch-like extensions or dendrites (see Figure 5.1, The Nervous System). The axon serves as the main exit point for the information transmitted from that cell. Some neurons are specialized to

- receive sensory information from the external environment (visual, auditory, pain, pressure, temperature, smell, taste);
- receive sensory impulses from the internal environment (physical balance, chemical balance);
- transmit impulses from one neuron to another; and
- transmit nervous impulses to muscles to initiate motor responses.

Each dendrite terminates on a dendrite of another neuron and each cell receives dendrites from hundreds of other neurons. The minuscule space between any two dendrites is called a 'synaptic gap.' Information is transmitted within the neuron as an electrical impulse and across the synaptic

Figure 5.1
The Nervous System

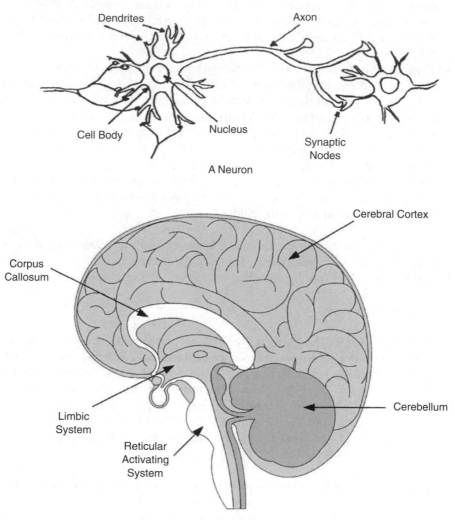

Dendrites

Axon

Cell Body

Nucleus

Synaptic
Nodes

A Neuron

Cerebral Cortex

Corpus
Callosum

Limbic
System

Reticular
Activating
System

Cerebellum

Cross-section of the Brain

gap by chemicals or neurotransmitters. The surge of biochemical information across a synapse is 'awe-inspiring in its volume and complexity' (Buzan
& Buzan, 1995).

The combined electrical impulses of the neurons in the brain can be measured as brain waves. The frequency of the brain waves at any given time
determines one's level of conscious awareness and focus of attention (Boucouvalas, 1993). There are five levels of brain waves:

1 *Gamma waves* are very rapid (26–40 cycles per second, or cps) and are associated with such states as agitation, distress, high anxiety, and euphoria. While the individual's attention is on the outside world, that attention is narrowed by focusing almost exclusively on the figure at the centre of the perceptual field. Little learning goes on at this level of consciousness.
2 *Beta waves* are rapid (13–26 cps) and are associated with conscious awareness and alert attention to what is occurring in the outside world. This level is associated with conscious learning and daily activities.
3 *Alpha waves* are slower (8–13 cps) and are associated with the individual's being awake but relaxed and not engaged in deliberate thought; attention is balanced between the outer and inner worlds and the individual moves in and out of 'consciousness.' This state of diffuse attention is associated with creativity and the use of imagery.
4 *Theta waves* are slow (4–8 cps) and are recorded when attention has been withdrawn from the outside world and consciousness during reverie, deep meditation, or dreaming sleep.
5 *Delta waves* are very slow (3–4 cps) and are recorded in deep sleep, anaesthesia, or coma. This is the state of being 'unconscious.'

The Brain

The easiest way to understand how the brain functions in learning is to view it as having three levels, each having its own form of memory, its own way of gathering information, its own sense of space and time, its own intelligence, and its own means for controlling behaviour. This triune brain as a whole works through a precarious, constantly changing balance among the three levels (Caine & Caine, 1991; Hart, 1983; MacLean, 1990). The three levels are referred to as

1 the reticular activating system or 'reptilian brain,' so-called because it is found in reptiles, as well as birds and mammals.
2 the limbic system or 'primitive mammalian brain,' so-called because it is found in birds and mammals.
3 the neo-cortex or 'modern mammalian brain,' so-called because it is found only in the highest order of primates.

The *reticular activating system* is the lowest level of the triune brain and consists of brain structures formed by the swelling of the top of the spinal cord (the brainstem) at the point where it enters the skull. It is both the lowermost and the innermost part of the brain. The reticular activating system is a relay station between nerves entering and leaving the brain and those within the brain. It can suppress or augment stimuli moving in either direction on the basis of individual needs for survival and safety, specifically for the primitive emotions driving the basic functions of feeding, fighting, flee-ing, and sexual behaviours.

When faced with conflicting stimuli, the reticular activating system will always augment those that enhance survival and suppress those that might provoke increased threat. If this relay station does not 'turn on' (become acti-vated), the higher brain centres will not be activated (Hart, 1983). The reticu-lar activating system is suppressed in sleep and is affected by biorhythms and the chemical balance of the blood. That is, it is sensitive to changes in the internal environment through blood chemistry, nutrition, hormone level, and so on, but not to changes in the external environment. The various func-tions of the reticular activating system are instinctive (Ferro, 1993; Pinker, 1997). Its memory relates to survival and threat.

What this part of the brain understands as being a threat may have no connection to what higher levels of the brain understand as threatening. The reptilian brain plays a large role in managing stress responses; it is impervi-ous to learning as we understand it. The reptilian brain is a unitary structure that is not divided laterally (right and left).

The *limbic system*, the middle level of the triune brain, is part of the mid-brain and is dedicated to the gentler social emotions such as are found in parenting (Ferro, 1993; Pinker, 1997). 'Only those creatures [birds and mam-mals] which have a limbic system are devoted to the care and raising of their young' (Ferro, 1993, p. 26).

The stimuli for all experience first pass through the limbic system before patterns are identified and meanings developed in the neo-cortex. That is, the emotional content of experience is processed before meaning is pro-cessed, and is under the control of brain structures below those responsible for thinking and reasoning. The limbic system controls the individual's basic value system, enhances or suppresses the short-term memory (strategies for remembering what happened in the past twenty-four hours), and has a marked effect on what we store in long-term memory (Hart, 1975; Pinker, 1997). The limbic system determines how the brain will respond to all infor-mation received. New experiences trigger memories to which feelings and values are attached. If the experience that originally created the memory was associated with positive feelings (happiness or pleasure), then the response to the new experience will also be positive. If the experience that originally created the memory was associated with negative feelings (pain, anxiety, or fear), then the response to the new experience will also be nega-tive (Ferro, 1993).

The limbic system judges all experience on the basis of pain and pleasure. When we behave in ways that enhance our self-preservation, the limbic sys-tem registers pleasure; when our self-preservation is threatened, it registers pain. This part of the brain is relatively impervious to change through learn-ing but can be changed through some forms of psychotherapy, particularly those that do not rely on verbal dialogue. New learning is mostly restricted to expanding existing values and registering new experiences. The primitive mammalian brain is not divided laterally and has no direct speech functions except for guttural sounds that register pain or pleasure (Hart, 1983).

The *neo-cortex* is the highest level of the triune brain and consists of the cerebral cortex, which is divided laterally into two cerebral hemispheres, and the corpus callosum, which connects the two hemispheres.

The cerebral cortex houses the intellect. Virtually all the learning we are concerned with in formal education and informal learning occurs in the cerebral cortex. All verbal speech functions originate within it (Pinker, 1997). It reasons, plans, worries, writes poems, makes lists, invents engines, paints pictures, and programs computers. Its products are foresight, hindsight, and insight; it is the 'mother of invention' and the 'father of abstract thought' (Hart, 1975). It co-ordinates our relationships with the outside world through its centres for vision, hearing, taste, smell, bodily sensations, and motor responses. Its memory has kinesthetic components (skin sensations, muscular movements, balance), iconic components (images, sounds, tastes, smells), and words or verbal components (Hart, 1983).

The neo-cortex has control over conscious activity and thought; but it is dependent on the lower levels of the brain to pass on information, yield control over various activities, and keep the entire system activated. Waking activities bring the cerebral cortex into action. Whenever sensory stimuli implying a threat to the individual are received, consciously or unconsciously, from the inner or outer environment, the brain will down-shift, taking direct control over cognitive functions away from the neo-cortex and giving it to the limbic system or the reticular activating system (Hart, 1983).

When down-shifting occurs, self-preservation becomes more important than learning and the cerebral hemispheres are put on hold. To reactivate the learning process, the lowest two levels must be satisfied that the threat to self has been resolved. In Chapter 6 I will discuss the effect of stress on learning in terms of emotional responses. Here we see that both real and perceived threats have a direct effect on brain functioning by causing the brain to down-shift, thereby stopping normal learning processes.

The Cerebral Hemispheres

The cerebral hemispheres are connected to each other through the corpus callosum. Research done on patients in whom this connecting bridge has been severed indicates that, in most humans, the hemispheres are specialized for different mental functions (Bogen, 1977; Pinker, 1997). Being of 'two minds' appears to have a physical basis. The left hemisphere controls most of the sensory input and all of the motor responses for the right side of the body, and the right hemisphere for the left side of the body. For most people, the left hemisphere is specialized for language and the right for nonverbal pattern recognition.

Hemispheric specialization is reversed in some people, particularly those who are left-handed. Specialization, or lateralization, is rarely complete in the majority of normally functioning humans. The left hemisphere usually retains some capacity to process nonverbal information and the right hemisphere some capacity to process verbal information.

The left hemisphere is more highly activated during language tasks in men than in women; more women use both hemispheres in language tasks. The cerebral hemispheres of the average man may be more highly lateralized than those in the average woman. On average, women outperform men on verbal tasks and men outperform women on spatial tasks (Blakemore & Frith, 2000).

Whether mental functions other than those for language and pattern recognition are lateralized to one hemisphere or the other is open to question. Writers in this field do not always agree about which functions are lateralized to which hemisphere and to what extent. Most researchers believe that experience is processed and memories stored somewhat differently in each hemisphere (Bogen, 1977; Springer & Deutsch, 1985). Figure 5.2, Functions of the Cerebral Hemispheres, lists those functions about which there is some agreement. This list should *not* be understood to mean that all verbal functions reside in the left hemisphere and all nonverbal functions in the right hemisphere. Mental functions are distributed across both hemispheres, although one hemisphere tends to dominate in the use of specific functions. Further, each hemisphere differs among individuals in terms of abilities and capacities to perform selected functions (Buzan & Buzan, 1995).

The list in Figure 5.2 tells us that there is more than one way to process and store experience and that each person's model of reality has both verbal and nonverbal, temporal and spatial components. We also know that normal human functioning requires the coordination and collaboration of both hemispheres. For example, language is a very complex process requiring

- semantics or words (a left hemisphere specialization) assigned to meaningful patterns (a right hemisphere specialization).
- syntax or grammatical rules (left hemisphere).
- the use of metaphor or imagery (right hemisphere), and
- sensitivity to sound (both hemispheres).

The spoken word calls for the use of auditory discrimination of sounds, visual discrimination of body language, and controlled motor responses of the vocal cords, mouth, and tongue for pronunciation, as well as language. The written word calls for the use of visual discrimination of symbols, fine motor skills, and eye-hand co-ordination, as well as language. That is, both

Figure 5.2
Functions of the Cerebral Hemispheres

Left Hemisphere Functions	Right Hemisphere Functions
Verbal	Nonverbal, visual-spatial
• turns experience into words that name, describe, and define it • recognizes language • stores information in linguistic or symbolic form	• recognizes patterns • keeps information in original form (e.g., visual, auditory, kinesthetic)
Logical, analytical	Gestalt, synthetic
• figures things out sequentially, step-by-step and part-by-part • reduces wholes to meaningful parts • uses rules of logic to draw conclusions	• sees experience or ideas whole rather than in parts • perceives global properties of patterns • integrates parts into meaningful wholes
Temporal	Spatial
• keeps track of things in time-ordered sequences	• keeps track of things in spatial arrangements
Sequential	Nonlinear
• links ideas in sequences so that one thought directly follows another logically	• figures things out simultaneously
Digital	Analogical
• uses words for cognition	• uses analogues for cognition

Sources: Adapted from Springer and Deutsch (1985), Edwards (1979).

spoken and written language require many different mental, sensory, and motor processes that are not necessarily specialized to the same hemisphere.

The current fashion of labelling people as 'left brain' or 'right brain' is dysfunctional. Much has been made of the assumption that formal educational institutions educate only one side of the brain. This assumption is false (Springer & Deutsch, 1985). Clearly, sensory information is received by, and motor responses are sent out from, both sides of the brain. One reason for believing that formal educational programs educate only one side of the brain is that such programs tend to evaluate, and hence reinforce, the kind of knowing and learning accompanied by language, for which the left hemisphere is specialized. It is more difficult to assess learning outcomes that reside in the mute right hemisphere (Springer & Deutsch, 1985).

Astronomer-biologist Carl Sagan (1977), in describing the role of the two hemispheres in scientific thinking, tells us that the search for patterns (right hemisphere thinking) without critical analysis (left hemisphere thinking) leads to incomplete science. Sagan suggests that scientists, like all humans, see what they want to see and identify patterns that, in fact, may not be supported by the information available. All identified patterns, therefore, must be subjected to critical analysis. All learning, as well as the effective pursuit of knowledge, requires the functions of both hemispheres.

Brain-Compatible Learning

Steven Pinker (1997) reminds us that the brain processes information and that thinking is a kind of computation. However, the brain should not be thought of as a complex computer. For one thing, a computer processes information serial fashion, doing one thing at a time; brains process information in parallel, doing many things at once. For another, computers are assembled according to a blueprint; brains assemble themselves through human development. Because the brain is a parallel processor, we need to be mindful of the rules that control and constrain the brain's activities and to ensure that our facilitating strategies do not violate these rules (Caine & Caine, 1991). Let's consider five principles of brain-based learning.

First, because the brain is a parallel processor, it is always doing many things at one time. We are aware of less than 25 per cent of the brain's activity. While you are engaged in conscious learning, your brain is monitoring and managing all your bodily functions and dealing, at some level below awareness, with the current concerns dominating your daily life. The brain is also on the alert for any perceived threats to the well-being of the individual. Good facilitation should take into account the possibility that any of these out-of-awareness concerns may become of greater concern to the learner than the task of learning. The use of time must be flexible enough to allow for varying individual concerns.

Second, to learn, the brain needs to be processing information. Delivering information only in a linear, sequential fashion is counterproductive. In such situations, the learner may begin to attend to information not being delivered by the facilitator, such as the temperature of the air, the comfort of the chairs, the strange hair colour of someone sitting in front, the sunset or rain seen through the window, or even the next weekend's activities. Good facilitation should be understood as a process of orchestrating the learners' experiences through providing a variety of activities and resources (Caine & Caine, 1991).

Third, the brain allows for both conscious and out-of-conscious learning. Individuals can learn how to calculate probabilities in their statistics class at the same time as they are learning to hate and fear statistics. We remember our experiences and the sense we make of them, not just what we are told. Learners need to learn how to become aware of, and benefit from, out-of-conscious learning through processing the total experience and not just the information presented by the facilitator (Caine & Caine, 1991; Reardon, 1999). The facilitator needs to know how to help the learner to do this

Figure 5.3
Activating the Brain Hemispheres

Left Hemisphere	Right Hemisphere
• Taking notes, writing outlines, listening for the facts	• Making mind maps, drawing, doodling, guided imagery
• Comparing patterns, analysing information	• Identifying patterns
• Planning, setting priorities, clarifying objectives	• Going with the 'flow'
• Eliminating extraneous ideas	• Being open to new ideas, brainstorming
• Using closed, convergent questions to obtain 'right' answers	• Using open-ended, divergent questions to explore possible answers
• Analytical listening	• Empathetic listening
• Crossword puzzles	• Jigsaw puzzles
• Puns, irony	• Cartoons, visual humour
• Adopting the attitude of challenging the ideas of others, debating	• Adopting the attitude of accepting ideas of others, opening up to 'irrelevancies'
• Making the mind do 'mental push-ups'	• Dreaming, daydreaming
• Focus on time, numbers, money	• Awareness of colours, odours, surrounding space
• Concentrating on the meaning of words	• Using repetitious sounds, rhythms, actions
• Staying focused on 'reality'	• Depriving self of food, sleep, and/or sensory stimulation
• Sitting still	• Extreme physical comfort, relaxation
• Describing emotions	• Feeling emotions

Sources: Developed from Wonder and Donovan (1984), Edwards (1979), Buzan and Buzan (1995).

and must be willing to listen to both negative and positive feedback about the experience of learning. In fact, since facilitators' brains are also parallel processors, they need to develop some awareness of their own out-of-conscious responses to any teaching-learning interaction. For me, walking out of a class session muttering to myself that 'they didn't seem to get it' is only the first step in understanding implications about my facilitating strategies.

Fourth, whatever we learn is embedded in the context in which we learn it. The 'context' consists of many components, including social interactions, physical environment, personal comfort, the language being used, and the information being learned. The brain processes all these contexts, not just the information to be learned. Learning experiences can be enhanced when the facilitator takes this embedded quality of learning into account. Facilitating success depends on having learners use all their senses and immersing learners in many different, complex, and interactive experiences over time (Caine & Caine, 1991).

Fifth, all facilitating activities have an effect on both cerebral hemispheres; however, some have a stronger effect on one hemisphere than the other. Figure 5.3, Activating the Brain Hemispheres, describes facilitating strategies that can be used to encourage the level of activity in each hemisphere. The left hemisphere responds best to activities depending on time-ordered sequences, the use of words and numbers, and organized analytical thinking. The right hemisphere responds best to activities depending on the use of visual, nonverbal materials and on simultaneous presentations with lots of redundant information.

LEARNING AND FACILITATING PRINCIPLES

A learner's personal model of reality is composed of both verbal and nonverbal components and integrates memories stored in both hemispheres. Learning is more effective when ideas, information, and knowledge can be learned and stored in both verbal and nonverbal forms.

> *Facilitating is most effective when ideas can be presented in both verbal and nonverbal forms.*

To function at top efficiency, the brain requires the individual to be in good physical condition. This includes being in good health, well rested, well nourished, and physically fit. The brain also requires that learning activities be carried out in a physically supportive environment in which the learner is reasonably comfortable, the temperature and lighting are suitable, and the air quality is good.

> *Good facilitators ensure that the physical environment is comfortable and that learners are not overly tired or hungry. Avoid having learners sit for extended periods of time. Plan learning activities that will allow learners to move around periodically.*

When learners are distressed, control of brain activity down-shifts from the cerebral cortex to the limbic system. When down-shifting occurs, learners becomes more concerned with self-preservation and self-protection than with learning. Once the brain has downshifted, learners stop using both logical and holistic thinking processes. Stress affects both cerebral hemispheres equally.

> Good facilitators are aware of signs signifying down-shifting and take time to help the learner deal with the associated distress. Distress will be considered in greater detail in Chapter 6. Down-shifting is similar to the disorienting phase of learning discussed in Chapter 3.

Processing information through verbal functions is time consuming but logical and analytical; processing information through nonverbal functions is time conserving but analogical and holistic. Effective learning involves both logical and analogical, analytic and holistic approaches. Effective learners and sound critical thinkers use the functions of both hemispheres to engage in learning and thinking.

> Facilitating activities calling for collaboration and integration of the activities of the two hemispheres are more likely to promote sound learning than activities drawing on the specialized talents of only one hemisphere.

The opposite of logical (left hemisphere) thinking is analogical (right hemisphere) thinking, *not* illogical or nonlogical thinking. Analogical thinking makes use of pattern recognition through metaphors, images, and the like. Nonverbal, analogical, holistic learning sometimes appears to be nonrational because it is not linear, not sequential, and frequently nonverbal.

> Good facilitating activities should include opportunities to engage in nonverbal, analogical, visual activities. The use of humour is a particularly effective way to encourage such activities. Laughter is good for learning.

The time taken to process information during learning involves processing it in both hemispheres, communicating between hemispheres, and integrating the results. If one hemisphere works faster than the other, the learner may accept the first answer that comes to mind, an answer that may not be the best answer. Learners should be encouraged to think twice before generating final learning responses.

> Good facilitators should not be too quick to judge first answers or initial learning attempts.

The Mind and Cognition

Pinker (1997) states: 'The mind is not the brain but what the brain does, and not even everything it does such as metabolizing fat and giving off heat' (p. 24). If the brain processes information in parallel and through two different hemispheres, we should expect to find corresponding processes within the mind. We experience the collective electrical and chemical activity of the brain of which we are aware as cognition – perceiving, remembering, thinking, problem solving, decision making, planning to act. We know about cognition because we are sentient, capable of being aware of and thinking about our own thinking.

The concepts we have developed to describe cognition are many. Here I will consider three basic groups of cognitive processes, those related to the strategies of perceiving, remembering, and thinking. We will address the role of emotions in these cognitive processes in the next chapter.

Perception Strategies

Perception is the process through which incoming sensory information is interpreted based on one's previous experience and personal model of reality, in preparation for the more complex mental activity of thinking. Two important processes used in perception are pattern recognition and attention. Whether these two processes occur one before the other, and if they do which occurs first, are matters of considerable debate. I will assume that they operate in tandem.

Pattern recognition involves comparing incoming sensory stimuli with existing patterns of information already stored in memory. Patterns can be recognized by analysing the features of incoming stimuli, one feature at a time, and comparing each to existing patterns; or by comparing incoming stimuli holistically to stored templates or mental copies of patterns. Feature-by-feature analysis is typical of the analytic cognitive style discussed in Chapter 4, while the use of templates is typical of the holistic cognitive style. Most of us can use both strategies but prefer one over the other.

A Finnish friend once asked me why Canadians gave so many different names to five-petalled flowers (garden pansy, winter-flowering pansy, dog's tooth violet, horned violet, sweet violet) when all of them, in her opinion, were violas. I didn't know the answer then, but have since learned that in North America 'viola' is a botanical name while 'pansy' and 'violet' are common names. I struggle to distinguish between violets and pansies by comparing incoming information, feature by feature, to patterns I already hold in memory; she holds a holistic template for five-petalled flowers for which no further analysis is needed. And then there are individuals who can instantly identify cars and trucks by make and year – a form of feature-by-feature analysis. My pattern recognition of other vehicles on the road is based on two holistic categories: those that can be overtaken by my car and those that cannot.

Attention involves selecting patterns for further processing. Attention is accomplished through scanning the perceptual field (what can be seen or heard) and selecting those parts that require further processing. When we scan a perceptual field, our attention is like a beam of light. A wide beam, or diffuse scanning, allows us to take in as much information about the field as possible all at once. A narrow beam, or limited scanning, allows us to take in selected information about the field at any one time.

Within that part of the perceptual field that is 'lit up' by our scanning, we can select a main figure from the incoming information as the central focus of our analysis while screening out other parts of the field. The screened-out parts are perceived as irrelevant information or 'informational noise' and retreat into the background behind the figure. Or we can keep as much of the perceptual field as intact as possible without any detailed analysis to create a more diffuse image that is not separated into figure and background. Limited scanning and figure differentiation support the analytic cognitive style; diffuse scanning and figure-ground integration support the holistic cognitive style.

I once had the unfortunate experience of having the police arrive at my door on a Sunday afternoon to investigate a complaint from a neighbour that my sons (then six and four years old) were disturbing the peace. The boys were in the backyard building a fort. I had heard the sounds, but all I really heard was that they were not fighting, a sound dear to my heart. My neighbours heard only the hammering and assumed that the boys were deliberately disturbing their peace. My neighbours and I were attending to different parts of the perceptual field and coming to quite different conclusions.

The preferred perceptual strategies used by individual learners will greatly affect what they attend to when information to be learned is presented to them and what parts of the information they will select for further analysis. A facilitator can assist in this process by providing advanced organizers – a teaching strategy that could include handouts or skeleton notes – to help direct the learners' attention to selected information; or through vocal or visual emphasis.

Memory Strategies

Memory is a cognitive process that allows us to maintain a reasonably complete record of our life experiences. Information is stored in memory so that it can be easily retrieved when we need it. One way to understand memory is to examine the basic cognitive strategies associated with the form in which information is stored or represented in memory, the manner in which information is organized, and the strategies involved in retrieving the stored information.

Information can be re-presented in memory using *verbal-analytical codes* or *visual-analogical codes*. Bits of information about a single activity can be stored in both types of code. I could describe my home to you as 'a big grey house with a red roof down by the river' or I could describe it as 'a two-storey, Georgian-style house with Palladian windows.' The first description is visual-analogical and uses broadly defined categories. The second is verbal-analytical and uses narrowly defined categories. Both descriptions are accurate, but to recognize the house using the second description you would need to know something about my narrowly defined categories. The analytic cognitive style is best served by verbal-analytical codes; the holistic cognitive style by visual-analogical codes.

Information can be organized in memory using *narrowly defined categories* based on a high degree of differentiation and little overlap among the categories and the patterns or ideas they represent; or using *broadly defined categories* based on similarities and considerable overlap among the categories and the patterns or ideas they represent. Both types of categories become interconnected as part of a conceptual network. David Hunt (1971, 1987) describes a conceptual network in terms of its complexity or conceptual level. At low levels of complexity, categories may have few interconnections, resulting in categorical or discrete thinking. At high levels of complexity, categories are widely interconnected, resulting in integrated and relativistic thinking. The analytic cognitive style is best served by narrowly defined categories; the holistic cognitive style by broadly defined categories.

Retrieving information from memory involves searching the conceptual network for the information needed. The analytic cognitive style is best served by search strategies that are *convergent* in nature. These strategies narrow the search for relevant information by attempting to find the single 'correct' bit of information through increasingly narrowing and sequencing the search. The holistic cognitive style is best served by search strategies that are *divergent* in nature. These strategies broaden the search for relevant information through retrieving a wide range of information, some bits of which are more relevant than others. Learners who use divergent strategies like to brainstorm, almost always coming up with many more answers to the question being asked than are needed; those who prefer the convergent strategy will brainstorm until they have identified the 'right' or 'best' answer.

Another way to understand memory is proposed by Tulving (1985), who describes long-term memories as involving habituated, episodic, and semantic memories. *Habituated memory* stores the knowledge and skills we use in everyday life. For example, use of the alphabet to find information in a telephone book, dictionary, or encyclopedia involves habituated memory.

Habituated memory stores strategies and information for such tasks as tying your shoelaces, driving your car, writing letters, and so on. Without habituated memory we would all spend far too much time figuring out how to solve repetitive problems. Habituated memory serves both analytic and holistic cognitive styles.

Episodic memory is a store of life events, still more or less in their original form as specific impressions. Sometimes a familiar smell will trigger a complete scene or episode from your life. For example, the smell of apples baking might recall a scene from childhood in which you can see and taste your mother's apple pie. The memory likely comes complete with sounds, sensations, and feelings. Episodic memory stores raw data that has gone through a pattern recognition process but the patterns may not have been assigned words or abstract meanings. Episodic memory serves the holistic cognitive style,

Semantic memory is a store of the meanings and facts we construct and acquire as a consequence of our life experiences and our learning. If I asked you to think of what represents 'love' for you, you might tell me one of the symbols is your mother baking an apple pie – a meaning assigned to a scene stored in episodic memory. Or you might provide a dictionary definition of the word. Semantic memory serves the analytic cognitive style.

To give you some idea of how your memory is organized, think of a home in which you lived as a child, one that you can recall vividly. Before you read any further, figure out how many windows were in that home.

If you walked through the home from room to room or around the outside, counting windows as you went, you are probably drawing on your episodic memory. You may have encountered other memories as you did the task.

If you recalled that each room had one window and there were seven rooms, then you are probably drawing on semantic memory and did not recall any other 'facts' about your home. You may even have had an argument with yourself about whether or not you should include the patio or porch door as a window.

I regularly teach a course in adult development. In the past, I have asked course participants to write a partial autobiography or life narrative as one assignment. My instructions to them are to begin the process by recalling their lives using an analytic strategy that involves listing dates and events from birth to the present time and then adding details for each event. Many students find this impossible and switch to a more holistic strategy. Birren and Deutchman (1991) describe a course on autobiographical writing that begins with a more holistic approach. Participants are asked to identify a 'branching point' in their lives and to write everything they can recall of the conditions and events that surround it. This writing does not need to be chronological. I have recently amended the course in adult development by providing both analytic and holistic strategies as alternative starting points for the autobiography assignment.

Conceptual Networks

Information is assumed to be stored in long-term memory as part of a conceptual network. Any word or image can become a trigger to call up a network of associated words, images, sounds, and sensations. Buzan and Buzan (1995) advocate the use of 'mind maps' to retrieve information from conceptual networks. Their technique for drawing mind maps includes the use of words and phrases, drawings, icons, and so on (see Figure 5.4, Dorothy's Mind Map for Brain and Mind, for an example). The mind maps advocated by Buzan and Buzan are somewhat more free-form that the concept maps proposed by other writers (Deshler, 1990; Novak & Gowin, 1984). Mind maps clearly appeal more to highly visual learners; we need to think of ways to develop similar techniques that draw on auditory representations through music or poems for example, or kinesthetic representations through dances, games, or charades.

Conceptual networks can also be described in terms of their *cognitive complexity* (Harvey, Hunt, & Schroder, 1961; Hunt, 1971, 1987; Joyce & Weil, 1992). Cognitive complexity ranges from low to high. A learner who is using low complexity understands and stores information in discrete categories (black/white thinking). Two or three categories may be understood in relation to each other (right/wrong, good/bad), but connections between paired concepts are minimal. For example, an individual who uses low cognitive complexity might lump all 'adults' into one category and contrast this category with other categories, such as 'children,' and might assign all members of the category the same characteristic, such as 'self-directed.' In low cognitive complexity, truth is understood to be absolute and thinking is described as dualistic and unidimensional. A conceptual structure that depends on separate and distinct categories reduces the individual's ability to perceive similarities among categories (Joyce & Weil, 1992).

A learner who is using moderate cognitive complexity understands and stores any given concept in various combinations with other concepts (black-grey-white thinking), combinations that allow for several different ways of structuring the world, thus introducing problems of choice and probability (Joyce & Weil, 1992). For example, 'adults' and 'children' might be understood in terms of selected characteristics based on both similarities and differences. That is, self-directedness might be understood as a characteristic of some children, while some adults might not necessarily be self-directed. In moderate cognitive complexity, truth is understood as having

Figure 5.4
Dorothy's Mind Map for Brain and Mind

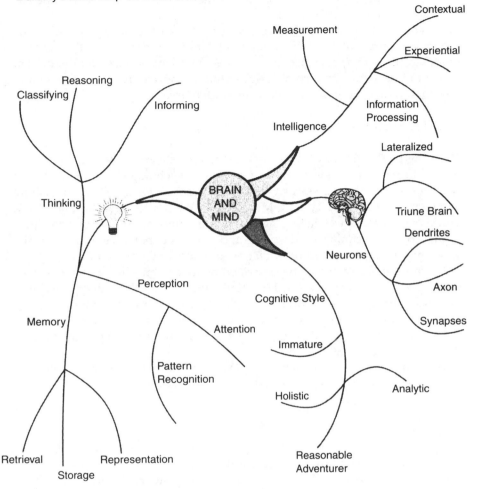

several different variations. That is, what I know to be true may not be the same as what you know to be true. Such thinking is described as multiplistic and multidimensional.

A learner who is using high cognitive complexity greatly increases the number of networks within which a single concept can be understood. In order to determine 'truth,' the individual must be prepared to select a context and specify under what conditions various versions of the truth are acceptable. For example, 'adultness' might be understood as having different meanings depending on the specific context in which the characteristic is observed. Truth and knowledge are understood to be relativistic – what is true in one context may not be true in another – and thinking is described as relativistic or contextualized.

Loevinger (1976), Hunt (1971), and Perry (1970), among others, define cognitive complexity as a developmental characteristic, one that can be modified through appropriate educational experiences. Most of us exhibit at least moderate cognitive complexity within our own area of expertise and low cognitive complexity in totally unfamiliar areas.

Thinking Strategies

Thinking processes are even harder to differentiate and describe than those related to perception and memory. Cognitive psychologists do not agree on the names of the processes or whether thinking styles are stable over time and contexts (Flannery, 1993; A. Miller, 1991). We can consider 'thinking' as a group of subprocesses (classifying, reasoning, inferring) that allows the individual to give meaning to, describe, and explain experience and to predict what might happen in future similar experiences or circumstances.

These processes can also be described as theory-building processes. Personal construct theory (Candy, 1990; Kelly, 1955) states that every individual builds his or her own theories to explain past experiences, predict future outcomes, and control present activities. Thinking consists of cognitive processes that help us to build our own theories about our own experience and thereby create our own model of reality.

Thinking in the *analytic cognitive style* involves processing bits of information sequentially, in a stepwise fashion. Such thinking is

- serial,
- systematic,
- logical,
- generally based on abstract ideas, and
- allows the learner to adopt an objective stance towards reality.

Explanations and predictions (hypotheses) are about specific, single attributes and are based on logical reasoning. The analytic thinker makes 'actuarial judgments' in which one attribute of a situation is considered at a time, with other attributes being held constant and irrelevant attributes being eliminated. Those who use this strategy 'worry away at difficulties until they have been mastered, in preference to leaving loose ends' (A. Miller, 1991, p. 58). The analytic thinker prefers literal analogies, rejects metaphors, avoids figurative speech, and may have trouble appreciating how one area of knowledge can be seen as analogous to another.

Thinking in the *holistic cognitive style* involves processing whole concepts or groups of concepts simultaneously. Such thinking is

- global,
- redundant,
- analogical, and
- allows the learner to adopt a subjective stance towards reality.

The holistic thinker develops explanations and predictions based not on single attributes but on collections of attributes, and on poetic analogies, idiosyncratic metaphors, and intuitive judgments. Holistic thinkers tend to juggle 'several ideas at once, hoping the situation will clarify itself in due course' (A. Miller, 1991, p. 59). They enjoy looking at things from several different points of view at the same time.

Narrative and Paradigmatic Thinking

Another way to think about thinking strategies is proposed by Jerome Bruner (1986), who describes analytical thinkers as using paradigmatic thinking and holistic thinkers as using narrative thinking. *Paradigmatic thinking* is based on propositions or logical arguments and seeks to establish context-free, causal relationships that explain why events happen the way they do. The truth of such ideas can be verified through empirical research, but the richness of the ideas is often sacrificed in the pursuit of accuracy. *Narrative thinking* allows us to store and describe information for which no clearly defined propositional knowledge is available. Such thinking uses story telling as a means for establishing themes of human behaviour describing human life in its social context, without offering explanations or causes. The truth of a narrative is based on credibility, and accuracy is sacrificed in favour of idiographic richness and coherence.

Narrative thinking is described in the literature under other labels, such as 'personal practical knowledge' (Connelly & Clandinin, 1985). This area is currently being explored by adult educators (Randall, 1995) as a means for understanding adult development and aging. Narratives are used frequently by individuals who are novices in an area of study, and provide a useful means for helping adult learners examine their sense of self and self-esteem and their early experiences as learners.

Thinking strategies, as with all strategies that contribute to cognitive style, are affected by normal age-related changes. Such changes in cognition have always been assumed to lead to deficits in thinking. This view is now changing. Berg et al. (1994) view holistic thinking strategies, particularly narrative thinking, as having adaptive functions in relation to age-related changes.

Paradigmatic thinking is concerned with accuracy in understanding texts and leads to better performance on text-processing tasks, such as recalling stories by remembering factual information. Narrative thinking is more concerned with metaphorical and psychological interpretations of texts and leads to poorer performance on tests requiring recall of factual information or propositional knowledge. Berg et al. (1994) claim that paradigmatic thinking is more typical of younger adults while narrative thinking is more typical of older adults, putting them at a disadvantage when performing on tests of cognitive ability. Narrative thinking may provide older adults with a more efficient means for storing and retrieving information and for transmitting information to younger generations.

LEARNING AND FACILITATING PRINCIPLES

No matter how information is presented to learners, each will process the information by using a personal cognitive style. New information, when combined with the individual's personal and unique model of reality, will rarely be interpreted and understood by the learner in the same manner as it is understood by the facilitator presenting the information.

> *Good facilitators will take the time to find out how learners have interpreted and understood the information that was presented.*

Cognitive styles are assumed to be stable characteristics and an integral part of personality. Individuals may have considerable difficulty changing their styles to match those being used by others.

> *Good facilitators will deliberately learn about other cognitive styles in order to better understand all learners. In making this effort, the facilitator may develop an integrated/synthetic style and become a 'reasonable adventurer.'*

Misunderstandings among learners or between learner and facilitator are often the result of differences in how a situation or information is processed through different cognitive styles.

> *Facilitators need to be aware of different cognitive styles in order to understand the origins of any misunderstandings among learners and between themselves and individual learners.*

Information needs to be presented to learners in a variety of perceptual modes: visual, auditory, kinesthetic, and verbal.

Assessment procedures generally favour analytic cognitive styles.
Assessment methods need to be designed to support holistic learners in their learning activities. Holistic thinkers would probably do
better on essay questions or questions based on case studies than on
multiple choice or true-false questions. If true-false questions must
be used, holistic thinkers could be asked to explain why an answer
is true or false (Flannery, 1993).

Narratives are stories that emerge from one's personal model of
reality, and therefore, are stories that relate to the 'self.'

> *Listening empathically to the narratives told by adult learners*
> *about their own learning is an excellent way to find out the*
> *best way to facilitate their learning and to affirm what they*
> *know and who they are.*

Intelligence

For most of us, intelligence is represented by a score on an intelligence test.
IQ scores may be statistically reliable, but they may also be irrelevant to normal daily living. However, 'intelligence' is a concept that we draw on to
describe the behaviour of others as well as our own. While we may not agree
with or approve of IQ tests and IQ scores, most of us know intelligent
behaviour when we see it, and most of us privately assess others in terms of
their intelligence.

Early writers on intelligence focused exclusively on the verbal and mathematical abilities important for success at school. Crucial components for
assessing intelligence were the use of symbols to solve problems but the
abilities to create a product – write a poem, stage a play, perform a dance,
manage an organization – were not included because these activities did not
lend themselves to short-answer tests. Recently, two influential writers –
Robert Sternberg and Howard Gardner – have expressed concerns that the
nature of intelligence goes well beyond the capacities examined in traditional IQ tests. Sternberg (1988) writes about triarchic intelligence and Gardner (1983) about multiple intelligences.

Sternberg's Triarchic Intelligence

Intelligence is a quality of mind that we use continually in our daily lives.
Sternberg (1988) defines intelligence as 'mental self-management – the men-

tal management of one's life in a constructive, purposeful way' (p. 11). Mental self-management, in Sternberg's terms, has three basic elements:

1 adapting to environments,
2 selecting new environments, and
3 shaping or modifying environments.

Intelligence, even in traditional definitions, involves the ability to adapt or to change one's behaviour to fit more easily into the environment. What is adaptive in one setting may not be adaptive in another. When an environment is unsatisfactory for a variety of reasons, it may be maladaptive to adapt and the intelligent choice may be to select a different environment. 'Trying again' or 'trying harder' may have merit, but individuals must also know when to stop banging their head against the walls of one environment and move on to another.

Sometimes neither adaptation nor selection is possible, and environmental shaping becomes the intelligent choice. Whereas adaptation involves fitting oneself into the environment, shaping involves fitting the environment to oneself. There is no single set of behaviours that is intelligent for everyone in every situation. What does appear to be common among intelligent people is their ability to capitalize on their strengths and compensate for their weaknesses in different environments.

Sternberg (1988) describes his theory of intelligence as a triarchic theory in which intelligence is conceived as having three parts: a fundamental or componential part forming the basis for learning and reasoning, an experiential part, and a contextual part.

The *componential part* deals with fundamental components of intelligence or underlying cognitive processes. Sternberg proposes three types of cognitive components or strategies:

1 *Knowledge acquisition or information-processing components* are basic cognitive strategies for learning, that is, for translating sensory input and information from life experiences into a personal, conceptual model of reality.
2 *Metacomponents* are overarching or executive cognitive strategies that allow one to use knowledge and information to reason, plan, and decide about personal actions and then evaluate those actions.
3 *Performance components* are basic cognitive strategies that allow one to turn plans into actions or motor outputs.

Intelligent behaviour involves an interactive relationship between these three fundamental components of cognition.

The *experiential part* of intelligence underlies an individual's responses to life experiences. These range along a continuum from highly novel experiences (never encountered) to highly familiar experiences for which responses have become automatic. Intelligence involves the ability to reason about and learn from new experiences, resulting in the development of new knowledge and skills and new executive strategies. Novelty can be a function of the context in which tasks are to be carried out or of the unfamiliarity of the tasks themselves.

Experiential intelligence involves bringing into play the fundamental components of intelligence in both novel and routine tasks (Sternberg, 1988). In adult education, for example, we are concerned about the transition from school to work and the transfer of knowledge from one context to another. Sternberg would define the ability to make such transitions and transfers successfully as aspects of experiential intelligence, or one's ability to retain composure in a novel situation.

The *contextual part* of intelligence underlies an individual's ability to be 'street smart' by

- adapting to, selecting, and shaping the environments in which he or she must function;
- knowing when to challenge others or change the environment itself, or, in the words of the song, 'know when to hold, know when to fold 'em, know when to walk away, know when to run' (Sternberg, 1988)

Individual differences in intelligence are partly a matter of genetic inheritance, partly a matter of personal preference, partly a matter of socialization and other environmental influences, and partly a matter of opportunity. The cognitive strategies we use are selected on the basis of our personal preferences from a full range of potential processes. The more one is able and willing to use alternate cognitive strategies, respond to novel situations, and adapt to and shape environments, the more intelligent one becomes (Sternberg, 1988).

Traditional IQ tests are based on the assumption that intelligence is the same thing for everyone. In some sense, intelligence is consistent across cultures because, for example, adaptation is always required. But what constitutes adaptation varies from one culture to another and what is acceptable as adaptation varies from one person to the next. Sternberg discusses the many ways in which early socialization in different cultures affects intelligence in children. And if intelligence is strongly affected by socialization, then the intelligence of adults can also be affected by socialization processes in workplaces, families, communities, and educational programs. To some extent, one can improve intelligence through learning.

Gardner's Multiple Intelligences

Gardner (1983) has proposed a theory of multiple intelligences. Each intelligence uses a characteristic set of psychological processes, and these processes need to be assessed in an 'intelligence-fair' manner. Gardner defines an intelligence as 'the ability to solve problems or to fashion products that are valued in at least one culture or community' (Gardner, 1999, p. 113). The seven intelligences that form the basis of Gardner's theory are (Gardner & Hatch, 1989):

1 Logical-mathematical – sensitivity to and ability to discern logical or numerical patterns; ability to handle long chains of reasoning;
2 Linguistic – sensitivity to sounds, rhythms, and meanings of words; sensitivity to the different functions of language;
3 Musical – abilities to produce and appreciate rhythm, pitch, and timbre; appreciation of the terms of musical expressiveness;
4 Spatial – capacities to perceive the visual-spatial world accurately and to perform transformations on one's initial perceptions;
5 Bodily-kinesthetic – abilities to control one's body movements and to handle objects skillfully;
6 Interpersonal – capacities to discern and respond appropriately to the moods, temperaments, motivations, and desires of other people;
7 Intrapersonal – access to one's own feelings and the ability to discriminate among them and draw upon them to guide behaviour; knowledge of one's own strengths, weaknesses, desires, and intelligences.

More recently, Gardner (1999) has proposed three additional intelligences: naturalistic, spiritual, and existential. While he now includes naturalistic intelligence as the eighth intelligence in his list, he still has doubts about whether or not spiritual and existential intelligences actually meet the criteria necessary to include them in his list. These three intelligences are defined as:

1 Naturalistic – capacity to recognize and classify flora and fauna, recognize instances as members of a species, distinguish among members of a species, recognize the existence of neighbouring species, and chart the formal and informal relations among several species;
2 Spiritual – capacity and desire to address the ultimate issues of existence, to understand ourselves in all our aspects and relations within the cosmos, and to create a system for understanding who we are and how we fit into the world;
3 Existential – capacity to locate oneself with respect to the most existential features of the human condition: the significance of life, the meaning

of death, the ultimate fate of the physical and psychological worlds, experience of love for another human being, or total immersion in a work of art.

Assessing Intelligence

Each of the three aspects of intelligence and the associated knowledge and strategies proposed by Sternberg (1988) and the eight intelligences proposed by Gardner (1983) can and should be assessed differently. Traditional IQ tests measure the knowledge acquisition and executive aspects of componential intelligence (Sternberg) and the logical-mathematical and linguisitic intelligences (Gardner). Academic achievement relates closely to such measures.

Schaie (1977–8) directs our attention to the fact that as we develop and change our social roles and responsibilities over our lifespan, our need for intelligent behaviour also changes. While we need all three forms of intelligence throughout life, the emphasis changes. As youth, before entering the workplace and starting families, we need to have the intelligence necessary to acquire knowledge and skills for future occupational and professional roles. The aspects of intelligence that we would use most often in this process would be the fundamental components.

As young adults, when we enter the workplace and start families, we need to use experiential and contextual intelligence as well as the fundamental components. If we have had no opportunities to practise such behaviour, we may have trouble making the necessary transitions. Assessing intelligent behaviour in this stage of development could involve, for example, performance appraisals by supervisors or responses to case studies rather than traditional cognitive tests.

As middle-aged adults, many of us assume responsibility for managing the affairs of our families, workplaces, and communities. To do this we need to draw on our creativity and responsiveness, behaviours that Sternberg identifies as beyond intelligence (1988, p. 240). Responsiveness involves the ability to co-ordinate the behaviour and performances of two or more persons as they carry out co-operative activities on behalf of the family, workplace, or community. Creativity involves developing new ways to understand or do things (Schaie, 1977–8). Assessing intelligent behaviour in this stage of development could focus on performance appraisals from coworkers and peers and responses to complex case studies.

As older adults, we need to be able to draw on wisdom, a form of behaviour that also goes beyond intelligence (Sternberg, 1988). Schaie (1977–8) describes this stage as involving reintegrative intelligence. Assessing intelligence at this stage seems counterproductive unless it is done by colleagues and peers in the same age group and focuses on contextual intelligence and the adaptiveness of behaviours developed to deal with age-related changes in oneself and in the environment.

LEARNING AND FACILITATING PRINCIPLES

We have all been socialized to believe that certain behaviours indicate intelligence and other behaviours indicate lack of intelligence. Definitions of what constitutes intelligent behaviour vary by subgroups within each culture. What is viewed as intelligent behaviour for men may be quite different from what is viewed as intelligent behaviour for women. Differences also exist between social classes, racial and linguistic groups, and so on.

What facilitators believe demonstrates lack of intelligence may be indicative of highly intelligent behaviour in a different culture. Facilitators need to consider carefully what types of behaviour they use to assess an adult learner's intelligence.

Cognitive Development

Until very recently, our understanding of cognitive development was based on the belief that this development was complete by the time we reached adulthood, and that any subsequent changes were age, accident, and disease related and involved declines and deficits. In the past twenty years, psychologists, gerontologists, and adult educators have carried out considerable research that refutes this claim. Traditional beliefs held that when individuals reached adulthood, they were capable of

- performing cognitive operations on mental representations of experience;
- identifying patterns among these representations;
- assigning meanings to these patterns in the form of symbols, words, and signs;
- using these meanings to think (solve problems and plan actions);
- identifying patterns among these meanings and assigning increasingly abstract meanings to them; and
- using these abstract meanings to think

Mental operations performed on abstract meanings can become highly complex and sophisticated.

Cognitive development from birth onward results in an organized set of mental constructs, our personal model of reality. This model consists of both the processes of cognition (attending, selecting, representing, storing, retrieving classifying, reasoning, inferring, etc.) and the structured concepts or results of cognition (stored systems of generalized knowledge, special-ized dimensions of knowledge, as well as the skills and knowledge to be activated in specific contexts). The development of both the processes and structures of cognition proceeds through two basic processes: differentiating (analysing) and integrating (synthesizing) (Kegan, 1982).

- When the integrating process results in expanded concepts without changing their essential meaning, the process is called *assimilation*.
- When the integration process results in transformed meanings, wholly new meanings, or new cognitive strategies, the process is called *accommo-dation* (Kegan, 1982) or *transformation* (Mezirow, 1991).

Those transformations that are accompanied by a major shift in the way the individual perceives, remembers, and thinks about the world are viewed as marking transitions from one stage of cognitive development to another.

According to Piaget (as cited in Hunt & Sullivan, 1974, pp. 131–8), the developing individual goes through four stages of cognitive growth:

- sensori-motor thought,
- representational or pre-operational thought,
- concrete operational thought (mental operations that convert concrete information into abstract ideas), and
- formal operational thought (mental operations that convert abstract ideas into more abstract and increasingly complex ideas).

These four stages are assumed to be necessary to attain the abstract thought perceived as typical of adults (Kegan, 1982). Each new cognitive stage cre-ates a more adequate and more logical set of concepts and processes for knowing the world. According to Kegan, Piaget viewed 'more adequate' cognitive processes and structures as those that would allow the individual to adopt an increasingly less egocentric stance from which to perceive, dif-ferentiate, and integrate increasingly more complex and interrelated mean-ings based on accumulated experience.

Adult Cognitive Development

Piaget's four stages were once thought to be universal, to happen to every human being. It has since been shown that development of formal opera-tional thought is largely dependent on the influence of secondary and post-secondary educational institutions, and therefore is not universal. Evidence based on testing done with adults indicates that many do not use formal operational thinking and that others use a form of dialectical thinking that is not accounted for by Piaget's description of formal thought.

Many writers now believe that there is a fifth stage of cognitive development that is typical of mature adult thinking, called *post-formal* (Sinnott, 1994) or *dialectical operational* thought (Basseches, 1984). The features of this stage must take into account the type of thinking that is typical of an adult's daily tasks. We know that any cognitive development during adulthood must take place in response to some or all of the following conditions and needs:

- Adults must transfer knowledge from one context to another, most often from a training context to a practical, applied context. *Transferability* involves the recognition of new instances in which existing knowledge and skills can be applied, a form of contextual intelligence and learning not accounted for in formal operational thinking (Kolb, 1984).
- Adults are called on to develop *specialized knowledge and skills*. Kolb (1984) describes specialization as a powerful developmental dynamic in which adults are encouraged, through professional, occupational, and role socialization, to develop personal characteristics deemed appropriate and acceptable to their field of specialization and that increasingly become an integral part of one's self and one's personal model of reality. When these characteristics become an integral part of personality, they may affect cognition.
- While children and adolescents spend much of their time solving problems and answering questions posed by others, adults must be able to *identify and formulate problems* before solving them, or *invent questions* before answering them (Arlin, 1986; Watzlawick, Weakland, & Fisch, 1974). While these tasks sound simple, many adults, even those in formal educational systems, cannot do them.
- Many adults live in work, family, and community environments where it is not clear what one's goals should be. *Indeterminate situations*, or *ill-structured problems* (Sinnott, 1994), call for the development of projective images of future possibilities (Schön, 1971). Such situations also require cognitive strategies allowing the individual to move back and forth between this future image and the current situation in order to monitor forward progress and modify actions before implementation.
- Adults must be able to deal with *uncertainties, doubts, and ambiguities*. Riegel (1973) criticizes the idea that formal operational thinking is the highest stage of cognitive development on the ground that uncertainty, doubt, and ambiguity cannot always be resolved through formal logic or rational thought. Therefore, it is logical to assume such situations call for cognitive strategies that represent a more advanced stage of cognitive development.
- Most adults must live and work within complex systems of roles and rela-

tionships and must learn how to manage the interactions and conflicts among them (Koplowitz, 1987). *Systems thinking* involves cognitive strategies for managing the complex interactions that typify most places of work and also the complexities of an individual adult's life.

- Adults need to be able to *reflect on their own actions* and change those actions even while in the process of acting (Argyris & Schön, 1974; Schön, 1987). The cognitive strategies required for learning how to learn and for reflective practice involve the development of executive cognitive strategies to guide and control other cognitive strategies. Executive cognitive strategies are not accounted for in formal operational thought.
- Adults need to be able to identify, through *critical thinking*, the assumptions that underlie ideas or systems of ideas (Brookfield, 1987). Critical thinking calls for the use of cognitive processes allowing one to think about or operate on formal thoughts. In every previous stage of cognitive development, similar shifts in ability are perceived as the beginning of a new stage of development.
- Adults need to be able to deal with *paradoxical situations*. Doubt, ambiguity, uncertainty, systems thinking, and self-reflective thought tend to give rise to paradoxes. It is reasonable to assume, therefore, that post-formal operational thought must allow the adult to develop strategies for dealing with paradox. A paradox is a conundrum raised when a rule, command, or generalization appears to contradict itself. 'All generalizations are false,' 'this statement is false,' and 'be spontaneous' are examples of paradoxical statements. A paradox can only be resolved by moving outside the frame of reference (or personal model of reality) that contains it, and beyond the cognitive strategies that are creating it. This requires shifting into a new frame of reference and using new cognitive strategies. This type of learning is called perspective transformation (Mezirow, 1991).

Development of Cognitive Complexity

Sternberg's (1988) triarchic theory of intelligence suggests other ideas about adult cognitive development. Clearly an adult needs to make full use of all three types of intelligence (information processing, experiential, and contextual). In North America, cognitive development in early adulthood probably involves the belated development of both contextual and experiential intelligence. Our current concern in many adult programs over such topics as job readiness, life skills, stress management, problem-solving skills, time management skills, and the like may be a reflection of formal education programs that do not necessarily foster the development of contextual or experiential intelligence at an earlier age.

Adult cognitive development probably involves an expansion of experiential and contextual intelligence by increasing the adult's experiential base, expanding the ability to reflect on experience and learn from it, and enlarging the number of contexts that one must adapt to, select, and shape. These changes most likely will be accompanied by changes in performance and the metacomponents of fundamental intelligence (reasoning, planning, organizing, deciding, etc.).

Speculatively speaking, what Schaie (1977–8) calls 'reintegrative intelligence' may involve an integration of the three aspects of intelligence, into a sort of global intelligence or wisdom in which mental processes become an integral part of the experience and context within which they are developed and used. Such a process would likely make older adults both more competent in familiar contexts and less competent in unfamiliar contexts. That is, the more the three forms of intelligence are integrated with each other, the more difficult will be the transfer of knowledge from one context to another.

LEARNING AND FACILITATING PRINCIPLES

Since cognitive complexity is a developmental characteristic, we can understand how best to facilitate learners by using the matching model discussed in Chapter 2.

> *For example, a comfort match for a dualistic thinker would be a facilitating style presenting knowledge as absolute truth, probably through lecturing. A developmental match for a dualistic thinker would be a facilitating style encouraging and supporting individualistic thinking, probably through group discussions.*

Adults may need assistance in learning the skills typifying the post-formal stage of cognitive development, including:

- finding and formulating problems;
- asking questions;
- recognizing instances in which transfer of knowledge or skills can occur;
- developing projective images of future possibilities and working towards them;
- dealing with uncertainties, ambiguities, doubts, and paradox;
- thinking critically;
- reflecting on action; and
- learning to learn.

6 Emotions and Motives in Learning

At the end of Chapter 1, we considered preliminary answers to a series of questions: Who is learning what from whom, how, why, and with what consequences? In Chapter 2, we discussed the characteristics of 'who' is doing the learning. The 'how' of learning was addressed by considering learning cycles in Chapter 3, learning styles in Chapter 4, and the functions and processes of the brain and mind in Chapter 5. Answers about 'from whom' one learns have been scattered throughout the first five chapters: adults learn from others – facilitators and enablers, guides and coaches, experts and sages, authorities and parents, colleagues and peers, teachers and self.

In this chapter, I want to consider 'why' we learn – what moves us to learn and what keeps us going when we falter. Learning requires energy, as well as motives that direct this energy towards immediate and long-range goals of some sort. In this chapter, I will discuss the body's energy system and how it becomes activated and directed towards learning.

Arousal, Emotions, and Stress

Learning involves the arousal and energy deployment system of the human body. Minimal arousal accompanies the body's processes for mobilizing energy and bringing the brain to attentive awareness. Higher, or optimal, levels of arousal and energy are required to create the internal conditions necessary for directed learning.

In physiological terms, the arousal response includes:

- increasing adrenaline levels in the blood,
- increasing heart and breathing rate,
- increasing blood pressure,
- increasing blood flow to the brain and skeletal muscles, and
- decreasing blood flow to the digestive system.

The result is an increasing ability to cope and adapt. Under normal circumstances, our arousal hovers around an optimal level for daily functioning, is assigned a positive or negative valence by the mind, and contributes to our sensation of mood.

Emotion is the term used to describe an arousal state exceeding optimal levels and having positive or negative meaning for the individual. An emotion typically arises in response to an event, either internal or external, and acts to organize cognitive, social, and physical behaviour in relation to the event and its consequences. Emotions are shorter in duration and more intense than mood.

Emotions, whether positive or negative, have the following features in common (More, 1974):

1 They are all special states of arousal or motivation.
2 As arousal increases, so does the emotional level.
3 As arousal increases, behaviour becomes increasingly motivated, organized, and directed towards accomplishing desired goals. Behaviour remains organized for some time even as arousal continues to increase towards a maximum level.
4 Then, if arousal continues beyond the individual's maximum ability to respond, motivation decreases rapidly, disorganized behaviour ensues, and physical collapse becomes a possibility.
5 Arousal is physiological and is interpreted in the brain's limbic system (midbrain) according to the situation involved and previous experience. This interpretation determines the type of emotion felt (Hebb, 1972).

If the situation giving rise to emotions is defined in positive terms – winning the lottery, meeting the mate of one's dreams, getting a raise, earning a coveted reward – then emotions are experienced as positive and are felt as excitement, happiness, hope, joy, love, or satisfaction. If the arousal level is very high, positive emotions may be experienced as euphoria. If the situation is defined in negative terms – being arrested, losing a loved one, not receiving an expected promotion, going into debt – then the emotions are experienced as negative and are felt as fear, anger, anxiety, sadness, shame, disgust, or dissatisfaction. If the arousal level is very high, negative emotions may be experienced as distress. Both euphoric and distressed adults may become totally engaged in their own feelings, often to the point of appearing to exclude or ignore others. Both euphoria and distress use up energy that is consequently not available for learning.

The term 'stress' was coined by Hans Selye in 1956 to describe a nonspecific arousal state occurring in response to perceived threats to the body or the self. Stress has been described as a bodily response that developed in primitive humans to prepare the body to fight or flee in the face of real threats such as an attacking lion or a stampeding herd of buffalo. In today's society, humans rarely encounter threats of this magnitude, but our bodies are still programmed for the stress response. We react to perceived threats – disapproval from a supervisor, failure on an exam, possible bad news from our physician – with a stress response that increases to distress when we cannot find a means for dissipating or eliminating the 'threat.'

At the beginning of the stress response, the body is initially brought to alertness with both mental and physical behavioural responses becoming more effective and efficient. Individuals who have good stress management strategies can usually deal with the perceived threat and thereafter lower the stress response. If the perceived threat increases or cannot be terminated by the individual's coping or adapting skills, the physiological response continues unabated; initial competence is followed by confusion, disorientation, and distortion of reality; then fatigue, muscle tension, anxiety, and irritability set in; and finally physical exhaustion occurs, accompanied by withdrawal, depression, and apathy (Adams, 1980; Brammer & Abrego, 1981; Brown, 1980; Hart, 1983; Hopson & Adams, 1976; Selye, 1956; Wlodkowski, 1985).

Anxiety is a nonspecific emotion that arises in response to an unlabelled fear or an unidentified source of danger (Rowe, 1975). The source of anxiety may be internal to the self but perceived as originating in the external world. Learning situations, schools, teachers, grades, tests, and the threat of failure, embarrassment, or exposed inadequacies represent, for many adults, memories to which anxiety has become attached (Kidd, 1973). Anxiety in learning situations can lead to disorientation, as we saw in Taylor's learning model in Chapter 3. As Marilyn Taylor (1987) suggests, such anxiety can be partially addressed by naming the fear or perceived danger, thus making it 'real' and less threatening.

Adults and Emotions

These definitions point out that emotions, stress, and anxiety share a similar physiological arousal process and have similar behavioural outcomes in the presence of continuing and unresolved threats to an individual. Hebb (1972) notes that adults and children both experience these arousal reactions, but the level, strength, and duration of the reaction increases with intellectual capacity and with age. He points out that adults are sheltered by a civilized environment, within which they are not much exposed to the causes of emotional disturbance. Such environments offer physical and psychological protection from emotional disturbance by reducing the causes to near zero. 'In a "civilized environment" [an adult] never has to be in strange places in darkness' (Hebb, 1972, p. 206).

Kidd (1973) tells us that adults have not fewer but more emotional associations with learning materials and activities than do children. We sometimes mistakenly assume that adults have fewer stress responses because their devices of control are more elaborate and more effective. In learning situations, adults may have more to feel threatened about than children because their self-concept is already well organized. They stand to lose much of their previous gains in self-esteem and self-confidence if they try to learn and fail. Many adults would prefer to not try at all, and therefore appear to resist learning. And many adults are as apprehensive of appearing to be euphoric as they are about appearing to be distressed.

Effects of Emotions and Stress on Learning

Emotional responses, stress, and anxiety affect adult learning in a number of ways. The energy mobilized through arousal can be channelled equally well into learning and ultimately into success and satisfaction or into increasing anxiety, distress, and resistance to learning. Most adults start new learning experiences under some stress and arousal, and do not generally require further arousal to motivate learning. If the facilitator further stimulates arousal or stress through demands created by information overload, competition, exposure of inadequacies, discounting of personal experience, and so on, the learner may withdraw or become self-defensive and appear to lack motivation. Excessive arousal and distress will negate the early benefits of limited arousal. Facilitators would be wise to spend some time during the first few learning sessions deliberately lowering anxiety to a manageable level (Knowles, 1970, 1990; Wlodkowski & Ginsberg, 1995).

One outcome of a prolonged stress reaction is reduced competence in communicating. Poor communicating can take the form of

- repeating phrases,
- not finishing sentences,
- not listening,
- excessive talking or excessive silence,
- omitting details,
- repeating questions that have already been answered, and so on.

Thistle (1968) indicates that the prospects for effective communication with persons in an angry, fearful, or hostile state of mind are mediocre and with those in an apathetic state of mind are very poor. Learning in this condition would be distorted learning at best. Adults who have reached this level of distress tend to appear child-like. They need a facilitator who will not misinterpret their behaviour as childish or immature and who will help them reduce their stress level before getting on with the learning activities.

Since the arousal response can motivate an individual to be a more productive learner, as well as to be a more defensive learner, stress and anxiety show up in both learning and resistance to learning. Presumably learning is more productive when there is an optimum level of arousal. In such cases, learners might appear excited, agitated, curious, restless, and perhaps anxious or frustrated. All these behaviours, as with those in prolonged stress responses, can be labelled as childish and immature. If the facilitator then proceeds to treat adult learners as if they were childish and immature, any motivation to learn will be diverted into defensiveness and resistance in order to protect the self. For adults to become fully engaged in learning, they must be aroused, feel relatively safe, and be willing and able to channel their motives into change processes. For these reasons, adults need a supportive and encouraging learning environment that does not threaten them. This is facilitated when relationships between the facilitator and learners are built on trust (Combs, 1974; Gibb, 1964; Kidd, 1973; Rogers & Roethlisberger, 1991).

Effects of Emotions and Stress on Information Processing

Work reported by O'Connor and Seymour (1990), Katz and Kahn (1970), Cropley (1977), and Toffler (1970) indicates that, in the presence of excessive amounts of information from the environment (sensory overload, overstimulation), the adult processes information in ways that delete, distort, oversimplify, and overgeneralize. The manner in which the overload is processed can vary from being highly productive (specializing) to highly dysfunctional (omitting, denying). The result is a set of corresponding deletions, distortions, simplifications, and overgeneralizations in the individual's personal model of reality. Lack of sufficient information, boredom, understimulation, excessive repetition, and nonproductive and irrelevant activities will produce the same result as overstimulation (Hart, 1983; Toffler, 1970).

Some individuals learn information-processing skills that are effective at all times but particularly in periods of overstimulation. These include employing multiple channels for processing information and learning how to learn.

Multiple channel processing involves allowing the brain to process information about a single event through multiple sensory channels, multiple memory resources, and multiple motor channels without super-imposing the single channel, verbal processing, semantic memory, and sitting still that is typical of formal schooling. Virginia Griffin (2001) has asked, 'Would you play a one-string guitar?' Her contention is that we spend too much time relying on our mental abilities for rational, verbal thought and ignoring our considerable capacities for physical, emotional, intuitive, relational, and spiritual learning.

Clear verbal thought requires a high level of mental attention (beta waves), a low degree of diversion and novelty in the environment, and the use of small amounts of selected and specific information. Verbal thinking is controlled by the sequence of the words and the grammar that guides it. Early errors in the sequence tend to be magnified in succeeding steps. Distress and information overload make this mode of thought difficult to maintain for any length of time. For example, most adults cannot listen to a lecture for more than fifteen minutes without taking a nonverbal break – if only in their own thinking.

Nonverbal thought requires the intake of large amounts and a wide variety of both relevant and nonrelevant information, a low level of direct attention (alpha waves), reliance on nonverbal forms of representation, simultaneous processing of information through multiple channels, and enough time to permit processing to occur without having to produce an output or reach an answer. In nonverbal thinking, order emerges as a result of thinking, not as a factor that guides it. When the same information is processed through several different channels, errors in one channel will be corrected by the results from another.

The brain, in fact, is quite capable of processing information it is not attending to even while it is attending to something else. For example, there is evidence that observing someone doing something activates a component of the brain's motor cortex without inducing an overt motor response. We may learn about and understand other people's intentions and desires by mentally imitating their motor actions (Blakemore & Frith, 2000). This tendency of the brain to learn things 'behind its back' makes the context or situation of the learning a crucial element. We will return to the context of learning in Chapter 10.

Several writers (Caine & Caine, 1991; Goleman, 1995; Hart, 1983; Marchese, 1997) suggest that the skills involved in employing multiple channels and in learning how to learn are normal mental activities that have been deactivated by the process of formal schooling. Such schooling places a higher value on sequential, verbal modes of thought than on simultaneous, nonverbal modes of thought. Whether the skills develop normally or are acquired through training is not clear. It is clear, however, that certain conditions increase an individual's capacity to make use of these skills in certain situations (Brookfield, 1987; Candy, 1990; Denis & Richter, 1987; Hart, 1983; Norman, 1973; Smith, 1990; Wlodkowski, 1997). These conditions include:

- the learner's perception of the situation as free from threat;
- material that is personally relevant to the learner and/or learning experiences and processes that are perceived as relevant to the learner's life experiences and current needs;
- presentation of information through a variety of sensory modes and expe-

riences, with sufficient repetitions and variations on themes to allow fine distinctions in patterns to emerge;
- effective two-way communications with others with primary emphasis on learner talking and self-reflecting and facilitator listening and reflecting; and
- individual learning styles or preferences in using learning strategies that support multiple-channel learning.

Learning how to learn involves a set of processes in which individual learners act, in whole or in part, as managers of their own change, and their focus needs to be on their own actions, ideas, and learning processes. This requires that learners recognize and be able to pay some attention to their own learning processes. They must also be willing to trust themselves to manage this process and to request help from someone else when necessary. Such learning can be carried out more productively in situations that do not threaten the learner (Candy, 1991).

Developing skills in learning to learn can itself create a challenge to the adequacy of the learner's existing meanings, values, and skills. At the point of change, the learner is likely to experience internal conflict as old and new meanings or values clash, to feel disconnected from past habits, and to feel disoriented as new skills require new behaviours. It is a point at which stress can increase and the learner might abort the learning process as too risky (Kidd, 1973; More, 1974; Pine & Boy, 1977).

LEARNING AND FACILITATING PRINCIPLES

Adults learn best when they are stimulated, aroused, or motivated to an optimum level through internal or external sources.

> *The facilitator can be most helpful by being aware of the symptomatic behaviours associated with stress, being able to make distinctions between stress-related behaviour and learning behaviour, and responding to both without labelling either as childish or immature.*

Adults do not learn when overstimulated or when experiencing extreme distress or anxiety.

> *The facilitator can be most helpful by making minimal demands on learners at the start of a learning activity, by avoiding information overload and boredom, and by making learning activities productive and relevant to learners' needs.*

Adults who are learning have more, stronger, and longer emotional responses to cope with than do children.

Adults learn best in environments that encourage the development of trusting relationships and provide freedom from threat.

Adults who enter into learning activities are often well motivated and generally do not require further stimulation in the form of pressure or demands from the facilitator or other learners. What they may require is assistance and support to channel their motives into learning rather than into defensiveness.

> *Facilitators should concentrate on reducing initial anxiety levels rather than increasing initial motivation levels. Anxiety is reduced when the learner feels satisfied, experiences success in learning, and perceives the learning situation to be nonthreatening. Anxiety is also reduced when learners know what to expect through a course outline, an agenda for a single session, an outline of how evaluation will be conducted, and instructions for contacting the facilitator if they encounter a problem.*

Adults who are experiencing extreme distress or anxiety may communicate poorly and process information in ways that delete, distort, oversimplify, or overgeneralize.

> *Facilitators can ease a distressful situation by helping to reduce anxiety levels through providing opportunities to talk and by compensating for any temporary decline in the learner's communicating skills.*

Stimulation or arousal can be channelled equally well into learning or into resistance to learning.

Stimulation or arousal can be labelled equally well as childish and immature behaviour, as stress behaviour, or as learning behaviour, depending on other aspects of the situation and the perceptions of the facilitator.

Adults who can process information through multiple channels and have learned how to learn are the most productive.

Adults learn best when information is presented through a variety of sensory modes and experiences, with sufficient repetitions and variations on themes to allow distinctions in patterns to emerge.

Adults learn best through effective two-way communications

emphasizing learner talking and self-reflecting and facilitator listening and reflecting.

Adults have developed well-organized strategies for defending
against threat and for covering emotional reactions. These may
mask stress or anxiety but rarely completely alleviate it.

The consequences of learning can lead to disorientation and conflict
that, in turn, can lead to further learning or can lead to increased
distress and decreased learning.

> *Facilitators may need to reassure learners that confusion has a
> function in the learning process and be prepared to halt learn-
> ing activities periodically to help learners clarify issues, prob-
> lems, and concerns.*

Motives for Learning

'Motivation' is an all-purpose term defined as a tendency within a person to
produce organized and directed behaviour. This organized behaviour
allows individuals to move in response to their internal or external environment to ensure their own and their communal groups' survival and satisfaction. In biological terms, human behaviour is motivated by four primary
drives (Lawrence & Nohria, 2001):

1 the drive *to acquire* by providing for hunger and thirst, collecting
   resources, and exchanging goods and services with others;
2 the drive *to bond* by finding mates, creating family units, and caring for
   loved ones;
3 the drive *to defend* by providing shelter and security from outside threats
   for self and family;
4 the drive *to learn* by reducing uncertainty through exploring all aspects of
   the environment, explaining natural phenomena, and figuring out ways
   to predict the consequences of future actions.

While these drives are not the only human drives, Paul Lawrence and Nitin
Nohria (2001) claim they 'exist as hard-wired mental modules in the brains
of all modern humans as primary drives ... [and] fulfilling one drive does
not fulfill any of the others' (p. 20). Each person must satisfy all four drives.
Interaction among the drives – sometimes competitive and sometimes com-
plementary – generates the complex behaviour that typifies daily living in
individual, social, and cultural terms.

Motivation in learning can be described as being either a drive to reduce uncertainty and meet unmet needs or a drive towards positive growth through exploring the unknown.

Reduction of unmet needs describes those motives that arise when something is absent or deficient in the individual's life, when threat (real or perceived) is present, or when insufficient information is available to support full understanding of a situation. Adults who engage in learning to reduce unmet needs may arrive at the learning experience feeling threatened by others (whom they may see as controlling them), feeling powerless or incompetent to change the conditions of their lives, or feeling confused and uncertain.

They may indeed be threatened, and may be there as nonvoluntary learners. Nonvoluntary learners include those mandated by the justice system to attend driver (re)education courses, substance abuse programs, or anger management workshops; those required by social policy to attend training programs to retain eligibility for social assistance; those required by the economic system to learn a new language or work-related skills; and sometimes those who are required to attend continuing education to retain professional certification. Such adults may require structured learning experiences, extensive help in determining their own directions, and prolonged support. They need both feedback and positive reinforcement from the facilitator. Once their initial feelings of threat or anxiety have been resolved or reduced, they can be assisted towards taking increasing responsibility for their own learning.

The drive towards positive growth presupposes, not an aversive set of existing conditions that need to be changed, but a potential positive outcome that will reward the individual as it is sought and obtained. Maslow (1971) suggests that people cannot move towards these positive goals until aversive conditions have been reduced. He describes aversive conditions as 'deficit needs' and positive goals as 'growth or being needs.' Deficit needs focus on the survival and security of individuals and their family units. Growth needs focus on belongingness, self-esteem, and self-actualizing tendencies. Deficit needs can be met through such learning activities as child or elder care training, grief workshops, anger management, job search skills, language programs for immigrants, job training for displaced workers, alcohol and drug rehabilitation, driver education, and so on.

Gibb (1964) indicates that deficit and growth needs are not mutually exclusive, and that as one increases in strength and priority the other decreases. Facilitating strategies can focus on reducing deficit needs first, thus freeing the learner to pursue growth goals, in turn enabling the learner to deal with future deficit needs. Facilitating could focus on some combination of these.

Growth needs relate to such personal goals as improving job skills, getting a salary increase, developing professionally, meeting new people, developing trust relationships, learning for the pleasure of learning, expanding knowledge, extending oneself, and so on. Kidd (1973) suggests that adults who attend learning experiences on the basis of personal growth in the direction of positive goals tend to be relaxed, do not require much structure or direction from facilitators, and are able to negotiate and plan their own structure, directions, feedback, and reinforcement with minimal assistance.

Motives Are Organized around Two Action Tendencies

Another way to conceptualize motivation, apart from the deficit and growth needs perspective, is to see individuals' motives as being related to two major tendencies: a tendency to function autonomously or independently in the environment, and a tendency to function harmoniously in interdependent relationships with others in pairs or groups (Jones, 1968).

In the literature, the tendency to autonomous, independent behaviour is variously referred to as achievement needs, instrumental participation, career-oriented learning needs, and self-confidence needs, among others. This tendency is accompanied by the need to reduce threats to autonomous functioning; to reduce feelings of powerlessness and incompetence; to build competent, skilled performance; and to improve self-esteem and self-concept. Independent behaviours do not necessarily benefit only the individual, but are often used in the defense or support of others.

The tendency to interdependent behaviour is variously referred to as affiliation needs, expressive participation, social-oriented learning needs, and acceptance needs, among others. This tendency is accompanied by the need to reduce threats to one's secure place within communal groups, to reduce isolation and alienation, to build and improve interpersonal relationships, and to create and maintain communal and collaborative groups. Interdependent behaviours can benefit the individual by providing a secure base from which to launch autonomous behaviours.

Some adult educators assume that all adults have put dependency needs behind them, and view needs for interdependency as a disguise for immature dependency needs. In fact, most adults use dependent behaviours in situations that are perceived as novel, critical, or traumatic. As we have seen in Chapter 2 in the section on self, autonomy-seeking motives may be more salient for men than for women, while relationship-seeking motives may be more salient for women than for men.

Each tendency can be thought of as a continuum of behaviours ranging from too-much-need at one end to too-little-need at the other. For example, Hunt (1971) describes too-much-need for independence as counter-dependency, and too-little-need for independence as unilateral dependence. If we understand behaviour to extend across a continuum, then we can perceive most adults as using behaviours that occupy the middle range of that continuum (Morstain & Smart, 1977).

The Role of Success and Satisfaction in Learning

Motivation is connected both to success (or failure) in reaching desired outcomes or changing adverse conditions and to the feelings of satisfaction (or dissatisfaction) that attend such progress. Satisfaction and success are not separate issues. Both are related to progress away from entry conditions and towards anticipated or desired outcomes. The deficit needs, growth needs, and motives with which learners enter a learning program determine their initial participation in the activities. Thereafter, their motives for continuing in the program will depend on whether they feel they are successfully and satisfactorily moving towards their anticipated or desired outcomes.

To be able to see their own progress, learners must receive frequent information about changes in their behaviour relative to what they anticipated or desired. Information that describes the results of change is referred to as 'feedback.' When feedback is specific in describing changes relative to planned outcomes, it leads to an awareness of success or failure. Knowledge of success or failure is accompanied by feelings of satisfaction or dissatisfaction, and it is these feelings that then become powerful motives for further learning or withdrawal (Jones, 1968).

We should not assume that entry-level motivation will be maintained through a learning program. Motivation levels within each learner are based on how they resolve competing drives. As time passes, learners with family, work, or other responsibilities find that competing drives place conflicting demands on their time, energy, and activities. Alice Home (1995) reports that female learners with both family and work responsibilities – especially single parents, those on low income, and full-time students – experience considerable stress related to role conflict and role contagion. Role conflict arises when individuals are required to deal simultaneously with several incompatible demands. Role contagion occurs when individuals have difficulty performing one role while worrying about their responsibilities in another. Home et al. (1995) advise facilitators to recognize role conflicts and contagion among adult students, increase flexibility in the pace of learning, increase access to available resources, and encourage women learners to join together in networks to support each other and to advocate on their own behalf.

What seems most clear from the literature on motivation is that the action tendencies that are labelled 'motives' arise from within the learner. Motives are not something added on by an external agent or facilitator, although the actions of the facilitator may tend to help or to hinder existing motives. Despite encouragement from some writers about 'motivating learners,' a facilitator cannot do this directly. The behaviour of the facilitator, in response to learner behaviours, must be viewed as contributing either to feedback or to reinforcement and by this route indirectly to further motivation.

The most suitable facilitator functions, as defined by Wlodkowski (1985), are:

- discovering, through consultation, the prime motives and specific learning needs of each learner;
- assisting the learner to establish specific objectives that can be translated into specific behaviours and hence into specific feedback;
- providing feedback on the basis of these choices; and
- allowing the feelings of success and satisfaction from these processes to be the major reinforcers of subsequent learning.

Feedback can come from the facilitator, other learners, nonhuman resources (as in biofeedback), or learners' observations about their own behaviour and environment. Feedback that is spread throughout the learning program can assist in maintaining learner motivation levels (Wlodkowski & Ginsberg, 1995).

Feedback can only be provided following activities that permit the learner to test out new behaviour. Feelings of success, therefore, are available to the learner only after that point in the learning process. If this point comes early in the session, then the good feelings from success will motivate the remainder of that session. If this point comes at the end of a session, then the good feelings may have dissipated before the next session.

If feedback is delayed from one session to the next, the learner may have trouble connecting it to the behaviour that was tested out previously. As the time lapse between action and feedback increases, the impact and reinforcement from feedback decreases, as does its value for further motivation (Wlodkowski & Ginsberg, 1995).

Involving adults in clarifying their own ambiguous needs and in defining clear learning objectives is acknowledged as an important aspect of adult learning (Knowles, 1990). Most adults, however, have little experience in verbalizing their own needs, let alone turning them into learning objectives. They are often embarrassed about expressing their needs in front of others and do not communicate them unless there is some personal crisis or external reason for doing so. If adults are asked to complete a needs assessment instrument, they are likely to respond as an 'average adult' rather than as themselves, or to give answers they assume the assessor wants to hear. Therefore, adults may need considerable assistance and support in verbalizing, clarifying, and specifying their learning needs (Wlodkowski & Ginsberg, 1995).

LEARNING AND FACILITATING PRINCIPLES

Motives can be the needs that learners feel when starting a learning activity. They may relate to unmet needs or unwanted conditions in life or to the pursuit of positive growth towards desired goals. As learners proceed towards meeting unmet needs, resolving unwanted conditions, or reaching desired goals, their motives for learning tend to change in relation to feelings and experiences of success/failure and satisfaction/dissatisfaction.

Adults who begin with motives related to unmet needs or unwanted conditions within their life are likely to feel threatened and require facilitator support, structure, and extensive assistance in clarifying and establishing their directions and goals.

Once directions and goals have been clearly identified, objectives specifying anticipated or desired outcomes can be developed to guide learners and facilitators in seeking and giving feedback. This feedback contributes to feelings of success or failure and satisfaction or dissatisfaction, and also provides information to guide further learning.

> *Learning is facilitated when feedback is provided immediately, or as soon as possible after the behaviour being assessed.*

Success and satisfaction become reinforcers for learning and motives for further learning.

While adults have the verbal capability to clarify and specify their own learning needs, they are often reluctant to do so and may need assistance in the process.

Adults who participate in learning activities on a voluntary basis are more likely to be positively motivated than those who are participating on a nonvoluntary basis.

> *Learning is facilitated when facilitators are aware of which learners are participating nonvoluntarily and/or have entered the program with unmet needs. These learners should be provided with additional assistance and support in identifying their own needs and goals for the program.*

Emotional Intelligence

In Chapter 5 we considered the multiple intelligences described by Howard

Gardner (1983). The work of Daniel Goleman (1995) informs us that emotional intelligence is a meta-ability that determines how well we use whatever skill sets we have. He compares his concept of emotional intelligence to Gardner's personal intelligences (interpersonal and intrapersonal). Goleman defines emotional intelligence as the ability to motivate oneself and persist in the face of frustrations, to control impulses and delay gratification, to regulate mood and keep distress from swamping one's ability to think, to empathize with others, and to hope.

Peter Salovey and John Mayer (1989–90) outline a long history of concepts related to emotional intelligence going back to the first century, when Publius Syrus warned, 'Rule your feelings, lest your feelings rule you' (p. 185). They discuss social intelligence as the ability to understand and manage people. They define emotional intelligence as a subset of social intelligence that involves the ability 'to monitor one's own and others' feelings and emotions, to discriminate among them and to use this information to guide one's thinking and actions' (p. 189). They also conceptualize emotional intelligence in cognitive terms, while Goleman (1995) attempts to move away from an exclusively cognitive definition.

Emotional intelligence appears to have five components:

1 *Knowing one's own emotions* through self-awareness, recognizing a feeling as it happens, and being able to monitor both positive and negative feelings in an ongoing way. Those who are emotionally intelligent can more accurately perceive and respond to their own emotions and better express these emotions to others.
2 *Managing one's emotions* through monitoring, evaluating, and regulating both moods and emotions; handling feelings as they occur, in appropriate ways; keeping distress from affecting one's ability to think; being able to shake off anxiety, gloom, or irritability; and controlling impulses and delaying gratification. Emotions can overwhelm thinking by swamping the mental capacity called 'working memory' or the ability to hold in mind all the information relevant to the task at hand.
3 *Motivating oneself* through marshalling emotions in the service of a goal and persisting in the face of frustration. Individuals differ in their abilities to harness their own emotions in order to solve problems. Positive emotions may facilitate the generation of multiple future plans and alter memory organization so that cognitive material is better integrated and diverse ideas are seen as more related. Positive emotions facilitate both mastery and creativity. Negative emotions may focus attention on the self rather than the problem.
4 *Recognizing emotions in others* through the capacity for empathy and being attuned to the social signals that indicate what others want or need. Individuals with skills in this area would be perceived by others as genuine

and warm; those lacking these skills would appear oblivious and boorish.
5 *Handling relationships* through managing emotions and moods in others
and responding to others in effective and appropriate ways. An emotionally intelligent facilitator can evoke emotions in others through both
verbal and nonverbal skills. One can evoke emotions in others charismati-
cally towards worthwhile ends or manipulate others to nefarious ends
(Salovey & Mayer, 1989–90).

In learning terms, the emotional brain (the limbic system) can direct, and
sometimes overpower, the thinking brain (cerebral cortex). Primary drives
(for survival and security, belonging to a supportive social group, and maintaining an acceptable sense of self) originate in the midbrain and emerge as
feelings, emotions, and unconscious biases that guide decision making.
Incoming information is coded in the midbrain in terms of its relevance to
these primary drives. This coding is sent to the prefrontal cortex – that part
of the cerebral cortex responsible for working memory and decision making
– where it is assessed and used in combination with long-term memories
and various skill sets. Lawrence and Nohria (2001) tell us that emotions are
essential for human survival. They state that 'reasoning does not work very
well without affective signals to provide goals, intentions, and ultimate
motives' (p. 46). This idea contradicts the 'conventional wisdom that emotions lead to impulsive and irrational behaviour that usually gets humans
into trouble' (p. 154).

Although affective signals are needed for rational thought, consistency,
and commitment, these signals can also overwhelm the learning process
under conditions that create distress, such as information overload, role conflict, fear of failure, lack of feedback about progress, and so on. Learners
who are anxious, angry, fearful, or depressed don't learn. They do not take
in information efficiently or make effective use of the information they do
have. Their attention is twisted towards their own preoccupations. Learners
who are happy and satisfied can learn almost anything. An individual with
a good emotional skill set is likely to be a good facilitator, a good learner,
and an asset in any group.

Unfortunately, writers on emotional intelligence do not describe how to
become an emotionally intelligent person. They do list some characteristics
that typify the emotionally intelligent person, including hopefulness, opti-
mism, positive thinking, and the ability to go with the flow (Csikszentmihalyi, 1990) – a state of self-forgetfulness and goal-directed activity that is
the opposite of rumination, worry, and self-obsession. Other characteristics
include the ability to be self-reflective and to keep thought and emotions
integrated.

7 Skilled Performance in Learning

There is not much written in the adult education literature about learning that is physical. The lack of literature on this topic suggests that adult educators may view physical learning as relatively unimportant in adulthood. This is not a sound conclusion given the range of skill training opportunities offered for the purposes of occupational and workplace training and for personal development through such things as hobbies, the arts, outdoor recreation, and physical fitness.

More and more adults are engaged in some form of learning that involves physical skill. Many of us will limit our physical learning to solving such problems as maintaining physical fitness, recovering from bone or muscle injuries, learning to use technological devices, doing inside and outside home maintenance, dealing with age-related changes, coping with newborn and elderly relatives who need physical care, and doing car maintenance; but eventually all of us will have to learn something that involves skilled performance.

During the 2002 Para-Olympics, I watched in awe as men and women flung themselves down steep icy mountains on one ski and propelled themselves around a hockey rink on ice sledges. Their skilled performances were inspiring. In the previous twelve months, I had struggled to learn to walk with replacement knees. I was proud of my progress but chagrined, in light of the exploits of adults without legs, that I was still walking downstairs one step at a time. I expect that, if I did research on the nature of the learning involved in skilled performance, the major obstacle would be learning to manage pain. When I walk downstairs, I anticipate the pain and stiffen up, thereby making the pain worse. I have not yet learned to walk through the pain.

Shortly after the Para-Olympics, I read a speech by Theodore Marchese, then President of the American Association for Higher Education, who talked about the newest concepts in learning. He reported that evolutionary psychologists have identified an approach to learning that has proved successful over the ages, and that we seem to have forgotten. That approach is apprenticeship. Only since the mid-1800s, when we moved to compulsory schooling, have we shifted to formal training as a means for preparing youth for valued adult roles. Marchese pointed out that only in the past six generations have we used the formal mechanism of schooling for this important task; 'for the figurative 994 generations that came before, young people learned what they learned through apprenticeship' (Marchese, 1997, p. 8).

One concept that has become part of the adult education literature – a concept that flows from the process of apprenticeship – is 'situated learning' (Lave & Wenger, 1991). We will consider situated learning again in Chapter 10; here we are interested in the associated learning and facilitating methods. Hilary McLellan (1996, pp. 7–12) reports that the key methods in situated learning are:

- *telling stories* as a type of expert system for storing, linking, and readily accessing information whenever a new situation calls for it;
- *reflecting* on what has been learned and how it can be used in alternative situations;
- using *cognitive apprenticeship* to enculturate learners into authentic practices through activity and *social interaction* in a way that is similar to traditional craft apprenticeship;
- using *collaborative activities* to encourage the use of collective problem solving, allow practice in multiple roles, and confront ineffective strategies and misconceptions;
- *coaching* to provide a 'guide on the side' who intervenes and provides scaffolding when necessary, then fades into the background to provide learners with opportunities for self-directed and self-assessed learning;
- using *multiple practice* sessions to help the learner move from supervised practice to working independently;
- encouraging learners to *articulate their strategies* by verbally stating what they are doing and why, thus helping them better understand their thinking processes; and
- using *technology* to replay skill-learning sessions for comparison and self-assessment by the learner.

The methods seem particularly appropriate for skill learning. The goal in these methods is to help individuals become independent learners, to aid them in learning skills in simulated or real-life situations, and to ensure that each understands the contextual meaning of the knowledge and skills being learned.

I believe we, as adult educators, need to know more about skilled performance. Since we do not have much literature of our own on this topic, we need to consult other literature sources, such as writings on rehabilitation, fitness and body training, sports and recreation, arts and crafts, home and workplace skill training, aging, and the use of technological devices.

Since there is very little theoretical information I will address some practical questions in this chapter: What is involved in physical learning? Who is engaged in physical learning and why? What are the characteristics of physical learning? How can we facilitate physical learning?

What Is Involved in Physical Learning?

We can categorize the physical aspects of learning as involving

- coordinating the body's functions;
- orienting the body in physical space, including balance;
- using tools and other resources effectively;
- improving muscular strength and flexibility,
- body-image, and general physical conditioning;
- learning new or improving existing skills in activities calling for physical performance – in the home and workplace, in sports, recreation, and arts and crafts activities;
- maintaining and improving eye-hand coordination and fine-muscle control, particularly in relation to using tools and technological devices;
- adapting existing skills as the need arises in response to age-related and other changes.

All skill learning does not necessarily involve physical learning, since the term 'skill' is also used to describe cognitive and interpersonal behaviours. In this chapter we will focus on physical skills.

Physical learning involves the co-ordination of sensory information and physical movement, as well as body-image. Sensory information is derived from specialized neurons that transmit information from outside the body (in the eyes, ears, tongue, and mouth, and skin receptors for pain, pressure, and temperature) and from inside the body (balance receptors in the inner ear, and movement and pain receptors in muscles and connective tissue).

Physical learning involves that part of your self-system that is commonly called the body-image. Your body-image develops in the same way as your self-concept and provides you with a sense of

- how your body will respond when called upon to learn physically,
- how you feel about your physical self,
- your awareness of your physical sensations and emotions,
- your physical experience of anxiety or stress,

- your sense of occupying physical space,
- what you think others see when they look at you,
- what you see when you look at yourself, and
- what you value (or not) about your own body.

Most of us have a body-image that is distorted. In part this is because we receive information about our body in ways that automatically distort our body perceptions. For example, if you look down at yourself, what you see is a foreshortened image of your body that may overemphasize or underemphasize physical attributes you do not like. If you look at yourself in a mirror, you are likely to see, not your body as it actually exists, but the body-image you expect to see, an image built up over a lifetime of scrutinizing your body for minor blemishes and defects. Few of us perceive our body exactly as it is.

Our body-image is a cognitive construct and is as likely to be based on distortions as any other set of concepts. For example, we hear our own voice as it is transmitted through the bones of the head and as our ears hear it. Since the bones do not transfer vocal quality and the ears are placed at the side of the head and behind the mouth, we do not hear the sound of our voice the same way others do. Body-image can be modified in the same ways that we modify other components of the self-system – through transformative learning.

Who Is Engaged in Physical Learning, and Why?

Adults of all ages, all sizes and shapes, all races and cultures, and both genders regularly engage in physical learning. Some reasons for engaging in physical learning are provided below. This list does not include all the various reasons for physical learning, and most could be categorized in different ways. Add your own ideas to the list:

- co-ordinating the body's functions, such as reactivation following stroke or serious injury, speech therapy following a stroke, sex therapy;
- orienting the body in physical space, such as walking on icy sidewalks, using crutches or a cane, riding a bicycle;
- using tools and resources effectively, such as learning to read Braille and use other devices to assist with vision impairments, learning to program a VCR or microwave oven;
- improving muscular strength and flexibility, such as fitness training, body building, weight training, relaxation (t'ai chi, yoga);
- improving body-image and general physical conditioning, such as dealing with anorexia or bulimia, losing weight, and learning to exercise within safe, appropriate, and effective limits;

- learning or improving skills in home-related activities, such as plastering, painting, paper hanging, outdoor maintenance, snow shovelling, gardening, cooking, baking, sewing, mending;
- learning or improving skills in work-related activities, such as using communication devices, learning about occupational health and safety;
- learning or improving skills in sports and recreation such as swimming, scuba diving, ice skating, roller skating, snow boarding, downhill skiing, cross-country skiing, water skiing, golf, tennis, squash, badminton, running, jogging, cycling, sailing, rowing, kayaking, wind surfing, canoeing;
- learning or improving skills in arts and crafts, such as woodworking, metal working, needlework, calligraphy, playing a musical instrument, singing, dancing, acting;
- maintaining and improving eye-hand coordination and fine muscle control, particularly in relation to using tools and technological devices, such as driving a car, using tools to augment movement of the hand and arm, learning to keyboard;
- adapting existing skills in response to age-related and other changes, such as adjusting to bifocal glasses, learning to move in spite of pain, assisting someone into and out of bed or a chair, learning to help someone else with basic personal activities.

Examples of Physical Learning

Many of these activities also include cognitive aspects of learning, as well as emotional, social, and spiritual aspects. Three examples might help in understanding the often strange relationships between physical and conceptual learning.

In the first example, an adult education student, who had recently completed a study of the adoption of high technology by forestry workers, took time to help them develop a curriculum for training workers to use new wood harvesters. The forestry workers with whom she worked insisted that one of the essential skills in which new workers should receive training was 'being able to drive a vehicle on a one-lane dirt road for 20 or 30 miles without breaking down and being able to get off the road fast when a fully-loaded pulp truck comes barrelling along from the other direction.' The pulp truck cannot stop, so the driver must be skilled enough to get the vehicle out of the way by driving into the bush.

In the second example, I co-facilitated sessions on teaching skills with graduate students who were working towards a certificate in university teaching. My colleague put us through voice training before we tried out facilitating strategies. We made our voices go up and down the scale, well beyond our normal range, with power, while we chanted nonsense syllables and tongue twisters. Somehow, our vocal exercises improved our facilitating skills, mostly by reducing stress.

In the third example, one of my recent classes benefited from the presence of a t'ai chi instructor as a class member. For fifteen minutes before the class started, we would line up along the hallway and follow her through traditional t'ai chi movements. We agreed it was a good way to get into our learning activities and divest ourselves of our daily pressures and problems.

I have often thought that we should take exercise breaks rather than coffee breaks during lengthy learning activities. Line dancing for ten or fifteen minutes would be a good way to relieve tension and increase energy levels. Many research studies report that individuals who participate regularly in physical activities learn more efficiently in cognitive activities.

What Are the Characteristics of Physical Learning?

Highly skilled physical performance has five characteristics:

1 fluency of movement,
2 speed of performance,
3 smoothly automated physical actions,
4 ability to do several different physical actions simultaneously, and
5 knowledge about when to use specific actions (Sloboda, 1993).

Fluency of Movement

Sloboda (1993) indicates that an action is fluent if the various subcomponents of the skill run together in an integrated and uninterrupted manner. For example, a fluent typist is one who can maintain a relatively even and continuous output of key strokes with a minimum of mistakes. Two things are involved in fluency.

First, the individual, in performing one activity, is preparing to do the next in the sequence. That is, in fluent performance, the individual does not have to stop and think about each activity before doing it. Second, several action sequences appear to be chunked into one global sequence, thereby reducing the number of actions that the mind must remember.

Fluency of movement can be severely affected by delaying feedback and by nervousness. For example, when an audience in a baseball stadium is being led in singing the national anthem, the leader singer will experience a time delay between singing one phrase and hearing the sound of the audience singing the same phrase. Inexperienced singers sometimes slow down as if this will allow the feedback to 'catch up.' Sometimes their pace slows so much that they forget the words. Delaying auditory feedback can cause stuttering.

Another example of delayed feedback occurs when I try to do work on the Internet. I expect that the letters I type on my keyboard will appear on my computer screen at the same rate they are typed; but the system is frequently so slow that I have typed well ahead of the computer's capability to enter the letters on the screen. Then I get frustrated and hit the enter key and everything becomes worse – a sort of 'computer stuttering.' And if, in frustration, I hit the enter key again (and again) to make the computer work faster, the entire program will stall.

Speed of Performance

Many physical skills rely on speed of performance or the ability to respond quickly. Skilled tennis players must be able to hit the ball smoothly and effectively, then move to the place where they think the return ball will arrive. All these actions must be made within seconds. Experts and novices differ in the speed with which they can perform a physical action and anticipate the next one. Both speed and fluency are adversely affected by the introduction of randomly occurring conditions that do not follow the anticipated pattern. For example, in a tennis game, if a spectator suddenly threw an extra ball onto the court in the middle of play, the players would become confused and stop play.

Smoothly Automated Actions

Another characteristic of an expert's skill is that it appears easy because the performer has smoothly automated the required physical actions. You may recall, in the discussion of experiential intelligence (Sternberg, 1988) in Chapter 5, that one aspect of intelligent behaviour is the ability to respond quickly to novel situations and later to automate such responses in frequently encountered situations.

Automated responses are important in physical learning. For example, as a car driver, think of how you respond to an amber light when approaching an intersection. The automatic response should be to put your foot on the brake. If you don't automatically make this choice, you may find that your foot seems to hesitate and doesn't 'know' whether to step on the gas or to come down on the brake pedal.

One means for testing whether a skill is automatic is to observe whether the individual can deal appropriately with an unexpected, but not abnormal, situation. If you are driving along the highway and you see a deer standing on the side of the road, the automatic response ought to be to slow down since deer have a tendency to bolt in unexpected directions. But some drivers speed up to get by the deer before it moves – often a fatal decision.

Sloboda (1993) describes a study in which experienced taxi drivers first were asked to describe the shortest route between points *A* and *B*. Then they were asked to drive the researcher from *A* to *B* by the shortest route. Most did not take the route they had described earlier. They took alternative routes depending on the flow of traffic and road conditions. The researchers concluded that the taxi drivers were capable of making on-the-spot choices without appearing to consciously think about them.

Performing Multiple Skills Simultaneously

A skilled expert seems to be able to do two or three things simultaneously. If you learned how to drive a car with a standard gear shift, you will recall that you had to be able to remember to take your foot off the clutch pedal while simultaneously pressing down on the gas pedal. When stopping and then starting the car on a steep hill, you had to ease off the clutch pedal, ease slowly off the brake pedal and step on the gas pedal before the car stalled or started to roll downhill. If you are now an expert driver, you no longer have to think about the complexities of driving a car. However, if you were to suddenly find yourself driving in a country in which traffic keeps to the 'wrong' side of the road, you would have to think very carefully every time you changed direction or turned a corner. The law in some jurisdictions forbids the use of hand-held cell phones while driving a car because the two tasks interfere with each other. The law, however, is silent on whether a parent should attempt to break up a fight between children in the back seat while the car is moving.

Knowledge about Actions

Skilled performance includes knowledge about *when* to use specific actions. This knowledge must be available when needed, in response to situations demanding its use (Sloboda, 1993). It is no use knowing that an amber light means 'slow down and stop' unless this knowledge is also an integral part of a skilled action.

For example, when I first acquired bifocal glasses, it took me several days not to think deliberately about lifting my feet every time I came to a curb while walking. The first day I had trouble seeing the curb and tripped on a few. I found myself walking along partly bent over so that I could see my feet clearly, and it took me several days to stop this behaviour and return to walking normally.

Learning skilled behaviour takes practice. We know that practice sessions should be spaced. It is almost useless to spend a number of hours continuously practising a new skill. Rather, practice sessions should be spaced apart, making each session short but intense. Research indicates that there are diminishing returns from practice sessions over a period of time. Initial improvement is rapid, then levels off to a point where improvement is minimal. For this reason, learning a skill takes determination and continuing motivation; it takes a long time to become an expert in most skilled behaviours.

How Can We Facilitate Physical Learning?

There are at least three basic methods for facilitating physical learning. We can let learners figure it out for themselves by providing opportunities for trying the skill with the necessary resources and giving feedback about results or possible alternative actions.

We can tell learners how to do the skill, demonstrate it, and provide specific instructions that, if followed, should lead to skilled performance. Then by observing the learner's performance, we can provide feedback to correct improper actions.

Neither of these two options, however, is viable for learning skills in situations where the consequences of performance may be potentially dangerous (a medical student learning surgery; an electrician learning to wire a house). Therefore, we need a process in which the learner performs the skill under supervision. Such a process, called 'cognitive apprenticeship,' can be used when learners are engaged in learning physical, cognitive, or social skills and is described as having five phases (Brandt, Farmer, & Buckmaster, 1993; Collins, Brown, & Newman, 1989; West, Farmer, & Wolff, 1991): modelling, coaching or scaffolding, fading, solo performance, and reflection and discussion.

The Modelling Phase

The process begins with the facilitator modelling the skill to be learned and the processes required to complete the task. While demonstrating the skill, the facilitator talks about or articulates what is being done and why. Such talk can be given before beginning the skill or after completing it if the talk interferes with performance. The commentary can include tricks of the trade and helpful hints for performing the skill more easily. Learners listen and observe. In learning cognitive skills, the modelling phase requires the articulation of internal (cognitive) processes and activities.

The Coaching or Scaffolding Phase

Next, the learner tries to approximate the skill by doing it with the facilitator observing and offering hints and support. While doing the skill, the learner talks about what is being done and why. As the facilitator listens to each learner's commentary on thoughts, feelings, and actions, problems can be corrected through immediate feedback and helpful suggestions.

If the facilitator is working with a group, one learner can perform the skill while others observe. The facilitator can ask individuals among the observing group to describe what the performer must do next and why. This serves to assist the performer and to keep the observers alert. The commentary can reflect on differences between the learner's performance and the facilitator's during the modelling phase, or between the current performance and previous ones.

This phase can be done several times until each learner seems comfortable. In a small group setting, one or two individuals can perform the task with commentary from observers.

The Fading Phase

Next, each learner tries the skill alone, in a safe and realistic environment. The facilitator observes and occasionally asks for out-loud commentary if the skill does not seem to be working.

In large groups learners can work in dyads, with one performing the skill and the other asking for the learner's commentary at various points in the process. The facilitator's role in this process is to circulate among the dyads and ask the observing partner to comment on what is happening in their role of surrogate facilitator. The facilitator can provide checklists to guide partners as they work, or the learners can develop and revise their own.

Solo Performance

In the fourth phase, the learner performs the skill alone. The skill can be performed in simulated conditions or in real situations within specified acceptable limits and with supervision available whenever necessary. In this phase the learner assumes responsibility for asking for assistance if the skill performance is not working.

The Reflection and Exploration Phase

In the final phase, the facilitator and learners discuss what has been learned and generalize about using the skill in different settings or with acceptable variations. This phase is essential if learners are to understand how and when the skill could be used appropriately in other contexts. It also encourages learners to frame questions and problems in using the skill in different contexts.

Brandt, Farmer, and Buckmaster (1993) comment that cognitive apprenticeship provides access to knowledge not available through traditional forms of instruction. This knowledge is tacit and is known by the 'just plain folks' who perform the skill in the real world (Brown, Collins, & Duguid,

1989). Asking people with real-world experience to state their thoughts about a skill out loud while they are performing it makes their tacit knowledge explicit.

The facilitator modelling the skill and providing the commentary about what is being done, and why, needs to think through the nature of the skill ahead of time, describing rather than prescribing and 'telling it like it is,' not 'like it ought to be.' Choices made by the facilitator in planning and implementing cognitive apprenticeship should make it likely that learners will

- quickly succeed in approximating the skill;
- pay attention to critical components and knowledge; and
- learn how to recognize and overcome flaws in their own thinking.

Cognitive apprenticeship can be used to help learners modify existing skills that are not working well or to improve existing skills.

LEARNING AND FACILITATING PRINCIPLES

Learners must have some understanding of their need to learn or modify the skill in question.

Facilitators may need to assist learners in assessing current skills and learning needs and in understanding the role of the skill in future learning.

Learners must have a clear idea of the behaviour to be attempted and learned.

Facilitators and/or learners need to establish clear behavioural objectives. Learners may know what must be learned but may need assistance in identifying learning objectives. Learning objectives serve as a means for assessing performance and providing feedback.

Learners must have opportunities to practise the appropriate behaviour.

Facilitators need to provide opportunities to practice the skill in nonthreatening environments. These environments should be as real-to-life as possible. Skills that are potentially dangerous must be performed first in safe environments.

Learners need feedback about how closely performance comes to accomplishing established objectives.

Feedback should be descriptive and nonjudgmental, task oriented and specific.

Some adult learners need reinforcement about their success to encourage them in further learning. Appropriate and useful feedback can be reinforcing in itself. Reinforcement can come from valued external sources or from the learner's own knowledge about success and feelings of satisfaction.

Appropriate resources and activities must be available for continuing learning. These can be planned through continuous reassessment of changing needs and new objectives.

Facilitators and learners should engage in ongoing, formative feedback through any learning program in which a skill is to be learned and later applied in real-life situations. Formative feedback assesses how the learning-facilitating interaction is proceeding and whether it is on-target.

8 Relationship in Learning

I tried a number of different titles for this chapter – gender in learning, connection in learning, relational and autonomous learning – but none seemed to convey my intended focus. I decided on 'Relationship in Learning' because my students have convinced me that very little learning occurs without relationship of some sort.

Our learning career begins in infancy and childhood within our relationships to caring adults and siblings. In this crucial learning period, we learn to walk and talk. Our literacy skills begin in this period in the company of adults who read to us, in intimate relationships based on trust and love. Later, for better or ill, we learn formally in the company of our peers. Formal schooling attempts to persuade us that we should learn alone and that we should assess our efficacy in relation to our independent actions. These formal schools hold us for twelve to sixteen, sometimes even twenty years. Then we go back to learning in the company of others – in families, workplaces, and communities. Some of us may remain strictly autonomous in our learning activities; many of us periodically engage in self-directed learning projects; but mostly we do our daily learning in relationships.

Roby Kidd (1960) describes the three R's of good learning and facilitating as relevancy, relationship, and responsibility. He goes on to say that relationship has two meanings.

1 Relationship refers to how knowledge from past experience connects to current learning, while relevancy refers to connections between current learning activities and the learner's present and future needs.
2 Relationship also refers to the learner's need to establish a sense of belonging within the learning environment by developing connections to other learners and to the facilitator.

To these two meanings, I would add a third: the learner-facilitator relationship is the primary context within which learning occurs. A positive relationship contributes to an environment in which the learner may feel secure enough to take risks; a negative relationship contributes to the learner's stress level and an environment in which motives for learning may be redirected into self-protection.

In this chapter, we will examine how formal education tries to convince us to learn alone, when during the rest of our life we actually learn in relationship. We will begin by looking again at the development of self and voice, then move on to consider sources of knowledge and alternative ways of knowing and learning.

Relationships in Adult Development

In Chapter 2, I examined women's difficulties in using traditional developmental theories to understand their own self-development. In the past three decades, female researchers have investigated this problem. Ruthellen Josselson (1992) comments that the most impressive aspect of these studies is the consistency of the findings that human interconnection and relatedness is a central plot of human development, certainly as central as the traditional plot focusing on autonomy and independence. We will look at how these two plots lead to four conceptions about adult development and to associated approaches to facilitating adult learning.

The first conception holds that there are at least two paths in 'normal' development that are equally valid and important, and that learning programs should support these two paths equally but separately. These two paths are:

1 the autonomous, separate or independent path typifying many men (and some women), and
2 the relational, connected or interdependent path typifying many women (and some men).

Whether these two paths originate in a biological imperative (nature) or early socialization (nurture) is probably irrelevant by the time we reach adulthood. Many female educators believe that women learn more easily and with less stress in gender-segregated groups (Weiler, 1988). Trade training or management development programs for women only typify this approach.

In the second conception, the two paths are viewed as diverging in early childhood but converging as we reach middle adulthood. If we view the two paths as two polarities in human development, then in mid-life, individuals who have developed predominantly along one path as young adults become aware of the other path through individuation (Borysenko, 1996; Estes, 1992; Jung, 1964; Levinson 1976; Neugarten & Datan, 1973). With awareness comes a need to distinguish behaviour associated with the other path, to test out these behaviours for oneself, and then to integrate them into one's self-system and model of reality. Some writers view maturity as occurring when individuals are capable of using both types of behaviour (Gilligan, 1982).

Advocates of this conception of adult development believe educational programs and learning activities should foster personal growth along the path of development not taken in early adulthood. When conducted with some groups, such as re-entry women, such provisions tend to be seen as remedial activities (Mezirow & Marsick, 1978) in which a gender-segregated group offers support and encouragement as individual women learn to function autonomously in other environments.

In the third conception, independence and autonomy form *the* central plot of human development, with interdependence and relatedness an issue only in terms of providing support. This conception is found in traditional concepts of development espoused by Erikson 1968), Kohlberg (1973), Levinson (1996), Loevinger (1976), and Sheehy (1976).

Advocates of this conception believe that educational programs and learning activities should foster autonomous behaviour through developing self-directed learning skills and encouraging self-directed learning projects (Knowles, 1970; Tough, 1971). Some female educators write that this approach to education programming creates barriers for learners who follow the relational path of development and sometimes excludes them entirely (Astin, 1976). Dependent behaviours are viewed as immature, and interdependent behaviours are sometimes perceived as cheating or second rate (Spender & Sarah, 1980). This approach is typically found in many universities and colleges.

In the fourth conception, human interconnection, relatedness, and interdependence form *the* central plot of human development, with autonomy, separateness, and independence developing within relationships. Josselson (1992) reminds us that 'relatedness is central to physical health, to longevity, to meaningful social life, and to the growth and development of the self' (p. 3). She urges us to turn our attention to how relatedness develops, how it becomes more differentiated and integrated over the lifespan, and how autonomy develops within relationships. This conception is supported by the work of feminist writers and researchers such as Clinchy and Zimmerman (1985), J.B. Miller (1986, 1991), and Surrey (1991).

Advocates of this conception of development believe that educational programs based on relational concepts can also accommodate learners who are following an autonomous path – or at least will not place barriers in their way (MacKeracher, 1993).

Relational and Autonomous Selves

These new concepts in adult development are associated with the idea that the self-system – comprised of the self-concept, self-esteem, self-ideal, and body-image – also develops along two paths. One path is based on the development of an autonomous sense of self and on seeing the self as separate from others. Development along this path is construed as occurring through a predictable sequence of behaviours or stages in which the individual moves from an immature self-system – derived from unequal relationships, feelings of powerlessness, and the use of dependent behaviours – towards a mature self-system supporting equality in relationships, feelings of empowerment, and the use of independent behaviours (Caffarella & Olson, 1993; Erikson, 1978; Levinson, 1978; Sheey, 1976; Vaillant, 1977).

The second path is based on a relational sense of self based on connectedness to others and interdependent action. Development along this path is construed as occurring through multidimensional and complex processes emerging from life's expected and unexpected events and changes (Schlossberg, 1987). The self-system is defined and discovered through interacting with others around mutual concerns for each other's well-being and through responsiveness to each other's needs (Caffarella & Olson, 1993; Gilligan, 1982; Lyons, 1988; J.B. Miller, 1986).

The two different self-systems are gender-related but not gender-specific. Research indicates that most individuals use a combination of the two self-systems to create their own unique self-system, while a smaller number use one system almost exclusively and show little or no development in the other. Lyons (1987) reports that in most men autonomous components of the self-system are more likely to dominate, while in most women relational components are more likely to dominate. Further, those whose self-concept is exclusively based on autonomy are men, while those whose self-concept is exclusively based on relationships are women. How individuals perceive themselves in adulthood depends on

- their early socialization,
- their accumulated life experiences, and
- the adaptations they have made over time.

Lyons reports that the autonomous self-system is based on concepts derived as a result of an individual's seeing the self as if through the eyes of significant others, even when those others are not present. In this self-system, one internalizes the opinions of significant others in childhood and early adulthood. Individuals can affirm and reaffirm aspects of their self-system even when they are alone because they carry the internalized standards within their ideal self.

Figure 8.1
Comparison of Self-Systems

	Autonomous or Separate Self	Relational or Connected Self
Major focus of self-definition	• Autonomous in relation to others • Focus on independence	• Connected in relation to others • Focus on interdependence
Basis for self-definition	• Through seeing self as if through the eyes of another	• Through interactive relationships with others
Relationships between self and others	• Experienced through reciprocity • Others assumed to be more similar than different in comparison with self and others, making reciprocity possible • Maintained through impartiality, objectivity, and increasing distance between self and others	• Experienced through interdependence • Others assumed to be more different than similar in comparison with self and others, making reciprocity necessary • Maintained through responsiveness to differences between self and others, concern for others' well-being, understanding needs and contexts of others, and reducing distance between self and others
	• Based on report-talk	• Based on rapport-talk

The relational self-system is based on self-concepts derived as a result of engaging in interactive relationships with significant others. Such a self-system allows the individual to affirm and re-affirm aspects of their self-system in the company of others. A comparison between the two modes of self-definition is provided in Figure 8.1, Comparison of Self-Systems.

Conversational style contributes to the two types of self-systems. Tannen (1990) reports on two ways of carrying on a conversation: report-talk and rapport-talk. Report-talk is a means for preserving independence and for negotiating and maintaining status in a hierarchical social order. It is more typical of the conversational style of men than of women and is used mainly in the public sphere. Report-talk involves exhibiting knowledge and skills, holding centre stage through verbal performance by such means as giving information and telling jokes or stories, and exercising control through authority.

Rapport-talk is a means for establishing connections and negotiating relationships. Tannen indicates it is more typical of the conversational style of women than of men and is used mainly in the private sphere. Rapport-talk involves sharing and comparing experiences, as well as sharing power.

Women are typically more talkative in private conversations while men are more talkative in public ones. Men often express frustration when women use rapport-talk in the public sphere, complaining that 'she takes too long to get to the point' or 'she wastes time on personal matters.' Women often express frustration when men use report-talk in the private sphere, complaining that 'he never listens to me' (Tannen, 1990, p. 78).

The research that has led to the understanding of the two self-systems is paralleled by research into the ways of knowing that typify women (Belenky et al., 1986) and into comparisons of how men and women engage in learning activities (Baxter Magolda, 1992; Clinchy & Zimmerman, 1985). The self-system is central to an individual's model of reality. How each individual develops and combines the autonomous and relational aspects of self will have an important effect on how that individual prefers to engage in the learning process.

Ways of Knowing

In recent years, research into cognitive development has resulted in an increasing interest in 'ways of knowing.' The assumption is that there are many ways of knowing and that each is associated with different kinds of processes. We have already seen, in Chapter 4, that Bruner (1986) identified paradigmatic and narrative ways of knowing or thinking. Other ways of knowing include personal practical ways of knowing (Connelly & Clandinin, 1985), spiritual ways of knowing (Huebner, 1985), and interpersonal ways of knowing (Berscheid, 1985). And in Chapter 7 we discussed 'physical ways of knowing.'

In this chapter, we will focus on ways of knowing that affect and are affected by the self-system (Belenky, Bond, & Weinstock, 1997; Clinchy & Zimmerman, 1985; Goldberger et al., 1996). The term 'women's ways of knowing' comes from the research of Mary Belenky, Blythe Clinchy, Nancy Goldberger, and Jill Tarule (1986). These women investigated whether Perry's (1970) model of intellectual development, derived from research focusing exclusively on university men, could be applied to women. Perry outlined nine positions or phases in intellectual development that can be combined into four major phases: dualistic thinking, multiplistic thinking, relativistic thinking, and integrated thinking.

The research into women's ways of knowing did not identify phases of thinking and knowing that contradicted those proposed by Perry but did add important concepts to our understanding of learning. These concepts include (Goldberger, 1996):

• the importance of voice in learning and knowing and as a reflection of the individual's self-concept and self-esteem;

- the importance of personal experience in knowing;
- different sources of knowledge;
- the nature of connected and separate procedures in learning;
- the need to keep passion connected to knowledge; and
- the experience of feeling silenced and disempowered.

We will consider each of these concepts in turn.

The Concept of Voice

Belenky and her colleagues (1986) use the concept of 'voice' to describe forms of knowing and attitudes about self. They equate the concept of voice with feelings of empowerment and self-efficacy.

The concept of voice can refer to the 'inner voice' or the 'outer voice.' The inner voice informs us of what we know and think, how we judge ourselves and our environment, and what we value. You may experience this inner voice as 'talking with you' or 'talking at you.' The inner voice can 'speak' in words, sounds, images, metaphors, sensations, and emotions.

The outer voice can be understood as having two components:

1 The outer voice we hear as if it were emanating from others, such as the strident voice of our conscience sounding like a sergeant-major in our mind, or the gentle voice of a caring parent. We 'hear' this voice as if it comes from an external source but, in reality, it is the voice of others that we have internalized in our conscience and personal model of reality.
2 The outer voice we actually use in talking with others. With this voice, we share our ideas and feelings through speech, body language, writing, drawing, dancing, performing, and so on. This voice can range from strong to weak.

Both inner and outer voices need to be positive and strong if the individual is to have a strong sense of self-efficacy.

Our inner voice tells us about ourselves based on our personal experiences and subjective knowledge. I am a good teacher – I have known this bit of subjective knowledge since I was seventeen, when I taught an older woman how to swim.

Our outer voice repeats back to us the received knowledge that comes to us from others. My outer voice tells me: 'you're such a klutz' (my brother's voice); 'you'll never be a good cook' (my mother's voice); 'if something is worth doing, it's worth doing well' (my father's voice); 'don't settle for being a nurse; you're smart enough to be a doctor' (a teacher's voice). Notice that the inner voice speaks in the first person singular and the outer voice speaks in prescriptions, platitudes, maxims, and the third person.

We convey our ideas and feelings to others through our outer speaking voice. We seem to use several different voices, each conveying a different aspect of our multiple identities. My prescriptive, parental voice sounds very much like my mother. My teaching voice sounds the most like the me I know I am. My social voice is quiet and unobtrusive. Occasionally the curious child in me pops out to ask embarrassing questions or to propose half-baked ideas.

The Role of Personal Experience

The model proposed by Belenky and her colleagues (1986) describes five ways of knowing. Each corresponds to a different world-view, each promoting a different understanding of knowledge and truth, the role of authority, and the nature of self. The authors specifically tell us that these five world-views do not necessarily describe a developmental process or sequence of developmental stages, although their supporters identify a direct correlation with the four major phases proposed in Perry's (1970) stages of intellectual development, and hence with an implied developmental sequence.

Belenky and her colleagues did not conduct their research with men; therefore, they are careful not to attribute their ways of knowing to male learners. Conversations with male students, however, have convinced me that men experience similar ways of knowing. The five ways of knowing are: silence, received knowing, subjective knowing, procedural knowing, and constructed knowing (Belenky et al., 1986). An individual uses one of the five ways of knowing as a basic viewpoint from which to relate to others and the world. Belenky and her colleagues refer to this basic view as a way of being. Individuals' ways of being change as their ways of knowing evolve.

Some individuals can use only one way of knowing, some use two or three, and some use all five. The more ways of knowing one can use, the more one becomes a flexible, effective, and efficient learner.

The descriptions of the five ways of knowing provided by Belenky and her associates leave me feeling frustrated because they offer no consistent means for understanding how a facilitator could help learners develop alternative ways of knowing. Therefore, I tend to think of the five ways of knowing as involving four dimensions of learning behaviour. Two describe sources of knowledge – received and subjective – and two describe the information-gathering and -processing procedures – separate and connected – used for knowing and learning (see Figure 8.2, Ways of Knowing, p. 165).

Sources of Knowledge

The two dimensions of learning behaviour that I am describing as 'sources of knowledge' include both received knowledge (right side of Figure 8.2) and subjective knowledge (left side of Figure 8.2). The learner can rely on both these sources of knowledge or on only one. *Received knowledge* comes from external sources such as family members, teachers, colleagues, authors, experts, and authorities. Such knowledge is generally conveyed in words. *Subjective knowledge* comes from internal sources and is based on personal experiences, feelings, and intuitions. Such knowledge frequently remains unarticulated, wordless.

Those who rely almost exclusively on received knowledge, termed 'received knowers,' tend to assimilate knowledge from external sources as if it were their own and to reproduce it without any substantial deviation or correction based on personal experience. These individuals tend to

- perceive authorities as powerful and infallible, as the major and only acceptable sources of knowledge in their world;
- view truth as absolute, factual, and concrete;
- search for the *one* right answer, then interpret it literally and use it as a guide for action without assessing it in practical and personal terms;
- be good listeners but have weak outer voices and often cannot find the 'right' words; and
- identify themselves as 'good persons' (as long as they have the right answers) who are trying to live up to expectations.

Those who rely almost exclusively on subjective knowledge, termed 'subjective knowers,' often do not know how they know that something is true. It is sometimes called intuition and is frequently discounted as nonrational, particularly when used by women. Subjective knowledge is problematic in a learning situation because most of it is unarticulated and unassessed. Subjective knowers tend to

- see authoritative or received knowledge as irrelevant since there are many personal truths, each one equally valid;
- value their inner voice and the spontaneous expression of feelings and opinions, believing that truth cannot be reduced to words;
- see no need to revise or even assess their ideas;
- often appear to be listening, but may be attending to their own thoughts;
- describe themselves as confident persons who know what's what; and
- speak with a confident outer voice.

Sometimes individuals need assistance in sorting out what part of their knowledge comes from external sources and what part comes from internal sources. Maturity in learning and knowing increases as individuals are able to integrate the two sources of knowledge and begin to construct their own knowledge. Those who facilitate adult learning need to help all learners to

- become aware of their subjective knowledge, find appropriate words to describe and share it with others, and assess it against received knowledge and reality;
- assess received knowledge against both reality and personal experience; and
- modify and integrate both types of knowledge.

Procedures for Knowing and Learning

The two dimensions of learning behaviour that I am describing as 'information-gathering and -processing procedures' include both separate procedures (top of Figure 8.2) and connected procedures (bottom of Figure 8.2). Learners can be skilled in using one set of procedures or both – or neither in the case of silenced knowers – and this skill can vary from high to low.

Those who are skilled at using such procedures, who can access both received and subjective knowledge, are called 'procedural knowers.' Procedural knowing involves a world-view based on learning and problem solving. Procedural knowers are described by Belenky and her colleagues (1986) as

- using the 'voice of reason,'
- speaking well with strong voices,
- using words easily,
- listening to others carefully,
- communicating and learning effectively, and
- identifying themselves as confident persons who know how to get things done.

Belenky and her colleagues divide procedural knowers into two types – 'separate' and 'connected' – each representing different ways of engaging in rational thinking. Both types of procedures draw on both received and subjective knowledge.

Separate procedural knowing encourages the knower to detach what is known from the person who knows it, or from the experience that generated it. Separate procedural knowers (often referred to as 'separate knowers') tend to generalize ideas so that they can detach themselves from real-life experiences, and decontextualize knowledge, thereby making it readily transferrable to other situations. Those who rely heavily on separate procedural knowing tend to

- be concerned with mastering and controlling their environment,
- adopt a highly critical adversarial stand when disagreeing with other persons, and
- force a choice between opposing versions of truth.

This process is sometimes referred to as the 'doubting game' (Elbow, 1973), which is described by Clinchy and Zimmerman (1985) as a strategy allowing the learner to doubt the truth of an idea until convinced by the logic of the argument supporting it. Those who doubt exclude ideas from their personal model of reality until an idea becomes a proven truth. Knowledge and truth are always backed up by logic and rational thinking.

According to Wingfield and Haste (1987), separate knowers are independent, tend to use analytical thinking styles, test for truth by looking for consistency and logic in knowledge, and prefer to hold thoughts and feelings separate from each other. When separate knowers ask 'Why?' they want an answer that will justify the logic or worth of an idea. Baxter Magolda (1992) uses the term 'autonomous' to describe college students, both male and female, who use separate procedures for learning.

Connected procedural knowing encourages the knower to connect what is known to the person who knows it or to the experience that generated it. Connected procedural knowers (often referred to as 'connected knowers') tend to keep ideas connected to their real-life experiences and keep knowledge contextualized and situation specific, but not necessarily generalizable or transferrable to other contexts and situations. Those who rely heavily on connected procedural knowing tend to

- be concerned about remaining connected to others within the environment;
- adopt a narrative or descriptive stance when they disagree with other persons; and
- search for ways to incorporate the ideas of others into a larger conceptual scheme.

This process is sometimes referred to as the 'believing game' (Elbow, 1973), which is described by Clinchy and Zimmerman (1985) as a strategy allowing learners to believe the truth of another's idea and to search for ways of including it, or a variation of it, in their personal model of reality. Knowledge and truth emerge from integrating different perspectives on an idea.

According to Wingfield and Haste (1987), learners who use connected procedures are interdependent, tend to use holistic thinking styles, test for truth by looking for believability in knowledge, and prefer to keep thoughts and feelings integrated. When connected knowers ask 'Why?' they want to know how ideas were developed or constructed, preferably by hearing a description of the specific situation or experience from which the ideas emerged. Baxter Magolda (1992) uses the term 'relational' to describe college students, both male and female, who use connected procedures for learning.

Maturity in learning and knowing increases as the learner becomes skilled in using both separate and connected procedures. While the two subsets of procedural knowing may become integrated, it is more likely that a mature learner will use each subset in different contexts and situations. Facilitators of adult learning have two functions in relation to procedural knowing:

1 to help separate procedural knowers recognize the need to contextualize some knowledge by connecting it to personal experience and to keep knowledge connected to the experiences in which it is grounded; and
2 to help connected procedural knowers generalize some knowledge so that it becomes transferrable to other contexts and to look for logic in knowledge.

Finding examples of separate and connected procedural knowing is difficult. I am usually content to go about my learning using procedures that could be classified as separate. I read; I consult authoritative sources; I present rational arguments to myself and try to find my errors in logic. When I am trying to solve a personal problem, however, I begin to annoy those around me by insisting on talking about the situation ad nauseum, alternately seeking advice and just venting my feelings. Something happens as I talk – I hear myself giving voice to ideas and feelings I was unaware of and proposing solutions that actually make sense. What I need most at such times is empathetic others who are very good listeners.

Constructed Knowing

Constructed knowing is described by Belenky and her colleagues (1986) as a mature way of knowing and being. *Constructed knowing* occurs when learners rely on, and integrate, both subjective and received sources of knowledge, and are willing and able to use both separate and connected procedures for knowing and learning. These learners understand that

• all knowledge is constructed by persons;
• all knowledge is contextualized and based on real experiences;
• some knowledge can be transferred to alternate contexts;
• one's own experience can be used to generate knowledge equally well as another person's experiences; and
• knowledge can and should be assessed against reality.

Those who can be described as 'constructed knowers' assume responsibility for examining, assessing, and developing systems of thought, for caring about thinking and thinking about caring (Belenky et al., 1986). They are willing to see themselves as authoritative sources, able to engage in collegial and collaborative activities rather than subordinating themselves to authority figures. They are capable of engaging in multiple dialogues. They describe themselves as persons who are confident, integrated, and capable of working alone or with others.

Silence

Belenky and her colleagues (1986) also describe 'feeling silenced' as a way of knowing and report that it is associated with a personal history of abusive relationships. Feeling silenced is the experience of having no voice, of feeling mindless and voiceless, and of being subject to the whims of external authority. This sort of silence can become a way of being in the world.

Silence as a way of knowing is experienced not only as a lack of an outer voice, but also as inner silence, accompanied by feelings of being suppressed, of being deaf and dumb, and being powerless. It seems to involve a lack of reliance on any source of knowledge, whether internal or external, and an inability to use either connected or separate procedures for learning.

The women who regularly use this way of knowing are rarely able to generalize from personal experience, but rather view each experience as separate and unconnected to other experiences.

- They perceive authority figures as arbitrary and punitive, as all-powerful but mute, as sources of punishment rather than sources of knowledge.
- They do not gain knowledge through words, since words were often used as weapons in chronic verbal abuse.
- They experience themselves as having no words.
- They may describe themselves as worthless nobodies.
- They tend to be poor learners who must first regain their ability to communicate and to trust others.
- Some have poor literacy skills and many are often found in basic education programs.

Facilitators of adult learning need to be able to identify silenced learners and offer them special and often extensive support services (Belenky, Bond, & Weinstock, 1997).

Many learners, however, use silence selectively and deliberately in response to arbitrary, ambiguous, or punitive authorities. Such learners use silence, not as a way of being in the world, but as a choice to be exercised when they feel unable to communicate their knowledge, in the absence of appropriate words or the presence of threats. The experience is described as 'feeling dumb' and frequently is accompanied by feelings of being depressed (rather than suppressed) and disempowered.

Variations on Ways of Knowing

The drawings in Figure 8.2, Ways of Knowing, attempt to depict how I see the two sources of knowledge and two procedures for knowing changing as a result of learning how to learn. It is difficult to convey the theory underlying women's ways of knowing because it is still a work in progress. Try to avoid reading Figure 8.2 as implying that received and subjective knowing, connected procedural and separate procedural knowing, are the opposite ends of behavioural continuums.

Received knowers can become more mature as learners by assessing their received knowledge against personal experience, and by developing and confidently using both separate and connected procedures for knowing and learning. The shaded circle representing their starting point in Figure 8.2 would expand to the left as well as up and down.

Subjective knowers can become more mature as learners by finding appropriate words to describe and share their subjective knowledge and assessing it against reality and received knowledge, and by developing and confidently using both connected and separate procedures for knowing and learning. The shaded circle representing their starting point in Figure 8.2 would expand to the right as well as up and down.

Separate procedural knowers can become more mature as learners by learning connected procedures for learning and recognizing the importance of experience-based knowledge and the need to contextualize some knowledge. Since they already use both received and subjective sources of knowledge, the shaded circle representing their starting point in Figure 8.2 would expand downward.

Connected procedural knowers can become more mature as learners by learning separate procedures for learning and recognizing the need to generalize some knowledge, so that it becomes transferrable to other contexts. Since they already use both received and subjective sources of knowledge, the shaded circle representing their starting point in Figure 8.2 would expand upward.

Silenced knowers would need to expand in all directions by first learning to trust others and by developing their communication skills.

In this way, all learners could eventually become constructed knowers, able to integrate both received and subjective sources of knowledge and to use both connected and separate procedures for knowing and learning.

Criticisms of Women's Ways of Knowing Model

Both feminists and educators have identified four problems with the Women's Ways of Knowing Model (Goldberger, 1996).

First, because the book was entitled *Women's Ways of Knowing*, some critics

Figure 8.2
Ways of Knowing

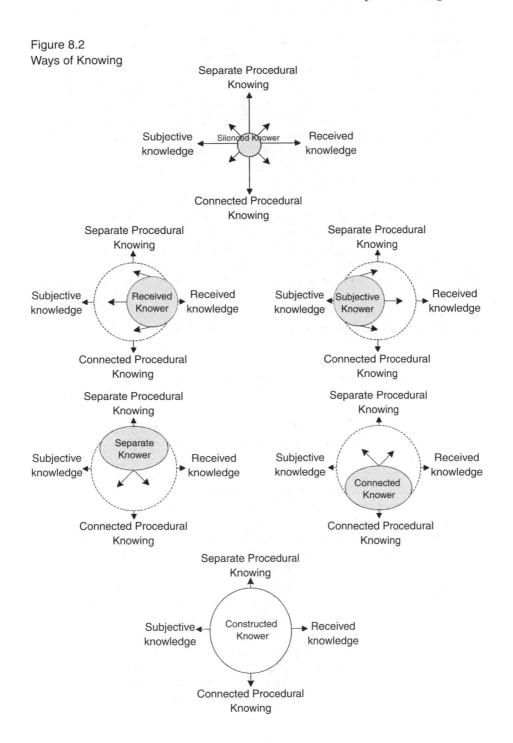

assumed that Belenky and her colleagues were implying the existence of contrasting men's ways of knowing. They were criticized as proposing biologically based gender differences transmitted genetically rather than socially constructed gender differences transmitted through socialization.

Goldberger (1996) concedes that the ideas described in their book (Belenky et al., 1986) would have been better received if the word 'women's' had been omitted from the title. Because the research was conducted with women, the writers were scrupulous in not generalizing their findings to men. Goldberger goes on to acknowledge that the identified ways of knowing also describe ways used by men.

Second, the model is seen as having been developed by 'white' feminists, and therefore as excluding the ways of knowing used by women of colour. Critics point out that categorizing women into five ways of knowing, without paying particular attention to race and class, does a disservice to poor women, women of colour, and women from different cultures.

Goldberger (1996) acknowledges that, while the original research included poor women and women of colour, the authors did not do a separate and comparative analysis of the data from these subgroups. Ruth Ray (1999/2000) reports that most women use relational ways of knowing but that

- black women talk about their relationships in terms of race and class;
- lower-class women talk about their relationships in terms of hardship and survival; and
- middle-class women talk about their relationships in terms of effort and agency, the terms adopted by Belenky and her colleagues.

Third, the model is criticized as being anti-intellectual because it is perceived as endorsing the superiority of anti-rationalist, subjectivist procedures for learning and knowing. This view seems to be the result of confusing subjectivist knowledge with connected procedures. Clinchy (1996) counters this argument by stating that both connected and separate procedural ways of knowing can be based on both subjective and/or received knowledge and that both procedures are legitimate means for learning and creating knowledge. Further, she maintains that separate and connected procedures result in different but equal bases of knowledge, both of which can inform further knowledge development.

Fourth, while the authors did not propose the Women's Ways of Knowing Model as a developmental sequence, many readers insist that it should be read that way. To this concern, Goldberger (1996) indicates that readers are certainly entitled to their own opinion, but they should be prepared to back up their opinions with well-designed longitudinal research.

Other Variations on Ways of Knowing and Learning

Although the original research in the Women's Ways of Knowing Model was done with women, more recent research has examined the concepts with both men and women. The model of knowing and learning proposed by Belenky and her colleagues (1986) must be understood as related to but not dictated by gender.

Marcia Baxter Magolda (1992) conducted research, based on Perry's (1970) stages of cognitive development, that included college men and women as study participants. She found that men and women did not differ in what they learned, only in how they preferred to go about that learning. Women more often than men used connected procedures and relational strategies to gather and understand information, while men more often than women used separate procedures and autonomous strategies.

Baxter Magolda identified three additional 'story-lines' that contribute to the ways in which both men and women know, reason, and learn.

1 The first story-line relates to the development and emergence of 'voice' in which students move from repeating what others say to developing their own perspective and speaking out about their own ideas.
2 The second story-line concerns the changing relationship with authority figures in which students move from an initial reliance on authority to finally developing their own sense of authority.
3 The third story-line deals with the evolving peer relationships in which students gradually increase the value they attribute to others as knowers in their own right.

Kathleen Galotti and her colleagues (Galotti et al., 1999; Galotti, Drebus, & Reimer, 2001) conducted research to determine whether different ways of knowing correlated with traditionally measured intellectual abilities, and whether they were more like attitudes, colouring the comfort with which knowers approached or immersed themselves in different learning tasks. They created an attitude survey measuring an individual's use of connected and separate procedural knowing, and found that:

• Connected and separate procedural knowing are independent of each other rather than being simply opposite ends of a single continuum.
• Each way of knowing represents a different kind of learning or cognitive style, not an intellectual ability. Neither way of knowing was found to be significantly correlated with any measure of cognitive intelligence.
• The two modes of knowing are not mutually exclusive. They can and do co-exist within one individual. Learners can score high on both modes, low on both modes, or high on one and low on the other.

Figure 8.3
Comparison of Autonomous and Relational Learners

	Separate knowing Autonomous learning	Connected knowing Relational learning
Learning concerns	• Mastering content • Achieving as an individual • Identifying truth • Asking questions to prove truth or worth of ideas	• Connecting to other learners • Identifying differences between ideas and opinions • Asking questions to understand situations, contexts, and ideas of others
Learning activities	• Challenging ideas of others • Convincing others through logic • Maintaining order through explicit agreement to abide by rules • Resolving conflicts through detached imposition of rules • Doubting or excluding others' ideas until their worth has been proved • Attempting to reveal truth that is general, impersonal, grounded in rational, logical thought or generalized perception of reality • Prefers self-directed activities, competes in group activities • Maintaining objectivity through adopting frame of reference of discipline (e.g., biology, social work) or authority (e.g., the instructor) • Holding thought and feeling separate	• Listening when knowledge is uncertain • Convincing others through sharing particulars of personal experiences • Maintaining order through implicit agreement to avoid conflict • Resolving conflicts through reconciling differences • Believing others' ideas in order to expand one's own understanding • Attempting to create truth that is personal, particular, and grounded in first-hand experiences, unique historical/personal events • Prefers collective or collaborative group activities or learning partnerships • Maintaining objectivity through understanding frame of reference of other person(s) • Keeping thought and feeling together
Preferred cognitive style	• Analytical • Based on patterns and exemplars	• Holistic • Based on narratives and metaphors
Nature of truth and knowledge	• Truth resides in reliability and validity of knowledge • Knowledge understood as separate from knower	• Truth resides in believability or meaning given to experiences or interpretation of facts • Knowledge understood in relation to knower
Nature of evaluation	• Opportunity to correct errors in selection of facts and logic used in interpretation • Individual accountable for own learning	• Opportunity to demonstrate understanding of different sides of an issue • Individual accountable to others for learning

- Women had significantly higher scores on connected knowing than men; men had significantly higher scores on separate knowing than women.
- Men and women were equally represented in the high connected/high separate and low connected/low separate groups. Those in the high connected/low separate group were disproportionately likely to be women; those in the low connected/high separate group were disproportionately likely to be men.
- Learners with high scores on connected knowing described the ideal teacher as being in control, accepting, facilitating, helpful, understanding, emotional, patient, open, thoughtful, purposeful, flexible, assertive, responsive, and tolerant.
- Learners with high scores on separate knowing described the ideal teacher as being demanding, enthusiastic, critical, analytical, and low in spontaneity and tolerance.

Goldberger (1996) comments: 'Knowing is not insular. How one knows is determined within the array of relationships that define the self ... Knowledge is co-constructed' (p. 14). She goes on to say that individual learners are situated in 'communities of knowers in which the dynamics of power and status are often controlling factors in how one knows and what one knows' (p. 15). We will address situated learning and issues of power in Chapter 10.

Without attributing relational/connected or autonomous/separate strategies to either men or women or to any cultural groups, and without judging the value of one set of strategies over the other, I have provided an outline of known or expected distinctions related to these two strategies in Figure 8.3, Comparison of Autonomous and Relational Learners. My advice to the reader is to think of the overall distinctions between relational and autonomous learners as contrasting behaviours. An individual might be more relational in some contexts, more autonomous in others, and demonstrate a mix of behaviours in still others.

LEARNING AND FACILITATING PRINCIPLES

Learners who feel silenced, or who use silence as a way of knowing, need opportunities to share their feelings and perceptions with others; to share how they perceive themselves and their learning environment and how that environment is silencing them.

Facilitators need to be alert to the possibility that some learners feel silenced. For those who use silence as a way of knowing, facilitators need to ensure that supportive services are made available. For those who are experiencing temporary silencing, facilitators need to provide opportunities to talk about the personal experiences that have led to feeling silenced.

Some learners attend only to the knowledge coming from authoritative sources.

When an exclusive focus on received knowledge is inappropriate, facilitators need to help learners think critically about such knowledge and assess it against personal life experiences.

Some learners attend only to the knowledge derived from their interpretation of their subjective experiences.

When an exclusive focus on subjective knowledge is inappropriate, facilitators need to help learners think critically about such knowledge and assess it against the shared knowledge of other learners and of experts.

Most adult learners have developed learning strategies supporting either separate procedural knowing or connected procedural knowing.

Facilitators can help adults become more effective learners by encouraging separate procedural knowers to develop the skills of connected knowing and connected procedural knowers to develop the skills of separate knowing.

Some adult learners have fully developed skills in using and understanding all ways of knowing.

The best facilitators can do is to avoid putting obstacles in their way and to act as collaborative colleagues in their learning endeavours.

Adults learn best in environments able to support both connected and separate procedural knowing.

Adults learn best when their experience and sense of self are validated in the learning process.

Both connected and separate procedural knowers are capable of learning the same things, but how they go about doing the learning differs.

Learning experiences that facilitate predominantly autonomous learning or separate procedural knowing tend to create considerable difficulties for those who tend to use relational learning or connected procedural knowing. Relational learners in autonomous programs tend to form informal groups outside the learning program to support their need for relationships.

> *Facilitating strategies that result in largely autonomous programs include lectures, debates, independent studies, computerized simulations, programmed instruction, large group discussions, and the like.*

Learning experiences that facilitate predominantly relational learning or connected procedural knowing create some difficulties for those who tend to use autonomous learning or separate procedural knowing. Autonomous learners in relational programs tend to do their assignments on their own even when they are working in groups.

> *Facilitating strategies that result in largely relational programs include small group assignments and activities, case studies and interactive games, storytelling, learning partnerships, talking circles, role playing, small group discussions, and the like.*

It is generally easier to be an autonomous learner in a relational program than to be a relational learner in an autonomous program.

> *Good facilitators need to be able to offer activities that support both relational and autonomous learning. Facilitating strategies that support both relational and autonomous programs include:*
>
> * *co-operative and collaborative learning structures such as small groups and learning partnerships;*
> * *co-operative evaluation techniques that encourage all learners in a small group to be accountable both for their own learning and for the learning of others;*
> * *co-operative communication styles in which each speaker recognizes and builds on the contributions made by other speakers; and*
> * *shared leadership that includes sharing responsibilities for listening to others, validating experience, synthesizing ideas, facilitating interpersonal interactions, and so on.*

9 Spirit and Soul in Learning

Concerns about 'spirit' and 'soul' are relatively new trends in adult education. When I first heard the terms 'spirituality' and 'spiritual learning,' I wondered what they meant. I found myself asking: Do I have spirituality? Am I doing any spiritual learning? How does my soul enter into my learning? I wondered if 'spirit' and 'soul' were similar or different concepts, how they were connected, and what their relationship was to other concepts such as 'religion' and 'faith.' In the previous edition of this book, I used the terms 'spirit' and 'soul' interchangeably; in this edition, I want to consider them separately and then attempt to bring them together. I will provide examples of soulful and spiritual learning at the end of the chapter.

I understand spirit and spirituality to be the experience of feeling expanded beyond the normal limits of my body and mind, of feeling connected to aspects of the external world that are of value to me – to others, to the earth, and to a greater cosmic being (Davis, 2002; Tisdell, 1999). Soul, on the other hand, calls on me to look inward at my individuality and personal substance. Thomas Moore (1994) tells us that soul is grounded in the ordinary details of everyday life, including the present mess the self is in. He goes on to say that spirit arises from a need to transcend the messy conditions of life to find 'an expression of meaning that will take one up and out of the quagmire of actual experience' (p. 5).

Spirit and soul, then, are related. In my understanding of the two concepts, the experience of soul is inward looking and allows the individual to find inner completeness, integrity, and serenity; the experience of spirit is outward looking and allows the individual to connect to relationships and realities beyond the immediacy of body and mind. The integrity of soul is essential if one is to look outward with any sense of self-extension; the possibility of spirit is essential for the individual to want to resolve conflicts within soul. Our spirituality gives purpose and meaning to our lives. It grows out of our soul or central sense of self; without a strong sense of self, we would have little inclination to move out into the world.

The noted adult educator Roby Kidd describes learning related to being-becoming-belonging in terms similar to those I have used to described learning that emerges from soul and spirit. He says that such learning involves 'the celebration, the affirmation, the enlargement of the full consciousness; the search for that part of the individual that is truly human, ... [that is] uniquely me, uniquely I' (1995, p. 198). Kidd goes on to say that such learning 'must be the heart and central goal of education' (p. 7). He tells us that learning for being-becoming-belonging

- involves both affective and cognitive components;
- involves a complete time dimension of past, present, and future;
- is about life and all of living; and
- happens not only through acquiring knowledge and skills, but also through self-discovery, self-expression, and self-fulfilment.

The separate discussions of spirit and soul that follow in this chapter are not meant as academic treatises on the role of spirit and soul in learning. They are meant to encourage both individual reflection and group discussion. Those who perceive spirit and soul as terms related to religion and faith will be disappointed: I prefer to leave discussions about religion and faith to those with more specialized knowledge than I possess. Leona English and Marie Gillen (2000) explain that 'religion is based on an organized set of principles shared by a group, whereas spirituality is the expression of an individual's quest for meaning' (p. 1). In this chapter I want to keep the focus on the individual.

The Soul and Learning

Soul is the very essence of our being, the centre of our individuality. It is not an entity or thing but an animating energy or process (J.P. Miller, 1999; Moore, 1992), a dimension through which we experience life and self. Moore (1992) tells us that the soul lies 'midway between understanding and unconsciousness and that its instrument is neither mind nor body, but imagination' (p. xi).

Much of the literature that discusses the soul uses terms derived from Carl Jung's work on the structure of the psyche. Jung (1964) described the human mind or psyche as having two components:

1 that part derived from personal experience that Jung viewed as including both the conscious and the personal unconscious; and
2 that part derived from the collective unconscious, a reservoir of primordial images.

The Ego, in Jung's terms, is an organizing force managing the boundary between the conscious and unconscious aspects of mind and determining what experiences, images, ideas, and memories will be brought forward into the conscious mind. Jung equated the soul with the collective unconscious and populated it with archetypes. An archetype is a preformed pattern for human behaviour, an image without content that is developed and filled out through experience. Three major archetypes are the Persona, the Shadow, and the Self.

- My Persona provides a mask I wear when I interact with others or play a particular role. It is an outward-facing archetype that promotes behaviour more visible to others than to me.
- My Shadow contains repressed and undeveloped behavioural possibilities that I do not want others to know about or that I do not want to know about. It is an inward-facing archetype that promotes behaviour more visible to me than to others.
- My Self is the central archetype of my collective unconscious, drawing to itself and integrating other archetypes and providing me with a sense of continuity and stability.

Jung originally conceived of the Self as providing the individual with a sense of 'oneness,' a singular personal identity that behaves consistently across different roles, relationships, and cultural contexts. Today, because of the work of poststructuralists (Clark, 1999; DeBold, Tolman, & Brown, 1996; Gergen, 1991), we are more inclined to view the Self as consisting of several different selves or identities. These different identities may offer little consistency in behaviours across an individual's different roles, responsibilities, and cultural contexts.

Soul work (soulful learning) involves an exploration of these various identities with a view to knowing them better, bringing their essence to consciousness, contemplating their ambiguity and mystery, and accepting them for what they are. Dirkx (1998) suggests as we become more aware of the inner forces of our psyche, 'by participating with them in a more conscious manner, we are less likely to be unwilling buffeted around by their presence in our lives' (p. 4).

The process of soul work usually begins with a deeply emotional image – a message from the soul that comes to us through visualizations, dreams, meditation, stories, myths, poetry, and the arts. All writers in the field caution that soul work cannot be accomplished by using rational, linear problem solving that seeks the right answer, but must rely on holistic contemplation that seeks a healthy answer (Dirkx, 1997, 1998; J.P. Miller, 1999; Moore, 1992, 1994, 1995; Tisdell, 1999). Moore (1995) states that when we try to live 'in an intellectually predictable world protected from all mysteries and comfortable with conformity, we lose our everyday opportunities for a soulful life' (p. 233).

Moore (1992) suggests that story telling is an excellent place to start learning about the soul. It helps us become aware of the themes that entwine our lives, the images that guide us, and the myths that we live. Taking an interest in our soul requires that we give over a certain amount of time and space for reflection and appreciation. Soulful learning also means not taking sides when a conflict arises and expanding the heart and mind wide enough to embrace contradiction and paradox. Moore suggests that an effective trick in soulful learning is to pay special attention to what the mind rejects and to 'speak favorably on behalf of the rejected element' (p. 16). The learning related to soul work takes time. It does not occur according to a plan or as a result of intentional intervention. If one attends to the soul with educated and steadfast imagination, change will take place without the individual being consciously aware of its happening. Moore concludes: 'A genuine odyssey is not about piling up experiences. It is a deeply felt, risky, unpredictable tour of the soul' (p. 230).

J.P. Miller (1999) writes that contemplation is the soul's main form of learning and knowing but is hardly ever encouraged in formal education. He states: 'by ignoring or denying contemplation, the soul is also denied. The soul hides while our minds analyze, memorize, and categorize' (p. 214). Education that nourishes the soul involves more than emotion and develops in the learner a creative, disciplined quality of mind. Such education begins through nurturing the imagination, not to create fantasies, but to discover the patterns that weave us together with the world.

Spirituality and Learning

Moore (1992) writes: 'In our spirituality, we reach for consciousness, awareness and highest values; in our soulfulness, we endure the most pleasurable and exhausting of human experience and emotions' (p. 231). The realm of the spirit in learning involves expanding our knowing beyond the previous limits of our self-system or model of reality and connecting with some new aspect of our world.

Leona English and Marie Gillen (2000) define spirituality as 'an awareness of something greater than ourselves, a sense that we are connected to all human beings, and to all creation' (p. 1). They argue that to omit the spiritual dimension of adult learning would be to ignore 'the importance of a holistic approach to adult learning as well as the complexity of the adult learner' (p. 2).

Spiritual learning helps us to:

- connect with a higher consciousness or cosmic being through what is described as 'transcendent' learning (Wilber, 1986);
- move beyond the limits of our model of reality through what is described as 'transformative' learning (Dirkx, 1997; Mezirow, 2000; Scott, 1997);

- move beyond the limits of our self-system to connect to others in meaningful ways through what is described as 'transpersonal' learning (Roberts & Clark, 1975);
- move beyond a separation of action and awareness to the experience of
'flow,' a holistic sensation associated with total involvement, intrinsic
rewards, and personal transcendence (Csikszentmihalyi, 1990).

These are not the only forms of spiritual learning, but are the most common
ones I have encountered in the literature.

Based on his work as a psychotherapist, Ken Wilber (1986) describes spiritual development as occurring through ten levels:

- The first three levels comprise *pre-personal development*. These levels –
sensory-physical, image, and representational – are based on Piaget's
model of cognitive development and describe the ability to represent
events, objects, and people in the mind as symbols, words, and concepts
(see Chapter 5).
- The second three levels comprise *personal development*. These levels – rule/
role, formal-reflexive, and vision-logic – are based on the concrete, formal,
and post-formal stages of operational cognitive development (see Chapter
5). Wilber seems to define spiritual development as paralleling cognitive
development, at least at the pre-personal and personal stages.
- The next three levels – psychic, subtle, and causal – comprise *transpersonal development*. At these levels, the individual learns to subtly and
reflexively inspect the mind's cognitive and perceptual capacities and
thus expand and transcend them. Both the individual's sense of self
and model of reality are expanded beyond their existing limits. By the
causal level, the individual's centralized sense of self becomes lost in
the largeness of being and is finally replaced by a feeling of a bound-
less universal self, an unlimited 'unity consciousness' pervading everything and everywhere. Unity consciousness is a kind of knowing in
which there are no distinctions between the knowing, the knower, and
the known.
- The tenth or *ultimate* level, the epitome of transpersonal development, is
one that few individuals reach and is based largely on conjecture. At this
level, Wilber describes the individual as reaching a sense of oneness with
the universe.

The literature on spiritual learning is divided on whether it occurs
through intentional activities at any stage of development, through seren-
dipitous events that begin with an altered or 'higher' state of consciousness,
or through some natural developmental process. Wilber's (1986) model
certainly implies that spiritual development in the transpersonal stages

involves higher states of consciousness and occurs only after an individual is capable of post-formal operational thinking.

Many educators, such as Leona English (2000), John Miller (1999), Jane Vella (2000), and Reg Wickett (2000), indicate that the use of appropriate facilitating strategies can encourage spiritual learning at any age and stage of human development. John Dirkx (1998) agrees but cautions that the content of such learning must be based, not on constructs and images arrived at consciously under the wilful control of the ego, but on messages and images that arrive from the soul. This places Dirkx closer to Wilber's model than to any other model proposed by adult educators. Indeed, Dirkx and Scott (1997) both challenge the cognitively based concepts of transformative learning (Cranton, 1994; Mezirow, 1991, 2000) as being too limited in scope to adequately describe spiritual learning.

Patricia Weibust and Eugene Thomas (1994), both psychologists, report that spirituality is age-related but not age-determined. They describe the normal age-related biological declines that lead to a general decline in abstract reasoning as providing the conditions necessary to engage in spiritual learning. One of the paradoxes of spiritual learning is that while an age-related readiness to engage in it does occur naturally, advanced spiritual development does not occur in all older individuals. 'While certain insights and learning are possible in the earlier years, the full fruition of spiritual maturity appears to come only after middle age' (Weibust & Thomas, 1994, p. 132).

Facilitating Spiritual Learning

By putting together ideas from a variety of sources, we can conclude that spiritual learning is more likely to occur when the following seven conditions are in place.

First, *spiritual learning often involves an altered or higher state of consciousness* (Weibust & Thomas, 1994; Wilber, 1986). We encountered ideas about altered states of consciousness in Chapter 5. The diffuse attention associated with alpha waves and the dreaming sleep associated with theta waves are the two states of consciousness most usually conducive to spiritual learning. The term 'higher consciousness' seems to refer to a reflexive awareness of the content and processes associated with one's own perceptions, thoughts, and memories and with how these relate to the perceptions, thoughts, and memories of others.

Whether an altered or higher state of consciousness is essential for spiritual learning seems open to debate. Strategies that facilitate altered states of consciousness include guided imagery, focused attention, visualizing, dream sharing, creativity (mental play), humour, and the use of metaphors. These activities encourage learners to turn their attention inward and allow themselves to be aware of thought, images, metaphors, analogies, feelings, physical sensations, and other experiences. The facilitator can help by providing a comfortable, nonthreatening, quiet environment and by guiding such activities in a quiet, leisurely manner. Once learners have completed the activity, the facilitator brings their attention back to reality and helps them debrief or share what has happened.

Second, *spiritual learning occurs more often among learners who are open to new experiences and new ideas* and who are willing to risk participating in learning activities that are, in outward appearance, the antithesis of traditional learning and education. Such activities can be described as nonsequential and sometimes chaotic rather than linear and orderly; imaginative and visual rather than verbal; analogical rather than logical; nonrational rather than rational. They include activities that are frequently labelled as 'crazy' and illogical by those who do not understand holistic learning.

Gisela Labouvie-Vief (1992) comments that normal human development has become equated with a decrease in playful, symbolic imaginative activities. In adults, these activities tend to be perceived as childish, even autistic, forms of thought and behaviour. Spiritual learning relies on such internal processes. Dirkx (1998) calls such processes 'mytho-poetic' in nature. Anyone who is not open to new experiences is unlikely to engage in spiritual learning.

Third, *spiritual learning favours those who are aware of their own state of consciousness* and who are alert to thoughts, images, metaphors, analogies, physical sensations, and other experiences associated with altered states of consciousness that might occur at odd times and places. Learners who want to engage in spiritual learning need to keep track, in some way, of the images that rise to their awareness. A dream journal is one such method. When the dreaming mind returns to normal waking consciousness and beta waves reclaim control of the mind, then the thoughts, images, and experiences that occurred during the dream will be quickly forgotten. It takes practice to develop an awareness of your own consciousness. If you start now and record your altered state experiences, in six months you will have expanded your awareness considerably.

Fourth, *spiritual learning occurs more often among learners who are able to avoid judging their thoughts or experiences.* To learn anything from one's own thoughts, images, and experiences, one must avoid judging their rightness or wrongness, goodness or badness. Dirkx (1998) says that the purpose of spiritual learning is not to analyse and dissect images and emotions but to imaginatively elaborate their meaning in one's life. Rather than asking 'how' or 'why,' questions that typify Mezirow's approach to transformative learning, one should simply ask 'what' – What does this image remind me of? What emotions accompany this image?

Everything is grist for the spiritual learning mill, but when something is judged the learning ceases. Surprisingly, agreeing or approving of a thought, image, feeling, or experience before it is recorded is also a form of judgment and equally likely to halt the learning process.

Fifth, *spiritual learning favours those who reflect on their thoughts and experiences*. Once the thoughts, images, and experiences have been recorded in some objective fashion, the learner can revisit them at a later time in order to contemplate them and give them meaning. Methods for making such records could include journal writing, drawing, writing poetry, writing stories, and so on. Revisiting the thoughts, images, and experiences sometimes occurs spontaneously – as if the unconscious mind has been mulling them over. When the conscious mind comes up with a meaning that makes sense, it is likely to appear in our awareness as an 'ah-ha' experience.

Learners also need to revisit their reflections deliberately. Even after the thoughts, images, and experiences have been given meaning, it may take time before the learner can understand how the new meanings fit with existing meanings or can be used in practical ways in work, family, or community contexts.

Sixth, *spiritual learning occurs more readily when learners share their experiences through interactive dialogues* (English, 2000; Tisdell, 1999; Vella, 2000). The expansive feelings that accompany spiritual learning are sometimes hard to share. Almost without fail, learners' enthusiasm for having reached out to touch a higher being or for having transcended themselves is heard by unbelieving listeners as palpable nonsense. So when you come to share your newfound knowledge, pick carefully the people with whom you will share your insights. You will want to talk to someone who is very good at validating your experiences, at listening empathetically and nonjudgmentally, at engaging in the mutual, side-by-side, 'looking on together' described by Jean Clandinin (1993) as essential to the mentoring process.

Seventh, *spiritual learning favours those who look for connections in unlikely places*, between apparently unconnected and disparate ideas and experiences. The process of revisiting altered-state experiences usually involves connecting their meanings to other concerns, ideas, and thoughts from other sources. Sometimes there is no apparent, direct link between the central meaning of the experience and the additional ideas that become connected to it. But connections are there, however well obscured they may be, and the meanings of these connections will emerge as time passes.

Weibust and Thomas (1994) quote the poet T.S. Eliot, who wrote that the end of our spiritual seeking is to find ourselves at the place where we began our journey and to 'know the place for the first time' (p. 125). In this sense, spiritual learning is paradoxical, a self-referential undertaking that results in a transformation of the premises that underlie one's model of reality and of the meaning perspectives through which one views the world and one's self. Paradoxes present the learner with ill-formed or divergent problems to be solved. The more the learner attempts to deal with the problem through convergent, logical methods, the more the problem diverges. The only solution is to transcend the problem, bringing the opposites into a single frame of reference, seeing them as mirror images of each other, and bringing them together as part of a larger whole.

LEARNING AND FACILITATING PRINCIPLES

To engage in soulful and spiritual learning, adults need:

- to be fully open to new ideas and new experiences. *Facilitators need to provide very safe, supportive environments in which openness to new ideas will not result in feelings of being discounted or devalued.*
- to be aware of their own state of consciousness. *Facilitators need to provide a variety of activities in which learners can become aware of and identify different states of consciousness. Some useful activities are deep relaxation, guided imagery, keeping a dream journal, sharing dreams, using humour, meditating, creativity, and mental play.*
- to avoid judging their thoughts or experiences. *In the same vein, facilitators need to avoid judging the ideas, thoughts, and feelings proposed by learners as a result of their spiritual learning. This includes avoiding agreement, approval, or rejection of both positive and negative ideas and feelings. For example, it is inappropriate to try to talk learners out of thoughts and feelings that are based on a negative view of self. One way to avoid making such judgments is to ask the learner if there is another way to interpret experiences.*
- to reflect on their thoughts and experiences, revisit their reflections, and share their experiences. *Facilitators need to provide opportunities and lots of time to reflect on and share thoughts and experiences following activities that involve an altered state of consciousness. This part of the process cannot be rushed and may take more time than can be provided within a formal class structure and timetable.*
- to look for connections in unlikely places, between apparently unconnected and disparate ideas and experiences. *Facilitators need to encourage learners to look for connections in unlikely places. This is not easy since many learners insist that insights from one experience bear no relationship whatsoever to other experiences and activities. This part of the process cannot be forced.*

A Personal Journey of the Soul and the Spirit

Providing an example of soulful and spiritual learning is difficult. I believe such an example should come from my own life rather than infringing on the privacy of others. In telling you about my experience, I first need to describe the image – a dream – that brought messages from my soul to my awareness and then describe the conditions in my life that prompted my need for these messages. Next I want to talk about my reflections about this image and the contradictions I identified in my life.

In the first edition of this book, I told a story about a dream I had prior to a trip to Sweden to participate in a workshop and to speak to several groups of educators. Rather than simply repeating this section from the first edition, I have edited the story somewhat and have provided some reflections based on the ideas about soulful and spiritual learning already discussed in this chapter.

The Dream

Dreams make interesting narratives but they need to be framed in some way to contextualize them. The dream I recount here occurred at a time when I was agonizing over the focus of the workshop and speeches for my trip to Sweden and over whether I was capable of doing these activities effectively.

I was being described in advertising for the activities as a distinguished adult educator with expertise on women, learning, and distance education, a description I would never have given myself. I see myself as competent and caring but not distinguished, a good teacher but not a good public speaker. In addition, I was not looking forward to the travelling. At the time I was afflicted with arthritis in my knees, and sitting and standing still for any length of time, as well as walking, made my knees ache. My body was grumbling about the travel, my stress levels were soaring at the prospect of speaking to strangers, and my thoughts were in chaos about what I would say and do; but one corner of my mind knew that I should make this trip as a contribution to my own professional development.

In narrating my dream, I have been guided by general advice I was given in counselling courses – dreams should be told in the first person singular and the present tense, as if the dream were occurring now (Dombeck, 1991).

It is a cold, crisp winter evening. I am in a hansom cab on my way to have dinner with the president. The driver is a man. I am accompanied by two other men. One is my father. I don't recognize the other man. My father insists on sitting on the roof of the carriage. I don't ask why. I am afraid he will fall off so I stand on the seat and hold onto him through a retractable roof.

We arrive at the president's house. His wife greets us at the door. She is very kind and gracious but I can tell she wasn't expecting us and she seems quite unconcerned about our situation. The president is away at a meeting. It's not clear whether he is coming back for dinner although I am sure this is the right night.

My father is too cold to walk, so I carry him into the house, into the front parlour. It is a cold, cheerless room. My father is now shivering and seems quite ill. I carry him upstairs to the family room where there is a fire and comfortable, overstuffed furniture. I lower him onto a sofa and wrap a blanket around him. I keep him company while the others go off to dinner with the president's wife.

Suddenly I am aware that the horses are free of the hansom cab and are running around and around the house, running closer and closer to the house. One runs at the front door, trying to get in. I rush to stop him but am pushed aside and am bowled over by his size and power.

I woke up from this dream feeling very sad and burdened but intrigued with why I had been carrying my father around, why a horse would want to get into a house, and why the president's wife was so unconcerned. I found myself repeating over and over: *Why* am I carrying my father around? No answers came immediately to mind, so I described my dream in my journal and let my questions go unanswered in the hope that the dream would make sense another day.

Contemplation and Reflection

At the beginning of this chapter, I wrote that soul work requires time for contemplation and reflection and that logical, linear thinking doesn't help a person understand an emotionally charged image or its meaning. I was also guided in my contemplations by the advice of dream therapists (Dombeck, 1991), who maintain that every part of the dream – every person, animal, and object in it – is part of the Self, and the meaning of each comes from my unconscious mind.

I let the dream sit around in the back of my mind for several weeks, revisiting it when I had time. I gradually realized the dream was partly about my academic expertise, partly about being a woman who works in an academic context, and partly about my sense of personal empowerment. I began to develop answers for my own questions

Why was I carrying the Father around? The Father in my dream seems to represent the theoretical or academic knowledge that dominates traditional thinking in the field of adult education. Much of this knowledge comes from male educators and conveys the impression that the education of males is more important than the education of females. While I teach this knowledge, much of it does not fit my life experience and does not coincide with the practical knowledge I have developed over thirty years as an adult educator. But then, women have carried the knowledge of their mythical Fathers as conceptual burdens since the dawn of patriarchy – why should I be any different?

Why did I work so hard to keep the Father from falling off the Hansom Cab and

look after him so carefully? I carry all my academic knowledge in my mind. Perhaps the Hansom Cab is my body and the Father is my mind, sitting on top of my body and exposed to the slings and arrows of public comment. I don't want to lose my mind and I certainly don't want to walk around with a sick mind. So I must hang onto it and take care of it.

This issue raises a contradiction in my life. Some of my ideas about adult education are unconventional, particularly my belief that autonomy is not the most mature form of human behaviour. I worry that expressing such thoughts might make me appear 'sick' – meaning ill-intentioned – and leave me open to criticism. I stubbornly hold to my unconventional ideas, but I cannot quite let go of all that male-defined conventional knowledge.

Why was the Horse trying to get into the House? The Horse seems to be a metaphor for power and seems to represent a powerful part of me that is trying to get into the House that is my self. I have made the Horse male. I know the masculine side of my psyche to be powerful in a way that sometimes overwhelms me. I cherish that feeling of power, but I cannot fully claim it every day and in every setting. The Horse is as much a part of me as the conceptual burden represented by the Father.

Why was the President's wife so unconcerned? This image I do not yet understand. Moore (1992) suggests that, in soul work, one should pay special attention to that which the mind rejects and to speak positively on behalf of that image. My immediate impulse is to reject the President's Wife. She seems ineffective and wishy-washy even though she is kind and caring. Perhaps I think this way because she doesn't turn us away even though she was not expecting us.

This is another contradiction in my life. I believe that the most mature form of human behaviour integrates both autonomy and caring, but using both simultaneously seems difficult. Maybe a mature person is capable of both types of behaviour and uses them appropriately depending on the situation. But I initially interpreted the caring response of the President's Wife as weak and ineffective. She seems to represent some uninformed and undervalued aspect of the feminine side of my psyche. I need to continuing contemplating this image.

The dream came to me when I was feeling burdened, inadequate, and incompetent as I thought about my trip to Sweden. I realize now I had been worrying in my mind and not allowing my feelings to be part of my thinking. I had not made my feelings and behaviours – represented in my dream by the Father, the Hansom Cab, the Horse, the House, and the President's Wife – an integral part of myself. By writing about the dream in the first person and active tense, I placed myself at the centre of the action, and this helped me to integrate my thoughts and feelings.

I only feel whole when my feelings and thoughts are firmly connected to each other and to my behaviour. I must be both subject and object in any story of my life; and when I cannot be both, or will not let myself be both, I cannot make sense of what is happening to me. My competence as an academic is only as great as the strength of the connections among my mind, my physical body, my feelings, my caring, my power, and my soul. This is a lesson I first learned when I was writing my thesis, but I never seem to remember it. I need to relearn it over and over again. Perhaps wisdom will come when the lesson has become an integral part of my knowing.

In contemplating the entire episode as a result of writing this chapter, I realize now that I have not completed the experiential learning cycle by using this knowledge in my daily life. I don't give myself time to contemplate my thoughts and feelings on a daily basis. Fortunately, my unconscious mind does this contemplation for me and sends my conscious mind urgent and emotionally charged messages through my dreams. I only need to listen more carefully to myself and my dreams to remain whole and competent.

Multiple Identities and Narratives

One of the topics I planned to speak about in Sweden was the use of story telling or narratives in the lives of women. In my extensive readings about narratives, I came across a quote from Ruthellen Josselson (1993) that intrigued me: 'Memory is where the self is held captive. Telling one's story is a means of becoming' (p. xi). To have no story to tell is tantamount to having no self. So beginning with a story about an image is a good way to begin to recognize the various identities that inhabit one's soul.

The identities in my dream seem to be adult identities that I have not encountered before in my dreaming. Over the years, I had become well-acquainted with identities more associated with the contradictions of my childhood and adolescence. While I have very few memories of my actual childhood, the presence of these child identities in my soul seems to make up for this lack. Now I have a new cast of identities to contemplate as part of my Self. Some of them – the Father and the Horse, for example – seem to parallel some of my child images. Others, particularly the President's Wife, are new. This gives me hope that someday my soul will be more integrated and whole and well-populated with identities of all ages.

The role of narratives in both soulful and spiritual learning is important. In terms of soul work, narratives about one's self provide images that can be contemplated to bring greater meaning and coherence to one's sense of self. In terms of spiritual learning, narratives put an individual in touch with others in a way that offers a personal connection – soul to soul, so to speak. I have told the story of my dream and the ideas I had developed in contemplating it to both individuals and groups. Each time, I heard fascinating stories from listeners. Many women, for example, have dreams in which images of power appear. Some expressed fear in response to these images. Sharing these images made them less frightening, and the process of sharing helped us feel connected to each other.

The more I learn about narratives the more I am convinced that they represent an important learning process crucial to both men and women. In Chapter 5, we encountered ideas put forward by Bruner (1986), who believes narratives are an important way of knowing. Other writers propose that narratives become more important as one grows older (Berg et al., 1994).

Certainly narratives are important to women. Tannen's (1990) work suggests that women are more likely to use 'rapport talk' than 'report talk.' Rapport talk takes the form of stories that illustrate ideas and help build relationships. A narrative implies a relationship between the teller and the listener. While story telling is not itself a dialogue, it can easily lead to reciprocal story telling and lengthy dialogues that are important to spiritual learning (English, 2000; Tisdell, 1999).

In this chapter, my story telling began as a way to help me learn from my dream and to engage in soul work. It eventually led to my sharing the story and what I had learned with others and to feelings that I had become connected with others. I consider my contemplative activities to be a work in progress that will lead to more insights and more stories. While I do not consider that my account of my activities represents a connection to a higher being, I am hopeful that I eventually will make that connection.

10 Environment and Context in Learning

In the past, concerns about learning have focused on the individual. Learning within this perspective is viewed as occurring internally, within the mind of the individual, with scant attention paid to how the environment affects this process. This perspective leads to the assumption that we can create a set of learning and facilitating principles to help all adults become more effective learners regardless of their background and circumstances (Caffarella & Merriam, 1999). Self-directed learning, transformational learning, memory and cognition, and brain-based learning are conceptual models supporting this individual perspective. Much of the content of this book has adopted this focus to help newcomers to the field of adult education understand how individuals learn.

More recently, concerns about learning have shifted to the environment within which learning occurs. The concepts of 'contextual learning' and 'situated learning' have become hot topics in the field of adult education. Until recently, the term 'learning environment' referred mostly to the physical and emotional comfort experienced by learners and facilitators. Now these collective terms refer to a variety of different ways of construing 'environment.' In the B-P-E model discussed in Chapter 2, the 'E' refers to everything occurring outside the individual – including the behaviours of other learners as well as the facilitator. Ongoing, periodic, and lifelong interactions between the Person (individual learner or facilitator) and the Environment have consequences for the resulting Behaviour or learning.

Sorting out the many terms used to describe 'E' in the B-P-E model is challenging. In this chapter we will discuss some of these different conceptions in terms of:

- the role of ergonomics and technology of learning – the physical environment;
- the invisible nature and role of culture in learning – the cultural environment;

- the role of power in teaching-learning interactions – the power environment;
- the role of hegemony and the nature of assumptions – the knowledge environment; and
- the role of context and situation in learning – the 'real-life' environment.

There is much overlap among these conceptions. A consistent theme throughout is that we always learn within environments and contexts that are both visible and invisible. We tend to ignore environment and context until they present us with barriers to our learning; they remain invisible and out of consciousness until they become unsupportive or problematic. Sometimes when the environment or context becomes problematic, we may have difficulty identifying the source of the problem. We need to learn to think critically about our learning environments and contexts before they become problematic.

In previous chapters we have encountered ideas related to variations in environmental, contextual, and situated learning, as well as ideas about creating a supportive and accepting environment. I will try to avoid repeating myself too much.

The Physical Environment

The physical environment generally refers to anything affecting the physical comfort and well-being of both learners and facilitator. I include in the physical environment the technologies used to aid in learning and facilitating, although they probably deserve an entire book of their own. The term 'ergonomics' refers to the study of factors modifying the efficiency of persons in their working environment; we can consider the learning environment as a working environment. The ergonomics of the environment can be affected by a number of factors, including:

- comfort of chairs and tables,
- sound quality,
- light and visual quality, and
- air quality.

Another aspect of the physical environment is the hardware or technologies used in learning and facilitating activities. These technologies range from the low tech of chalkboards to the high tech of computer networks and multimedia presentations.

Comfort of Chairs and Tables

We have all had the experience of learning while sitting in chairs that are too hard, too soft, too high, too low, too inconsistent with our body shape. Like

Goldilocks, we move around trying to find the chair that is 'just right.' Then there are tables that are too high, too low, too full of splinters, too sticky from someone else's drink spills. Facilitators have to contend with tables that are too heavy to move or too big for small group discussions, and chairs that are bolted to the floor. These conditions tend to create ineffective learning environments.

The arrangement of the tables and chairs also affects learning. The custodial staff in the building where I work like to have tables and chairs arranged in neat rows – I have always assumed for ease in cleaning. I have run afoul of these fine folk on many occasions when I have insisted on dragging tables and chairs into the abstract arrangements that enhance my facilitating style. All that dragging marks up the highly polished floors and disarranges things for the next class. Now there are signs posted cautioning us to leave the room arranged as we found it. While such problems do not directly affect learning, they play havoc with my usual facilitating style. I tell my students that a good facilitator is someone who is prepared to reorganize the room (and clean up any garbage) ahead of time and restore the room to its original condition (and clean up the garbage) at the end of a session. A good description of effective arrangements for tables and chairs can be found in Peter Renner's book *The Art of Teaching Adults* (1994).

Sound Quality

In Chapter 2 we discussed sound quality in a learning environment in relation to persons with hearing impairments. As someone who is gradually losing hearing acuity, I have become ultra-sensitive to the sound environment in teaching-learning environments. I teach many courses via audioconference and know that I am not the only person who is adversely affected by poor sound quality.

Some of the problems I have encountered in recent years include:

- meeting with a small group in a very large room with poor acoustics caused by hard surfaces, high ceilings, and a poor table configuration (long and narrow rather than round or oblong);
- poor-quality electrical and electronic devices that hum (fluorescent lights, air conditioners, computer data projectors); and
- individuals who speak with a soft voice or who let their voice drop as they speak.

In recent weeks I have had problems with audiovisual technicians who insist that my complaints about sound systems are unwarranted. If I am asked to work in a room with poor sound quality, I fight for improvements

or move to another room. I have learned that poor sound quality has a devastating effect on the social interactions that are essential to good learning.

With or without hearing difficulties, learners who cannot hear what is
being said will give up listening and start murmuring to others or withdraw
from the social interactions, and in some cases nod off. Learners who feel
they are not being heard will gradually lapse into silence or will regularly
seek permission to speak.

Dunn and Dunn (1978; Dunn & Griggs, 2000) define a preference for quiet
when learning as a learning style. Such learners are distracted by extraneous
sounds; some even hear sounds that others do not hear. Other learners can
block out sounds through becoming enmeshed in their own thoughts. A
third type of learner needs to hear sounds (from a radio, television, or CD
player) to block out other distracting environmental sounds.

Light and Visual Quality

In Chapter 2 we discussed light and visual problems for persons with visual
impairments. The quality of light in a learning environment is important.
Dunn and Dunn (1978; Dunn & Griggs, 2000) identify preferences for light
intensity as a learning style. They have found that learners who prefer a
dimly lighted learning environment also prefer activities that are typical of
the right hemisphere of the cerebral cortex. While individuals can modify
the light quality of their private learning environments, facilitators need to
pay some attention to the light quality for both small and large learning
groups.

I have worked in rooms in which some lights generated such a hum that it
was easier to work in semi-darkness; I have worked in rooms in which spot
lighting generated so much heat that everyone was soon sweltering; and I
have worked in rooms that could not be sufficiently darkened to show
slides. The bottom line is that facilitators must know about the light quality
in any room in which they are going to work. Check out the room in day-
light, at dusk, and at night; check the lights and whether the room can be
darkened for slide viewing; check whether a spectacular sunset or other outside activity will divert students' attention.

The rooms in which you do your facilitating and learning have other
visual qualities, including the texture and colour of the walls, window hangings, and floor coverings, and the visual 'art work' hung on the walls. I am
not markedly affected by colour or other visual qualities, but others are. So
check out the visual quality of any room in which you must work. If you
cannot change things, you may want to move to another room. One classroom in my building is bilious green. I feel oppressed in that room and I
refuse to teach in it.

Window hangings that are inappropriate or need repair are distracting and frustrating. Too much visual work on the walls can be distracting; too little is boring and depressing. Whatever is posted on the walls needs to be changed periodically. Other visual distractions are provided by learning and facilitating materials and resources left hanging or lying around a room by other facilitators oblivious to the effects of such distractions on others.

Air Quality

Learning can be adversely affected by poor temperature control and poor air quality. Air conditioning in warm months and heating plants in cold months often belch forth dust and various growing things that can cause asthma, allergies, and other respiratory ailments not conducive to good learning.

I work in a building with windows that can be opened and in an urban area with good air quality, so I can open windows to let out hot, stale air and let in fresh air. Open windows, however, bring mixed blessings. Until five years ago, none of our windows had screens. An open window in the evening became an invitation for wild life to fly in and create havoc. One enterprising bird started a new nest overnight. Flying wildlife does not affect learning in the same way as poor air quality but does tend to distract the learners.

Dunn and Dunn (1978; Dunn & Griggs, 2000) list preferences for higher or lower temperatures as a learning style. While no one lists air quality as being associated with any learning style, we can think of it as a health condition that can adversely affect all learning. Effective learning requires basic physical resources – good-quality air, a good heating-cooling system, good-quality sound, light and visual resources, and reasonably comfortable chairs and tables.

Technology in the Environment

In over thirty years of teaching adults, I have fought many battles over the quality of the technology made available for my facilitating activities. I have encountered chalkboards covered with a permanent film of chalk; white-boards on which someone has used permanent markers; overhead projectors with burned-out light bulbs; flip charts with only one sheet of paper or no markers; computer data projectors and audioconference equipment locked inside cupboards; computer equipment incompatible with prepared resources; audioconferenced sessions planned for rooms with no telephone outlet; and power outages in the middle of class sessions.

Facilitators must know how to use the available equipment, how to do easy repairs to equipment, how to make do when something doesn't work, how to contact technicians who can provide assistance, and how to get out of the building in the dark. If you don't know how, learn. In a recent course, the audioconference equipment at my site failed and we needed to contact other sites. I asked if anyone had a cell phone and was given one. That was when I discovered I didn't know how to use one! I learned quickly.

Technology that works as it is supposed to work becomes invisible; technology that doesn't work or that no one knows how to work becomes an insurmountable and highly visible barrier to both facilitating and learning. With the expanded use of computers, most of us need to take courses in effectively using associated technologies, and in solving difficulties when different technologies prove incompatible or are not working.

Another way to protect yourself from the vicissitudes of technologies is to make friends with the secretarial staff responsible for arranging for resources, the custodial staff responsible for ensuring appropriate room arrangements, and the technical staff responsible for keeping technologies in working order. That way, when you must call one after working hours, they will know who is calling and whom to chastise the next day.

My experiences and recent readings about using facilitating and learning technologies have yielded the following ideas:

- Any technology that appeals to only one learning style (sequential rather than random order) will be used by only half the learners. Any technology that enables users to exercise maximum control and freedom to use their own learning strategies is better than one that requires compliance and someone else's preferred learning strategies (Burge, 2000).
- Any technology that does not serve the goals of learning and the needs of learners is a waste of resources. For example, interactive videoconferencing is an expensive technology that is useful when it is essential to *see* what learners at other sites are physically doing or the materials and resources they are using. Otherwise videoconferencing is a distracting luxury.
- Multimedia presentations (images and sounds) should not divide learners' attention. Copying a complex (or even simple) diagram into notes is almost impossible while trying to listen to an explanation of the diagram. The two cognitive tasks conflict with each other, rendering both ineffective. Reduce divided attention by providing a skeleton version of the diagram that can be elaborated by the learner as the talk progresses (deWinstanley & Bjork, 2002). PowerPoint presentations can divide learners' attention unless a bare-bones outline is provided for note taking or the learners are instructed that notes will be provided after the presentation.
- Research has found that adding interesting stories to pad out an otherwise straightforward multimedia presentation is distracting to learners (Mayer, 2002).
- One of the unintended effects of asynchronous courses is the loss of the

sense of community associated with synchronous (face-to-face or voice-to-voice) courses. In Chapter 8 we discussed the fact that some learners require a sense of community if they are to be effective learners. On-line courses deliver information very effectively but fail to deliver features that are essential to some learning strategies (Heermann, Fox, & Boyd, 2000).

- On-line courses may be ineffective as a consequence of poor ergonomics, including poorly designed computer chairs and workplaces, often resulting in repetitive strain injury and eyestrain. Reading from a computer screen is less efficient than reading paper copies of the same material (Heermann, Fox, & Boyd, 2000).
- Some learners do better in on-line courses as compared to face-to-face courses; some do less well. Some learners express themselves well only in writing; some express themselves well only orally (Suessmuth, 1985).

I like the advice offered by Christina Olgren (2000): 'The role of technology is not to be a delivery system but rather to ... create a learning design that cues and supports the full repertoire of learning strategies' (p. 15). At this time, we are only beginning to understand how technologies can be used to design activities that support a full range of learning strategies.

The Cultural Environment

Invisible contexts surround us. These contexts derive from the cultural and social expectations that control and direct how people relate and work gets done in our various environments. Culture is a system of learned beliefs, values, assumptions, customs, language, meanings, and behaviours shared with groups of individuals, and a guide for organizing the lives of group members (Barer-Stein, 2001; Imel, 1998). Sheila Ramsey (1996) points out that

- large 'C' or objective culture refers to such organized activities as theatre, dance, music, literature, and art;
- small 'c' or subjective culture has to do with how we create meaning in our lives and how we behave according to those meanings.

Subjective culture provides a pervasive, habitual context in which we are embedded. We take our culture for granted until we become sojourners in another culture or we encounter, at home, persons from cultures differing from and conflicting with our own. As long as we live among people who share our culture, we remain largely unaware of its associated beliefs, values, customs, and behaviours. We become consciously aware of our culture only when we encounter persons who do not share it.

Culture is never neutral. It pervades the teaching-learning environment, brought there by both learners and facilitator. Our facilitating is always based on cultural values regardless of our awareness of their influence (Heimlich & Norland, 1994). In North America, adult education is based on a 'default' (unquestioned) assumption that favours individualism over collectivism, egalitarianism over hierarchy, action over 'being,' and change over tradition (Ziegahn, 2001).

Our culture is an integral part of our model of reality. We derived it from the various groups to which we belong – family, community, workplace, religion, race, age, gender, language, ethnicity, sexual orientation, profession or occupation, and so on. We integrate all these cultures into our model of reality, reconciling differences among them or behaving differently within each group. For example, I am not inclined to argue about the beliefs espoused within a religious community even if I disagree because to do so would be impolite, a belief derived from my family. However, within professional groups, I am quite prepared to challenge the beliefs of others and strongly defend my own.

Culture is an abstraction; like intelligence, it exists in the mind of the beholder. As culture becomes more thing-like in our mind, we may begin to perceive it as having an existence external to those who invented it. Once we have invested energy and time in creating and externalizing culture, we may feel compelled to defend it, export it, or become distraught when others assess it unfavourably.

And when looking at the culture of others, we may begin to stereotype those who come from that culture. It is important to understand the culture of others and to avoid developing stereotypes that can lead to ethnocentrism, racism, and so on. It is also important to be aware that our own culture may be invisible to us, but not to others.

Problems associated with invisible cultural contexts are many. Marilyn Noble (2000) describes the deeply ingrained and often invisible assumptions that accompany cultural beliefs as leading to four major problems.

First, unknown differences and uncertainty can increase our anxiety and stress when we encounter cultures that differ from our own. Edward Taylor (1994) describes learning to be interculturally competent as involving a five-phase process. In the first phase, the individual's past experiences and personal model of reality set the stage for encountering a new culture. In the second, the individual encounters 'cultural disequilibrium' or a period of dissonance between the learner's culture and the host culture. The emotional aspect of this disequilibrium is intensified by the learner's race and gender but muted by host language competency and previous experiences of being marginalized in another culture. The third phase involves cognitive (re)orientation through nonreflective activities (getting on with daily life) and critically reflective activities that examine the perspectives and underlying assumptions operating within one's existing model of reality. In the fourth phase, the learner uses behavioural learning strategies to begin to resolve the dissonance. These strategies include observing others, engaging in daily social activities, and sharing concerns with a friend from the host culture. In the fifth phase, the individual begins to develop an intercultural identity based on modified values and changed meaning perspectives. This learning model is not unlike the one developed by Marilyn Taylor (1987) to describe the learning cycle in an inquiry sequence (see Chapter 3).

The second assumption that accompanies beliefs is that we can sometimes use our personal model of reality to incorrectly interpret someone else's behaviour and inappropriately judge them or their behaviour (Noble, 2000). Amina Mama (2002), a West African educator, reports that in much of Africa there is no all-encompassing concept for 'identity' because there is 'no substantive apparatus for the production of the kind of singularity that the term seem[s] to require' (p. 8). In Euro-American cultures, the word 'identity' implies a singular entity, an individual who has clear ego boundaries and who is autonomous in behaviour. In African cultures, the individual would quickly follow any identity label with a qualifying communal term indicating ethnic or clan origins. Mama reports that she developed an awareness of her other-ness only when she was sent away to an English boarding school. There she was compelled to claim and assert an identity but was still treated as a 'black,' an orphan, and an immigrant and 'furthermore, ... was assumed to have an "identity problem"' (p. 8). She concludes that identity is, at best, an oversimplification of selfhood, a concept denying and negating the complexity and multiplicity of life found in most African communities; and that, for nonwhite persons, identity tends to be based on an awareness of difference within a white culture.

Third, when we do not understand cultural differences between ourselves and others, 'offence can be unwittingly given or taken' (Noble, 2000, p. 9). Gallos and Ramsey (1997, as cited in Imel, 1998) warn that in trying to increase cultural diversity in our facilitating activities, we may cause members of some socially defined groups to become 'othered [and] end up being seen as different in some way from the mainstream' (p. 45). In a learning situation, encouraging diversity and cultural pluralism by emphasizing differences can lead to stereotyping and the creation of other-ness. Encouraging a cultural 'melting pot' by emphasizing similarities can result in offending members of minority cultures or glossing over potential learning problems. Facilitators of adult learning need to be able to tread a fine and flexible line between these two extremes.

Fourth, differences between cultures are also accompanied by power imbalances (Noble, 2000). In any society, one culture tends to become more privileged than others, usually because of unexamined assumptions but also because of historical events and the exercise of power by one group over others. In North American society, privileged groups include the white race, English speakers, the male gender, and persons with money and education. We discussed some aspects of gender in Chapter 8. Any extended discussion of race, language, and class is well beyond the scope of this book.

Sue Shore (1997) describes the problem of whiteness as its 'absent presence ... as the invisible norm: always there yet never acknowledged' (p. 3). Peggy McIntosh (1989) describes whiteness as an invisible, weightless knapsack of unearned privilege. In her opinion whites are taught to think of their lives as morally neutral and average, but also as ideal, so that a white person's work to benefit others is perceived as helping 'them' become more like 'us,' thus eliminating any disadvantages and alleviating any privileges.

McIntosh lists twenty-six daily effects of white privilege in her life. Five of these effects are:

1 'When I am told about our national heritage or about "civilization," I am shown that people of my colour made it what it is.'
2 'I can do well in a challenging situation without being called a credit to my race.'
3 'I am never asked to speak for all people of my racial group.'
4 'I can take a job with an affirmative action employer without having co-workers on the job suspect that I got it because of race.'
5 'If my day, week, or year is going badly, I need not ask of each negative episode or situation whether it has racial overtones.'

McIntosh challenges us to redesign our social systems but points out that we need first to acknowledge their unseen dimensions. She indicates that men rarely admit to being overprivileged even though they may grant that women are disadvantaged, and that most men 'can't or won't support the idea of lessening men's [status]' (p. 1). The advantage of whiteness, like other advantaging systems, has both active forms that are visible and embedded forms that are invisible to members of the dominant group. She concludes, 'I was taught to see racism only in individual acts of meanness ... never in invisible systems conferring unsought racial dominance on my group from birth' (p. 2).

Becoming interculturally competent is a complex process. At its core, such competence calls for effective communication skills – listening actively, avoiding inappropriately projecting one's model of reality onto others, and letting others be different (Ramsey, 1996). Other skills are similar to learning to learn skills and transformative learning. Ramsey lists four:

1 accepting and working effectively with uncertainty and ambiguity,
2 accepting and working effectively with change,

3 thinking creatively by critically reflecting on the premises that underlie one's interpretation of new experiences, and
4 consciously managing one's emotional responses to new experiences.
   (p. 12)

To learn more about the effects of culture on learning, I recommend that you consult the excellent summaries prepared by Susan Imel (1998) and Linda Ziegahn (2001).

The Power Environment

The cultures that accompany each participant – learners and facilitator – into a learning group permeate the interpersonal environment. Each person brings their invisible knapsack containing not only their culture with all its beliefs, values, assumptions, customs, meanings, and behaviours, but also their day-to-day responsibilities and current life problems. They place that knapsack in front of them and may hide behind it or use it as a platform from which to interact with others. The resulting interactions among individuals create a learning context in which power, its sources and uses, become crucial elements.

We can look at power relationships from an individual perspective or from a social structuralist perspective. The individual perspective is a dominant theme in women's literature. Belenky and her colleagues (1986; Goldberger et al., 1996) use the concept of 'voice' to denote empowerment, knowledge, and personal development. In their model, women's development is associated with their increasing skill in expressing their knowledge in their own voice. The power of their voice increases as they move from the knowledge they receive from others to the knowledge they create based on their own experience, and then to the knowledge they construct by integrating knowledge from various sources. A similar knowledge development process has been identified by Baxter Magolda (1992) as occurring among both male and female learners. Both women and men feel more empowered as their skills and knowledge increase.

The individual perspective focuses on similarities among learners from diverse groups and encourages development in accordance with idealized models. This perspective also encourages the facilitator to provide an environment in which learners can find their voice in a supportive and safe atmosphere (Tisdell, 2000).

The social structuralist perspective argues that individual behaviour is 'influenced by the structural systems of power, privilege and oppression that inform our lives' (Tisdell, 2000, p. 166). The term 'positionality' is used to describe an individual's location within a shifting network of relationships defined primarily in terms of race, gender, and class (Maher &

Tetreault, 2001). An individual's positionality is a composite of his or her positions relative to others on the basis of each socially structured group.

Men and women relate to each other on the basis of the social structure of gender. If we add race to the relationships, we find we have four 'positions': white women, black women, white men, and black men. The relationships among these four groups is more complex than the relationships between men and women. And if we add class to the mix, the complexity increases again. Writers in the field of social structuralism contradict each other on whether race is more important than gender or whether class is more important than either race or gender.

The five items I selected from McIntosh's (1989) list of twenty-six privileges are all clearly racially based, but several items on her list are less clear:

- 'If I should need to move, I can be pretty sure of renting or purchasing housing in an area which I can afford and in which I would want to live': this could be racially or class based.
- 'I can go shopping alone most of the time, pretty well assured that I will not be followed or harassed': this could be racially, gender, or class based.

Structuralists perceive positionality as relational and as constantly shifting. Each member of a learning group brings their own positionality into the group. Those who occupy privileged positions may have no awareness of how their position affects or oppresses others. The entire matter of positionality calls on each member of a learning group to think critically about how their behaviour is affected by both visible and invisible privileges and oppression.

Caffarella and Merriam (2000) raise questions about who holds power in learning groups and how that power should and could be shared. They urge us to be critically aware of how our own positionality affects our behaviour as facilitators. They believe that both the individual and structural perspective should be integrated to create an inclusive and supportive learning environment.

In contrast, the black feminist educator bell hooks believes that the structural approach should encourage facilitators to challenge learners, especially those from oppressed or exploited groups (as cited in Tisdell, 2000). Such challenges should encourage learners to voice their ideas and opinions even in environments that may not be entirely safe, where 'they may feel afraid or see themselves as risk' (p. 167). Structuralists believe that facilitators should be prepared to analyse and confront power-related incidents in a learning group by calling attention to such dynamics when they arise. One problem for the facilitator is to recognize incidents that exemplify power relationships and positionality. The easiest approach to the problem is to use one's own positionality as the basis for any analysis and to encourage other members of the learning group to do the same. Analysing the behaviour of another person in terms of their apparent positionality is likely to result in blaming and bad feelings.

In teaching a recent course on women and education, I was concerned because three of the six audioconference sites had only women in the group, one site had one man and six women, one had two men and seven women, and one had three men and one woman. I was concerned initially that the men might dominate the course (six men to twenty-four women); they didn't. Then I became concerned that the strength of the women might overwhelm the men, who were mostly younger and less experienced. My concerns in this regard were unjustified. I should have been concerned about the solitary woman who met weekly with three men. She felt somewhat disempowered but did not share this fact with me until the course was over. Information about the learning environment at distant sites is one of the bits of information that I miss when teaching by audioconference. I must rely completely on the learners to tell me about the problems that arise in both the visible and invisible environments at their site.

The Knowledge Environment

An epistemology is a system of knowledge; the processes used to create and validate the knowledge generated are as much a part of the system as its content or knowledge. Some people believe a single epistemology exists that includes all truthful and verifiable knowledge. Such an epistemology might be espoused by a religion, a scientific community, or an indigenous community with no outside contacts. However, yesteryear's extensive exploration and colonization and today's profusion of communication technologies have convinced most of us that there are as many epistemologies as there are cultures, perhaps even one for every human. Your personal model of reality is as much an epistemology as mine.

Even if we never agree on a single all-encompassing epistemology, we should be able to agree on some of the characteristics of existing epistemologies.

- Each knowledge system is developed in response to observed occurrences of phenomena occurring within our natural world, including human interactions; and each is designed to describe these phenomena, explain how and why they occur, predict their consequences, and thereby provide the knower with strategies for responding to future phenomena.
- Each knowledge system is a *local knowledge system* (Harding, 1996) – local in the sense that we can figure out what group or groups were responsible for developing the system in the historical past and are responsible for maintaining and revising it in the present.

- Some knowledge systems are more powerful than others. Powerful systems can explain more, provide better predictions, and offer knowers more strategies for responding to future phenomena. Some are powerful enough to co-opt the knowledge found in less powerful systems, giving back little except oppression (Harding, 1996). When French and English explorers and settlers reached North America, their knowledge systems siphoned what was considered useful from the knowledge systems of the Native tribes and ignored what was considered useless. White settlers learned to hunt animals and cultivate local plants without also learning the cultural and ethical principles guiding the judicious use of such knowledge. The settlers viewed Native knowledge about herbal remedies as a kind of witchcraft and therefore suspect. We are only now learning the value of Native knowledge.
- All knowledge systems have been developed on the basis of local resources, natural phenomena, and human interactions. By extension, they are silent on phenomena not observed and resources not available. Knowledge systems developed by sea-faring groups differ from those developed by grassland dwellers. Knowledge systems developed by teachers and educators differ from those developed by psychologists and sociologists, even though such systems may share many commonalities.
- All knowledge systems have limitations, 'patterns of ignorance' (Harding, 1996, p. 444) based on overlooking some phenomena, deleting and distorting others, and making inappropriate and incorrect assumptions about such things as the type of persons best able to create, maintain, and revise knowledge and the type of knowledge most acceptable. Patterns of ignorance are more apparent to those standing outside or on the margins of the knowledge system that those standing inside it.
- All knowledge systems are political in nature in that they dictate both that which can be seen and commented on and that which is 'not supposed to exist' (Harding, 1996, p. 446). Gaining knowledge that is not supposed to exist requires a political struggle.

In North American society, the most powerful epistemology is derived from the Eurocentrism of Northern (European) sciences, philosophies, and histories. It was developed by upper and middle-class (well-to-do, educated), white male scientists, historians, philosophers, explorers, cartographers, settlers, doctors, law makers, and the like. Today, in every field of human knowledge, this dominant epistemology is being challenged by knowledge systems developed by marginalized groups without the power to change the system from the inside.

For example, by really listening to women's experiences of their own bodies and not devaluing their subjective knowledge, the women's health movement has been able to identify 'patterns of systematic ignorance in the dominant biomedical knowledge system' (Harding, 1996, p. 447). Similarly, the writings of Carol Gilligan, Jean Baker Miller, and Mary Field Belenky and her colleagues have identified blind spots in the developmental psychology knowledge system.

These female writers constitute a second wave of feminists. The first wave challenged the exclusion of women from the political arena and won. The second wave has challenged the dominant knowledge system by pointing out its limitations, particularly with regard to the life experiences of women. Now a third wave of minority group feminists is challenging the knowledge generated by the second wave by pointing out the limitations of the ideas we considered in Chapter 8. These minority groups include blacks, Native women, lesbians, Marxist feminists, women with disabilities, women living in poverty, and so on (Flannery, 1994; Poonwassie, 2001; Stone, 1992). African and Asian women offer challenges from the standpoint of women living in less developed and developing countries; African-Americans and other hyphenated groups offer challenges based on their experiences living within North America. Similar challenges to the dominant knowledge system come from racial minority groups.

Over the past fifty years, well-educated, white, male adult educators have developed an adult education epistemology that encompasses such concepts as andragogy (Knowles, 1970), self-directed learning (Tough, 1979), experiential learning (Kolb, 1984), and transformative learning (Mezirow, 1978). In the past ten years, both male and female adult educators have challenged the privileged position of these concepts by introducing such concerns as:

- the role of emotions in learning,
- the importance of relationships and interdependence in learning,
- the place of spirit and soul in learning, and
- community-based, organizational, and group learning

Today the challenge is to move these concerns from the margins of our knowledge system to the more central positions and to modify our existing epistemology accordingly. At the same time, new challenges will arise before any integration is complete.

When individuals participate in learning groups, they each bring their favoured epistemology with them. Conflicts may emerge between individual learners who espouse differing epistemologies.

- An adult learner expresses the opinion that adults today should all be able to read given the number of opportunities to learn to read that exist in most communities – a belief unacceptable to participants who labour diligently in literacy programs.

- Another adult learner comments that many older adults live in poverty – a 'fact' disputed by unemployed adults living in an economically depressed region where older adults are perceived as the only community members with a guaranteed income.
- A female learner shares a tentative idea, based on her experience, about why women living in abusive relationships drop out of upgrading classes – a speculation promptly dismissed by a male learner as 'rubbish.'

Only by listening carefully to the ideas brought forward from the margins will we come to understand the full range of natural phenomena and human interactions that might contribute to an adult education epistemology.

The 'Real-Life' Environment

The term 'situated cognition' describes an emerging body of ideas covering both the nature of learning and the design of learning experiences (McLellan, 1996). The ideas that inform 'situated cognition' are based on the notion that all knowledge is contextually situated and is fundamentally influenced by the activity, context, and culture in which it is developed and used (Brown, Collins, & Duguid, 1989). By extension, situated learning is always social or relational because it occurs with other people; is tool dependent because the context provides tools (computers, maps, texts, measuring instruments, and the like) that aid and structure the cognitive processes; and is always active in nature because the doing and the knowing are never separated in the learning experience (Wilson, 1993). What one learns in one context may not be easily transferrable to other contexts.

Some examples of situated learning might help:

- Prenatal classes are not necessarily helpful in preparing for childbirth because the learning program cannot duplicate, or even simulate, the experience of birth.
- On the other hand, classes for new parents are useful because the participants are up to their ears in the experience of caring for newborns.
- Learning a new language in a classroom may help with standard phrases and grammatical structures, but language fluency comes only with immersion experiences.
- Individuals who have developed 'math phobia' in school may have no problem calculating money transactions in everyday situations.

Schools and higher education institutions are also 'contexts,' and the knowledge developed, used, and learned within them is contextually situated. What one learns within an educational institution may not be transferrable to other contexts, although that is usually one of the goals of formal education (Lave & Wenger, 1991).

In adult education terms, situated learning theory would argue that the knowledge and skills related to adult roles and responsibilities can be learned most effectively within the actual contexts where they are used. While he does not use the term, Malcolm Knowles (1970) is referring to situated learning when he states that adults are motivated to learn in response to the tasks of their social roles, are concerned about the immediate application of knowledge, and prefer to participate in problem-centred learning activities.

Brown, Collins, and Duguid (1989) argue that situated knowledge is characteristic of practitioner knowledge. They point out that educational programs emphasize reasoning with theoretical models to reach unambiguous solutions to well-structured problems; but practitioners reason using situated knowledge emerging from their practice in response to ill-structured problems and ambiguous solutions (Schön, 1987). For example, an ill-structured problem might involve trying to figure out how, as facilitators, we can be responsive to the various learning styles of individual learners given that our own learning style can make us blind to our own limitations or to how we are affecting others. One mentor told me to stop trying to please everyone in the learning group and just 'get on with it' – a somewhat ambiguous solution but one based on a practitioner's knowledge.

Novice practitioners (newcomers) must gain access to the ways that skilled practitioners (oldtimers) impose coherence on ill-structured problems. Access to oldtimers' situated knowledge is available to newcomers through role modelling, coaching, and mentoring and through learning within a community of practitioners, rather than within an educational institution (Jacobson, 1996). As the newcomers act within a community of practitioners, they also learn the culture – the beliefs, values, assumptions, customs, meanings, and behaviours – that typifies that community. This culture, as we have seen, has both visible and invisible components. While newcomers might be able to learn the visible aspects of the culture through studying at a formal educational institution, they are unlikely to learn the invisible aspects unless they are learning at least at the margins of the relevant community of practice (Stein, 1998).

Situated cognition calls for learning experiences designed using the following features (McLellan, 1996, pp. 7–12):

- telling stories as a type of 'expert system' for storing, linking, and readily accessing information whenever a new situation calls for it;
- reflecting during learning activities (reflection-in-action) and following the activity (reflection-on-action) (Schön, 1987). Reflection-in-action calls for an awareness of the present moment and mindful learning (Caffarella & Merriam, 2000);

- using cognitive apprenticeship strategies (see Chapter 7) to introduce learners to authentic practices through learning activities and social inter-actions similar to those evident in craft apprenticeship (Brandt, Farmer, & Buckmaster, 1993);
- promoting collaborative activities among peers, including collective prob-lem solving and confronting ineffective problem-solving strategies and misconceptions;
- providing coaches and mentors who observe learners as they carry out tasks, act as a guide rather than an expert or the boss, provide scaffolding early in the learning process and dismantle it as learning progresses, and provide opportunities for new initiatives and self-directed problem solving;
- providing many different opportunities to engage in practice;
- articulating the skills to be learned by differentiating and describing the various components of complex skills and by having learners describe their thinking processes as they perform the skills to aid them to better understand their own problem-solving strategies;
- using technologies to stimulate learning through making available the tools used in the context, providing a highly realistic or virtual simulation of the context when the context itself is unavailable or too costly, or pro-viding a 'real-world' anchoring context such as a video, multimedia pro-gram, or field trip.

Situated learning brings to mind Kolb's cycle of learning from experi-ence (see Chapter 3). In Kolb's model, learning begins with experience and ends with new experience but remains essentially an internal process. The model makes no reference to the need for social interaction as part of the reflective process, nor does it address the issue of context. In the situated learning model, the learner learns *during* experience rather than merely *from* experience (Jacobson, 1996). In Figure 3.3, Kolb's Model Modified – Version 1, I emphasized reflective learning because reflective observation is part of my preferred learning style. My doodling of Kolb's model in rela-tion to situated learning has produced Figure 10.1, Kolb's Model Modified – Version 3. In this figure, I have kept the orientation of the four phases of learning the same as in the Kolb model, although I expect that those who espouse situated learning would place the action phase at the top of the figure. Figure 10.1 is quite similar to the model of action research described by Quigley and Kuhne (1997). Also note that the situated learning model incorporates two reflective activities: one during the active phase and one during the reflective phase.

Concepts related to situated learning show considerable potential for use in adult education. However, there are some problems that remain to be solved.

Figure 10.1
Kolb's Model Modified: Version 3 – Situated Learning

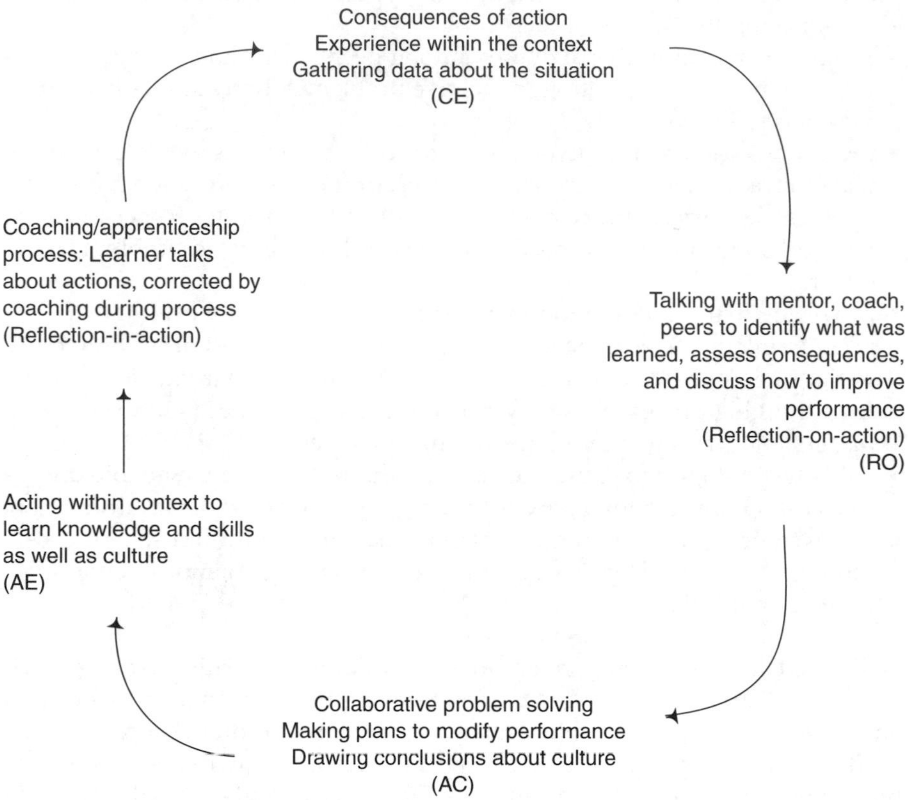

Consequences of action
Experience within the context
Gathering data about the situation
(CE)

Coaching/apprenticeship
process: Learner talks
about actions, corrected by
coaching during process
(Reflection-in-action)

Talking with mentor, coach,
peers to identify what was
learned, assess consequences,
and discuss how to improve
performance
(Reflection-on-action)
(RO)

Acting within context to
learn knowledge and skills
as well as culture
(AE)

Collaborative problem solving
Making plans to modify performance
Drawing conclusions about culture
(AC)

- Not all contexts are suitable for learning activities. Some, like training pilots to fly airplanes, are too expensive and too dangerous. Others, like training surgeons, require too much time and are also dangerous. The development of simulators to do these types of training is costly but well worth the investment, since a simulator can be used over and over.
- Not all contexts are willing to accept novice learners into their community of practice. Working with novices is time and energy consuming. Persons who act as mentors or coaches may receive no dispensation from their regular duties or compensation for their extra responsibilities. Those who take on the responsibility of working with novice learners may find that the work overload and potential role conflict soon result in their reduced effectiveness because of burnout.

- Not all coaches or mentors are equally competent to act as both model and guide for novice learning (Hansman, 1997). Some oldtimers become hostile when asked to assist a newcomer within their community of practice. Issues related to sexism and racism can occur in the interactions between poorly prepared oldtimers and the newcomers they are assisting.
- Learning through reflection-in-action requires that learners and facilitators have additional learning to learn skills and far more time than is needed for learning through reflection-on-action. Awareness of the present moment must be part of the skill repertoire, as well as skills in critical and reflective thinking.
- Situated learning can go by faster than the mind can grasp the details. We need to develop ways to slow the process down. Cognitive apprenticeship is one means for doing this.

In general, we are better at facilitating reflection-on-action and learning from experience than we are at facilitating reflection-in-action and learning during experience. This fact probably explains why the concepts of situated learning have not become as popular in the field of adult education as the potential effectiveness of the process would suggest.

11 Strategies and Styles in Facilitating

This chapter is only indirectly about learning. In Chapter 1, I described the learning-centred approach used in this book as one in which the learning process is assumed to be of paramount importance, while facilitating is regarded as a responsive activity adapting to the learner's activities and the natural learning process. In this chapter, I will describe facilitating models in terms of how each follows a set of assumptions about learning.

I will look at two different ways to understand facilitating and see how each corresponds to learning. First, I will examine three basic strategies or styles for facilitating – directing, enabling, and collaborating. These strategies are derived from the literature about working with adult learners. Second, I will briefly discuss four theoretical models of facilitating – behavioural, information processing, humanistic, and dialectical.

Basic Strategies for Facilitating

As facilitators, we can improve our facilitating strategies and styles by becoming more aware of our beliefs, intentions, and actions (Pratt, 1999). Only when we understand both sides of the learning-facilitating interactions in which we participate can we determine ways for improving and applying sound facilitating beliefs, implicit theories, intentions, and actions concerning learning.

Three basic strategies – directing, enabling, and collaborating – typify many approaches to facilitating. Each must be considered both as part of a continuum of facilitating behaviours and as unique by itself; each strategy has advantages and disadvantages. Good facilitators are able to use all three strategies in varying combinations depending on the material, the learners, and the setting of the learning activities.

There is considerable debate among adult educators as to which strategy of teaching is best suited to the needs of adult learners. In keeping with

Lewin's B-P-E formulation, each strategy is functional for some adult learners, in some learning contexts, and for some content; and no single strategy will serve all purposes (Cross, 1976; Hunt & Sullivan, 1974; Joyce & Weil, 1992; Knowles, 1990; Pratt, 1999; Smith, 1990; Thomas, 1991).

Directing

When using the directing strategy, facilitators:

- define and structure content;
- plan and direct the activities constituting the learning process;
- provide feedback and reinforcement to learners; and
- provide support, encouragement, and guidance as necessary.

The responsibility for these functions rests with the facilitator, but can be negotiated and shared with learners. The time required to complete the learning tasks will increase as the amount of negotiating and sharing increases.

The directing strategy:

- helps learners acquire specific skills and knowledge relevant and essential to specific tasks and performance, such as driving a car, speaking a foreign language, or becoming a certified plumber;
- works best with material that – by social convention, professional supervision, or law – is prescribed for certain roles and/or certification;
- works best with material that can be segmented into manageable parts and then organized into sequences or hierarchies to form complex units of knowledge and skill;
- is the best method when the learner is constrained to learn specific material within a short period of time;
- requires that someone – an 'expert,' the facilitator, and/or the learner – set the objectives, define the material, divide the material into segments, organize it into sequences and hierarchies, and provide it to the learner in a ready-to-use form;
- requires facilitators to provide immediate feedback and periodic reinforcement. The type and focus of feedback can be negotiated between facilitator and learner but is generally built into the program. Rewards or reinforcement can also be built into programmed material, but most adults also require additional support and encouragement from the facilitator or other learners;
- can be implemented in situations varying from a 'facilitator-less' programmed learning module to a group-based training program, or combined with other facilitating strategies such as micro-teaching programs.

Programmed modules provide direction through the design of the material and can be self-paced;

- must involve the learner, either explicitly or implicitly, in two critical aspects of the learning process. First, the learner must be willing to make a commitment to the objectives of the program and to the planned learning processes. Second, the learner must be willing and able to learn from the feedback and reinforcement provided;
- is relatively nonthreatening to facilitators provided they are expert in both the content and processes involved in the learning activities;
- may provide little opportunity for interpersonal involvement among individual learners or between the facilitator and learners;
- allows learners to acquire material in a relatively short period of time without having to discover it for themselves;
- provides a potential threat to learners at two points: (1) if the objectives and processes do not meet the learner's real needs and he or she cannot exit from the program; and (2) if the feedback is somehow threatening to the learner's self-system; and
- is most relevant for mastery learning and achievement needs and for enhancing self-esteem.

Enabling

When using the enabling strategy, facilitators:

- act as a catalyst in the learning process,
- provide content and process resources,
- serve as a reflective mirror or alter ego,
- act as a co-inquirer with the learners, and
- provide support, guidance, and encouragement to the learners.

The responsibility for these functions can rest with the facilitator or can be shared among facilitator and learners. The structure, objectives, and direction of the learning activities are negotiated; the content, in the form of personal meanings, comes from the learner.

The enabling strategy:

- proceeds through dialogue involving statement making, clarifying, probing, developing analogies and metaphors, and reflecting, among other activities. The dialogue is complete only when learners are satisfied with their personal understanding of meanings. Reinforcement is a normal part of the dialogue between two persons; and feedback is provided through reflecting, summarizing, and paraphrasing rather than through judging or evaluating;
- helps learners (1) discover personal meanings within knowledge and

skills already learned; (2) discover new meanings within experience; and (3) create new meanings, values and strategies from integrating new and old learning, for example, through self-discovery, consciousness raising, and transformative learning;

- works best with material that does not need to be learned as a logical sequence of parts in order to understand the whole, and allows the learner to develop personal perceptions about the parts and about their relationships to the whole as well as to each other;
- works best when the learner has few time constraints on the learning process;
- requires that someone – the facilitator, learner, or external resource – provide structured experiences to be shared by learners and used to generate knowledge or provide opportunities to share personal experiences from other contexts; and requires a communication process through which experiences can be shared, and/or a resource, such as a film, book, art object, photograph, artifact, and the like, through which the experiences of others can be described for the learners;
- can be implemented through activities varying from group experiential processes, to demonstrations and use of media, to one-on-one counselling;
- is relatively nonthreatening for facilitators provided they don't interfere with the content to be learned (the learner's meanings) and they become involved through their process skills, as manager of the learning process or as co-inquirer;
- can potentially be threatening for learners since their personal meanings and self-systems are open to discussion and possible disconfirmation. For this reason, enabling activities require time to build a trusting relationships among facilitator and learners; and
- is most relevant to belongingness and affiliation needs, to mastery learning requiring a sense of personal commitment to a set of values such as those found in professional development, and to improvement of the self-system.

Collaborating

The collaborating strategy calls for learners and facilitators to share as co-learners in the discovery and creation of shared meanings and values.

The collaborating strategy:

- requires that facilitators participate as co-learners with the same responsibilities and rights as other co-learners and with full membership in the group;
- works best with material in which all co-learners have a stake;
- works best in contexts that enable co-learners to grow individually and as

members of a team, for example, through community problem-solving groups or work-related project teams;
- works best with material defined by the co-learners, and through processes, structures, and directions negotiated by them and resulting in a group consensus;
- is the best method for building 'a community of learners,' but requires considerable expenditure of time and energy;
- requires co-learners to divide or share tasks on some mutually acceptable basis and contribute to leadership functions in both tasks and interpersonal relationships. Co-learners are expected to act interdependently;
- is relatively threatening and high-risk to both facilitator and learners because all are vulnerable within the process;
- requires a high level of trust; and
- is most relevant to belongingness and affiliation needs.

The collaborating strategy could be used for almost any learning need, but this would require that co-learners be willing to temporarily shift to another facilitating strategy to learn in relation to specific needs. For example, if a work team needs to develop computer skills, they may need to shift to the directing strategy to meet this particular goal.

Theoretical Models of Facilitating

The literature on adult education yields a number of models for designing the overall processes through which learners can be assisted to learn. Joyce and Weil (1992) define a model of facilitating as a set of assumptions about how learning and teaching occur that is used to design teaching-learning interactions and select resources for use in formal, informal, or individual settings. Each model is based on theoretical assumptions about the nature of learning and facilitating, and about the nature and characteristics of adult learners. In this chapter, we will discuss four basic models of facilitating: behavioural, information-processing, humanistic, and dialectical models. These correspond roughly to the four philosophical orientations – vocational, liberal, humanist and liberatory – outlined in Chapter 1.

These four models are by no means inclusive of all possibilities:

- each encompasses a wide range of possible designs;
- each tends to overlap with other models;
- each serves one part of the learning process very effectively and other parts less effectively;
- each can be used in combination with other models; and
- each can be adapted for group or individual learning.

If you wish to know more about models of facilitating, I recommend that you read *Models of Teaching* by Bruce Joyce and Marsha Weil (1992) or *Five Perspectives on Teaching in Adult Education* by Dan Pratt (1999).

Behavioural Models

Behavioural models (sometimes called *operant conditioning*) assume that what learners think and how they manipulate information are less important than how successful they are in achieving behavioural objectives, coping with the environment, or changing their behaviour (Boshier, 1975; Hoyer, 1974; Joyce & Weil, 1992; Skinner, 1971). Behavioural models assume that learning can be controlled from outside the learner by applying the correct stimulus for the desired response and by appropriately reinforcing that response to encourage its continued use.

Facilitating strategies are concerned with developing a contingency plan based on benchmark data about the nature and occurrence of the behaviour to be changed. The steps in developing a contingency plan are:

- identifying the behaviour to be changed, the contexts and conditions most often eliciting this behaviour, and the reinforcement most likely to be successful;
- establishing objectives stating the desired responses;
- designing learning activities through which learners will have opportunities to use this behaviour;
- identifying the conditions governing reinforcement; and
- monitoring and reinforcing behaviour on the basis of the plan.

The process involved is diagrammed in Figure 11.1, Behavioural Learning Model. The facilitator must have special knowledge about the stimuli likely to elicit the desired response and the reinforcers most appropriate for encouraging further use of the response. The learner is perceived as a more or less passive respondent; and not much concern is wasted on what, if anything, might be going on inside the learner.

The reinforcement or feedback can include:

- describing the learner's performance or its results without assessing or judging it as good or bad, right or wrong ('here's what you did');
- describing the learner's progress towards established objectives or criteria ('here's where you succeeded – or didn't succeed');
- advising the learner about ways to modify, improve, or augment the next response without actually commenting on the previous response ('next time do this');
- rewarding the learner by providing something extra the learner likes or wants (positive reinforcement) or removing an undesired condition (nega-

Figure 11.1
Behavioural Learning Model

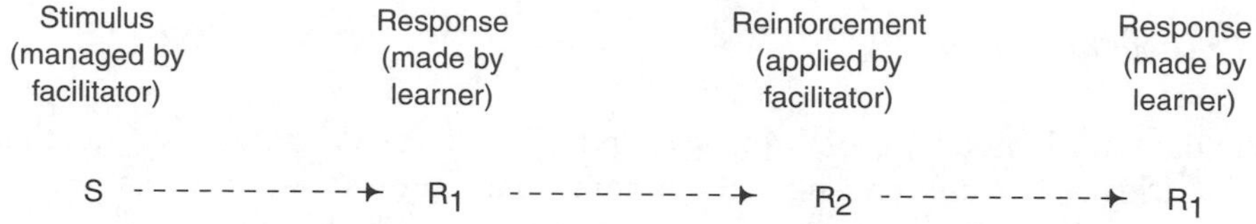

Stimulus (managed by facilitator)	Response (made by learner)	Reinforcement (applied by facilitator)	Response (made by learner)

$$S \; \text{---------} \to \; R_1 \; \text{----------} \to \; R_2 \; \text{----------} \to \; R_1$$

tive reinforcement); and/or punishing the learner by providing something extra the learner does not like (aversive reinforcement).

Positive reinforcement makes the response occur more often. A positive reinforcement could be smiling, giving the learner a 'pat' on the back, or administering a 'reward' such as grades or money. Negative reinforcement makes the undesired response occur less frequently. For example, a blood pressure cuff attached to the finger can be rigged to emit an aggravating sound when the individual's blood pressure rises above an unacceptable level. The individual must learn how to reduce blood pressure in order to make the sound stop. Aversive reinforcement has the same outcome as negative reinforcement but is less pleasant. Examples include docking pay for poor performance or deducting marks from an test score for poor spelling. Positive and negative reinforcements are usually more productive than aversive reinforcements.

The reinforcement or continency plan includes such details as:

• who will apply the reinforcer,
• what the reinforcer will consist of, and
• whether it will be administered according to a schedule (every time, every other time) or on a random basis.

When one is working with adult learners, an appropriate approach is to have the learner co-operate in developing the contingency plan, particularly in collecting the initial benchmark data and identifying the desired goal and reinforcement schedule; and to have the learner take over the reinforcement process as soon as possible. The adult learner must value both feedback and reinforcements, or neither will be effective. In many instances, the act of receiving reinforcement tends be more rewarding than the actual value of the reinforcement itself (Boshier, 1975).

I find that behavioural approaches, while they look rather impersonal, help me understand the most appropriate way to design learning resources (the stimuli), the importance of feedback, and the nature of reinforcement. Behavioural approaches are most appropriate when the learner is trying to learn physical or cognitive skills or modify inappropriate existing behaviour. The facilitator's role in these models is best understood as that of 'coach.'

Adult educators have a tendency to discount the value of the behavioural approach because the learner indirectly may learn to be other-directed rather than self-directed. However, the behavioural model does provide important insights into the intrinsic and reinforcing value of feedback, particularly when it relates to the learners' anticipated learning outcomes.

If any reader believes that behaviourist models have nothing to say to them, I would point out that behaviourist concepts underlie:

- the field of *instructional technology* encompassing the development of sound educational resources such as instructional manuals, self-instructed learning modules, videotapes, and so on (Albright & Graf, 1992; O'Rourke, 2000);
- the development of *programmed learning modules and computer-based training programs* to assist learners to acquire and master skilled behaviour, such as word-processing tutorials, computer-based simulations that teach pilots how to fly new types of airplanes, computer programs that help learners change nutritional knowledge and eating behaviours, and so on (Burge, 2000, Heermann, 1984; Heermann, Fox, & Boyd, 2000; Kerka, 2000);
- *programs designed to modify behaviour,* such as assertiveness training and anger management (Joyce & Weil, 1992); and
- *biofeedback programs* designed to help the learner change behaviours, such as those that cause high blood pressure, that are inaccessible to normal learning activities (Brown, 1980).

Information-Processing Models

Information-processing models (also called *cognitivist* or *mentalist* models) are related to:

- cognitive or intellectual development;
- cognitive activities for processing, storing, and using information; and/or
- the knowledge framework associated with a specific discipline or area of study (Brandt, Farmer, & Buckmaster, 1993; DiVesta, 1974; Flannery, 1993; Huber, 1993; Norman, 1973; Yanoff, 1976).

When facilitators use information-processing models based on a *learner's cognitive or intellectual development*, such as increasing cognitive complexity

(Hunt, 1987; Hunt & Sullivan, 1974), they may assume adults are capable of using certain cognitive skills and thinking strategies solely because of their age or experience. This assumption ignores the fact that some adults have never acquired these skills and strategies, and others have acquired them but do not use them. Cognitive development was discussed in some detail in Chapter 5.

When facilitators used information-processing models based on *cognitive activities for processing, storing, and using information*, they may rely on their own cognitive style to develop either analytical or holistic learning activities. One set of activities is likely to benefit only half of the adults in any typical learning group. Cognitive styles were discussed in Chapter 4. Cognitive processes were described in Chapter 5 as including:

- perceptual skills and strategies for sensing, attending, and recognizing patterns in information;
- memory skills and strategies for representing, storing, and retrieving information; and
- thinking skills and strategies for classifying, making sense of, understanding, analysing, synthesizing, and assessing information.

Information-processing models assume that if we understand how learners process information, we will also know how to present information as a stimulus for learning and how to sequence learning activities to support specific cognitive activities. Information-processing models are usually highly structured in terms of learning activities but vary widely in how the content to be learned is structured. Facilitators need:

- mastery of the content to be learned and of the best means for structuring learning activities;
- knowledge about individual differences in cognitive styles; and
- skills for facilitating the relevant learning strategies.

The content can be provided either by expert resources (books, the facilitator, films, etc.) or by the learner as a result of analysing personal problems and experiences.

When facilitators use information-processing models based on the *knowledge framework of a specific discipline or area of study*, they use, as guiding structures, both the concepts and the skills to be learned within the discipline. For example, in studying history, learners are encouraged to use the historical method of inquiry. In adult education, guiding structures might include learning theory, program planning and problem-solving models, small group development, or communicative processes, since these are basic conceptual structures in the field.

If a problem-solving model is to be learned, the learner usually solves one or two problems while 'walking through' the related problem-solving strategy. Then, through reflection, learners think about what happened and develop an understanding of what problem solving involves and how to transfer the strategy to other contexts. This understanding might include a conceptual framework, skills and strategies for further problem solving, a set of values about the process, and some methods for helping other learners solve problems (Joyce & Weil, 1992; Stouch, 1993).

Discipline-specific models are typical in professional development programs such as teacher education or medical training. Adults who are learning how to help other adults learn need to experience the relevant activities in the same way as the adult learners with whom they will eventually work. Much professional development of adult educators consists of doing an activity that involves the method being learned and then reflecting on that activity. In the vernacular of the field, this reflecting is referred to as 'debriefing' or 'processing the experience.'

I have found that information-processing models help me appreciate the complexity of cognitive processes and avoid taking for granted that all adult learners can use all cognitive processes. Facilitators who rely on these models, however, may look at adult learners from only a cognitive point of view, ignore emotionality and stress, disavow the importance of the social, spiritual, and physical aspects of learning, and not understand the holistic and integrated nature of learning.

Information processing models include, among others, such techniques as:

- *inquiry training* involving the process of investigating and explaining unusual phenomena through asking questions, gathering relevant information, and analysing the information logically (Joyce & Weil, 1992);
- *mind mapping* or *concept mapping*, a visual depiction of a network of ideas. A mind map uses divergent thinking, and usually has a central image, idea, or concept from which main themes radiate outward as major branches. Each major branch comprises a key image or word from which smaller branches radiate representing associated ideas or images (Buzan & Buzan, 1995; Deshler, 1990) (refer to Figure 5.4, Dorothy's Mind Map for Brain and Mind);
- *concept attainment* (or deductive thinking) involving the search for and listing of attributes that can distinguish examples of various conceptual categories from nonexamples; and
- *concept formation* (or inductive thinking) involving creating new categories through organizing uncategorized information or reanalysing already categorized information (Joyce & Weil, 1992).
- *advance organizers* providing 'intellectual scaffolding' that structures ideas

and facts related to a central concept and guides the manner in which the learner will think about this concept (Joyce & Weil, 1992). Outline notes for a single class session are one example of an advance organizer;
- *mnemonic devices* used as an aid to memory through the use of association techniques. Association techniques might link ideas to be remembered to visual images ('one is a bun, two is a shoe') or rhymes ('*i* before *e* except after *c*') (Norman, 1973);
- *lateral thinking* or 'the process of using information to bring about creativity and insight restructuring' (DeBono, 1990). Lateral thinking is concerned with restructuring or changing patterns of concepts, ideas, thoughts, or images so as to develop more effective patterns;
- *problem solving*, described by Koberg and Bagnall (1981) as a design process for improving existing conditions and finding a clear path out of dilemmas. To improve existing conditions, the learner must: (1) become aware of the problematic state; (2) identify the essential components of the problem; and (3) be able to use the skills and methods required to manipulate the problem condition into a better state. The same process works for finding a way out of a dilemma, but Koberg and Bagnall advise that one must also know how to keep a cool head (p. 8).

The vast majority of adult training programs and academic programs are designed using information-processing models. Such models are logical, and provide a clear sequence of planning activities for developing a lengthy program or curriculum. Information-processing models are based on understanding what goes on inside a learner's mind in order to provide facilitating activities that take an outside-in perspective.

Humanistic Models

Humanistic or person-centred models focus on the whole person, on learning involving body, mind, and spirit and cognitive, affective, and motor components. These models have two general overall objectives:

1 to help learners discover, explore, and create the personal meanings and values, skills, and strategies used to facilitate personal learning; and
2 to help learners develop a positive self-concept and high self-esteem, contributing in positive ways to further learning.

Humanists tend to view learning as an inside-out process controlled and directed by the learner rather than an outside-in process controlled and directed by the facilitator as in the information-processing and behaviourist models.
  Humanistic models assume that humans have a natural potential for

learning. They also assume learning is facilitated when learners participate responsibly and autonomously in the learning process through

- choosing their own directions,
- discovering their own learning resources,
- formulating their own problems,
- deciding their own course of action, and
- living with the consequences of their choices.

Further, they assume that learning involving the whole person is the most pervasive and lasting; and that the most useful learning is learning how to learn (Brookfield, 1990; Coleman, 1976; Joyce & Weil, 1992; Kidd, 1973; Knowles, 1990; Smith, 1990). In adult education, humanistic models tend to be based on the notion that adults prefer to be self-directing as learners.

Humanistic approaches shift facilitators' attention away from correct answers, achievement levels, extrinsic reward systems (grades and certification), reinforcement schedules, cognitive processes, and the technology of planning learning programs and resources. These models do not work well in contexts constrained by the prescriptive demands of occupational training or where the facilitator must work with very large groups of learners.

Humanistic approaches work best when working with individuals or small groups and when the learning outcomes can be flexible. Facilitating strategies associated with the model focus on what learners need and want from their learning activities. Learners are assisted indirectly through interpersonal relationships based on trust, rather than directly through a set of structured activities or laid-on content.

The humanistic model reminds me, as a facilitator, that I have important responsibilities to:

- create a climate valuing learning and reducing disincentives or obstacles to learning to a minimum;
- help learners to clarify learning needs, purposes, and objectives;
- organize and make available the widest possible range of resources;
- present myself as a flexible resource to be used by the learner; and
- behave in simultaneous roles – as a co-learner who can and will learn from and with the learners, an objective observer who can respond to the needs and feelings of individual learners, and a subjective participant who will act on and share feelings, needs, and personal values.

Humanistic models, therefore, demand that the facilitator be highly skilled in process facilitation and highly committed to personal involvement in the facilitating-learning interaction. Since much of the content is based on individual need, the facilitator does not need to be a content specialist, although it helps.

Humanistic models do not propose a planned sequence of activities, but favour emergent and flexible program designs.

- The facilitator usually waits to discover what learners need and want before learning activities and content are planned, although potential resources can be collected ahead of time.
- Learning processes and activities are shaped collaboratively as learners select and implement their own goals.
- Most humanistic models also include provision for some structured activities at the beginning of the learning program that assist both learner and facilitator to clarify learning objectives and directions. These objectives or directions may relate to any aspect of the learning process – content, strategies, processes, activities, experiences, resources, and so on.

Humanistic models are based on the value orientation that every learner is not only unique but also worthy of respect and acceptance and of being treated with dignity. This orientation suggests that the facilitator must be willing to acknowledge learners as a potential resource for learning, and that all share equal and reciprocal rights and responsibilities.

Since facilitators are expected to be able to respond to individual needs and learning styles, the most essential element of facilitating is learning about learners. Humanistic models call for skill in responding to individuals, developing supportive and responsive learning environments, and facilitating learning processes for both individuals and groups.

Suggestions on how to use humanistic models with children generally begin with the assumption that children do not have all the necessary knowledge and skills to be self-directing and that any program needs to provide opportunities for the children to develop these as part of their learning. Suggestions on how to use humanistic models with adults tend to emphasize the need to treat them as self-directing, autonomous individuals and to avoid perceiving them in child-like terms (Knowles, 1980). Adults who do not have the necessary knowledge and skills to be self-directing may not receive the support and direction they need, and may end up feeling child-like because of their inability to participate fully, even if they are not being treated in child-like terms. Humanistic facilitators who assume that all adults are both willing and able to be self-directing may not be fully responsive to the needs of those who are not. Further, little consideration may be given to how a facilitator would implement a humanistic model in a group setting where the individuals range from those with none of these skills to those with all of them.

Humanistic models are most relevant to the affective and social dimensions of learning and can lead to attitude changes, understanding and awareness of personal meanings and values, and changes in both self-concept and self-esteem.

Dialectical Models

In Chapter 1, I briefly discussed the dialectical nature of learning. Within dialectical models, learning is assumed to have three characteristics:

1 Learning is interactive because we make meaning through exchanging information with our environment, most particularly with other persons.
2 Learning is constructive or interpretive because we endow both ourselves and the world around us with social meaning, thereby inventing our own model of reality.
3 Learning is transformative because both our meanings and personal model of reality are changed during interactive and constructive processes (Basseches, 1984; Mezirow, 1991; Riegel, 1973).

THE INTERACTIVE ASPECTS OF LEARNING

Interactions can occur between the learner and his or her own model of reality, and/or between the learner and the facilitator, other learners, and learning resources. The effectiveness of interactive processes rests on communication skills, including active and empathic listening, responding to the other's ideas and feelings, sharing one's own ideas and feelings, and providing feedback. In effective dialogue, each person responds to the previous person's statement before adding something new. When effective communication skills are not used, a dialogue has a tendency to be reduced to two monologues in which neither participant listens to the other.

When interaction is effective, participation is based on equality, co-operation, collaboration, and shared power and control. Both facilitator and learner must understand that such characteristics are not based on some altruistic process in which one 'gives' equality, control, and power to the other. Rather, both must assume that the other is capable of exercising equality, control, and power while at the same time ensuring that resources, such as time and space, are shared equitably.

Further, all participants both learn and facilitate and need to be able to use effective communication and cognitive skills. Interactivity assumes learning and facilitating processes modify each other through a continuing dialogue over time. Since nothing stays the same for long, theorizing about interactivity is difficult. Two relevant theoretical concepts are exchange and empowerment.

Learning involves an *exchange* of information, meanings, energy, feedback, and reinforcements. Concepts about exchange hold that individuals will continue to interact as long as each person feels rewarded and these rewards are more valued than the personal costs incurred (Dowd, 1980). The rewards one person desires or needs may not be apparent to a casual observer and are rarely the same for both persons. For example, I once watched my young son engage in a relationship with an adult he did not like for the sole purpose of learning how to do something he really wanted to learn.

Another example is provided by persons who remain in abusive relationships when others think they should leave. Exchange concepts suggest that the abused person is gaining some 'reward' or avoiding some alternative 'cost' perceived as being greater than the pain of the abuse. On the reward side, abusers often provide support or care for the abused person, and the recognition inherent in the abusive act may be perceived by the abused person as important. On the cost side, protesting the abuse may escalate it; leaving the relationship may be perceived as leading to loneliness and difficulties in supporting oneself. When the costs of staying in the relationship increase above the level of the rewards being gained, or the costs of leaving the relationship are perceived as being offset by potential future rewards, the individual may feel able to leave the abusive relationship.

Empowerment involves growing personal confidence and feeling able to give voice to one's ideas and feelings in a confident manner within relationships. Empowerment in learning interactions is associated with a number of different processes:

- *Learning knowledge and skills* can enable the individual to be informed and skilled in new ways that can increase self-confidence. The conferring of credentials attests to this form of empowerment.
- *Reflective learning and critical thinking* can help a learner to become more self-reliant through learning how to learn, thus making them better able to direct, manage, and control their own learning processes (Candy, 1990).
- *Self-reflective learning* can enable individuals to become more self-confident and assertive, to believe in and value themselves more, and to perceive themselves as agents of their own actions, better able to shape their own destiny in small and large ways (Boyd & Fales, 1983).
- *Emancipatory learning* can enable marginalized groups and their individual members to understand how their own culture or experience has become submerged within a dominant culture and experience, to work towards recovering these submerged realities, and as a result to develop social actions designed to counter injustices and inequalities (Freire, 1973; Mezirow, 1991; Welton, 1995).

As a facilitator, I cannot give power to a learner, but I can set up an environment and use facilitating activities that help shift power to learners and encourage them to use their power on their own behalf.

THE CONSTRUCTIVE OR INTERPRETIVE ASPECTS OF LEARNING

The constructive aspects of learning provide an opportunity for individuals to share in the meaning-making process, to share personal meanings, and to use these activities to come to a better understanding of one's self and others. Meanings are negotiated between the interacting persons through communicative processes. In theory, at the start of every dialogue, all meanings are open to modification and negotiation. In practice, dialogues never start with new meanings each time.

We tend to operate with our existing meanings until they don't work – then we negotiate. This process leaves much room for misunderstandings. The meaning-making process proceeds most effectively if both persons can

- clarify their own ideas and paraphrase what they have understood of the ideas of the other;
- share their own feelings; and
- reflect the feelings of the other.

Whenever we interact in a learning-facilitating dialogue, we invest our self-system in the exchange of information and meanings. Between two persons, the possibility exists that self-systems will be challenged in some way as shared meanings are negotiated. To safeguard our own integrity, we tend to travel through life looking for exchanges that simultaneously enhance and reaffirm our self-systems. We also protect our self-systems through selective attention to what the other is saying and through distorting what we hear about ourselves. To be open to the possibility of learning in interactions with others requires that one be willing to take risks that what will be learned is of greater value than what is being protected from change.

As a facilitator, while I cannot create a completely risk-free learning environment, I need to help set up an environment and expectations that support and encourage everyone to negotiate meanings and express feelings as freely as possible.

THE TRANSFORMATIVE ASPECTS OF LEARNING

Transformations involve both changes in meanings schemes and changes in meaning perspectives or frames of reference (Cranton, 1994; Mezirow, 1991, 1995). A meaning scheme is a specific set of beliefs, knowledge, attitudes, and feelings that shape a particular interpretation (Mezirow, 1995, p. 43). A meaning perspective provides a general frame of reference and consists of an integrated set of meaning schemes, assumptions, and expectations through which we filter our experiences. Your knowledge and attitudes about specific learning styles constitute a meaning scheme; your assumptions and expectations about how learning styles affect learning behaviour and how knowledge about learning styles can be integrated into your facilitating activities constitutes a meaning perspective.

Both meaning schemes and meaning perspectives have cognitive, emotional, and mental dimensions. We use them to choose which experiences we give meaning to and how we give them meaning. Our frames of reference are composed of those we receive and assimilate from our cultural and social contexts, those we generate from our own experiences, and those we create by integrating other perspectives.

Our frames of reference are part of our model of reality and offer us stability, coherence, and identity. Because we have invested a lifetime in creating our frames of reference, they are emotionally charged and strongly defended. Those held by others and differing from our own are likely to be viewed as 'mad' (crazy, illogical) or 'bad' (unreasonable, wrong). When others call our frames of reference into question, our first instinct is to dismiss such points of view as distorted or ill-intentioned. Our second response may be to feel disconfirmed, followed by confusion (M. Taylor, 1987).

In Chapter 1, we encountered three types of transformative learning:

1 Meaning schemes – the content of our personal model of reality – can be transformed through modifying our knowledge, skills, or values.
2 Premises or habits of mind in our model of reality – processes of learning, how we come to know what we know and why we value what we value – can be transformed through reflecting on and modifying the strategies, processes, and values underlying our meaning schemes.
3 Meaning perspectives – the general framework of meanings and cultural values underlying our model of reality – can be transformed by reflecting on, thinking critically about, and modifying the underlying assumptions or premises.

Learning through perspective transformation involves transforming our personal model of reality and our frame of reference for viewing reality. Such learning begins when we encounter experiences, often in emotionally charged situations, that fail to fit our expectations and consequently lack meaning for us; or we encounter an anomaly that we cannot understand by either learning within existing meanings schemes or learning new meaning schemes; or we experience a growing sense of the inadequacy of our old ways of seeing and understanding something.

An example might help at this point. When I was still a graduate student in adult education, I was often told that I 'looked confident.' Since I never felt confident, I questioned the ability of anyone to actually judge someone else's confidence. Then I became involved in a peer counselling session that was videotaped. When the tape was replayed, my first impression on seeing myself was 'What a confident looking person!' Then I was trapped in an inner conflict based on an anomaly I couldn't immediately resolve. How could I present myself as a confident person on the outside when I felt very unconfident on the inside?

I reconsidered and reflected. Maybe, just maybe, I was able to do more than I had thought I was able to do. All my life I had seen myself as inadequate in interpersonal relationships, but maybe I had more skills than I was giving myself credit for. After that incident, each time I found myself feeling inadequate or lacking in confidence, I reassessed (through critical reflection) what I was doing and feeling. Eventually my perspective on myself changed, and with that change I had to change almost all aspects of my self-system.

The idea of a perspective transformation is hard to understand until you have gone through one. In my example, one small change – related to feelings of self-confidence – promoted a massive transformation to my self-system. Transformations at the level of meaning schemes can occur regularly through regular reflection on life experiences and through new learning. Transformations at the level of premises can occur through self-reflection on the ways we know and learn. Transformations at the level of meaning perspectives can occur through periodic self-reflection and critical thinking about the assumptions that underlie our beliefs, intentions, and actions.

FACILITATING DIALECTICAL LEARNING
Facilitating dialectical learning is more difficult to plan for than facilitating the other three models I have discussed. As facilitators, we can

- set up opportunities for interactions among learners or between a learner and a facilitator;
- promote the sharing of meanings and the development of shared models of interpreting reality; and
- encourage learners to assume control over their own learning and to see themselves as empowered to relate on an equal basis with others.

But transformations must evolve from within the learner.

The facilitator's tasks are to provide activities, information, and ideas; encourage critical reflection and self-reflection; participate in dialogues on issues of importance to the learner; and provide nonjudgmental feedback. But whether or not a transformation will occur is very much dependent on the learner's willingness to

- be open to new ideas,
- cope with ambiguity,

- accept potential feelings of disconfirmation and personal disorganization, and
- redefine the situation or problem in new ways.

Of greater importance to facilitating the dialectical model of learning are three ethical dilemmas confronting the facilitator in encouraging learners to engage in transformative learning (M. Taylor, 1990).

The first dilemma is whether I, as a facilitator, have the right to encourage you to think about introducing changes into your facilitating strategies and practices by thinking critically about them and about everything you read in adult education, including the ideas described here, without also doing something to change the fundamentally authoritative nature of educational institutions that tend to create obstacles for both facilitator and learner. The strategies I have proposed are cosmetic at best until we can work together to change the ways our institutions operate.

The second ethical dilemma is that the dialectical model carries with it the idea that the facilitator and the learner are equal in the learning-facilitating interaction; that the facilitator is also a learner engaged in learning about learners and about the nature of learning. The very best dialectical facilitators are concerned primarily about the learner's needs, goals, and styles, and adjust their facilitating strategies accordingly. This implies an altruism that may negate the very nature of the dialectical process and may fly in the face of its underlying assumptions. The balance of power in the resulting interactions is never equal if facilitators are unprepared to critically, collaboratively, and publicly examine their own personal model of reality and its underlying assumptions. I puzzle over how I can do that while, at the same time, continuing to be a productive, effective, and supportive facilitator and still meet the requirements of the institution where I work.

The third ethical dilemma is the frequently unquestioned assumption that all learners can benefit from transformative learning. Perhaps some learners do not benefit from such learning. Perhaps I, as a facilitator, have no right to deliberately encourage such learning through my facilitating strategies. This dilemma raises the question 'Empowerment for what?' and 'Transformation for what purpose?' I have no clear answers to these ethical dilemmas and would urge you to discuss them with your colleagues.

Other Facilitating Models

Two other groups of facilitating models are worth noting. Both bear some resemblance to the three facilitating strategies and four models already described in this chapter, but both introduce other dimensions to our overall understanding of facilitating strategies and styles.

Dan Pratt (1999) has proposed five perspectives on teaching based on research conducted in North America and Asia. His teaching perspectives address the actions, intentions, and beliefs of teachers in a variety of formal and informal contexts. His five perspectives are:

1 In the *Transmission perspective*, the primary focus is on the efficient and accurate delivery of content – the knowledge and/or procedures of a discipline or occupation. The dominant relationship in this perspective is based on the teacher's concern for and authority over what is to be learned.

2 In the *Apprenticeship perspective*, the primary focus is on the teacher as a role model of the knowledge, skills, and values of his or her community of practice. A major concern in this perspective is that teaching and learning be done in authentic social situations and contexts where the content to be learned is also to be applied.

3 In the *Developmental perspective*, the primary focus is on cultivating and modifying ways of thinking. Prior knowledge and ways of thinking form the basis of each learner's approach to new learning. The role of the teacher is to both accept and challenge prior knowledge and ways of thinking.

4 In the *Nurturing perspective*, the primary focus is on facilitating personal agency. Learning is much affected by self-concept and self-efficacy; therefore, teaching needs to provide a balance between caring for and challenging the learner.

5 In the *Social Reform perspective*, the primary focus is on a central core of ideals represented by the teacher's beliefs and values and presented to the learner as essential content. This core of ideals can be derived from an ethical code (such as equal rights for all, equal pay for work of equal value), a religious doctrine (such as the sanctity of God's law or the church's principles), or a political or social ideal (such as the need to redistribute power and privilege in society) (Pratt, 1999, p. 43)

Anthony Grasha (1993) proposes five teaching styles based on his research with faculty in colleges and universities. His styles are based on needs, beliefs, and behaviours that faculty members displayed in their classrooms. He states that few individuals use only one style, but use a primary cluster of these styles and a secondary cluster depending on the discipline they are teaching. His five teaching styles are as follows.

1 The *Expert style* is concerned with transmitting knowledge and expertise learners need to acquire. Those who use this style strive to maintain their status as an expert through displaying detailed knowledge and challenging learners to enhance their competence.

2 In the *Formal Authority style* the individual maintains status through

drawing on both knowledge and the role of faculty member. Activities focus on providing positive and negative feedback to learners, and establishing goals for learning as well as expectations and rules for the classroom. Those who use this style are concerned with doing things the 'appropriate' way.

3 In the *Personal Model style*, the faculty member believes in teaching through personal example and establishing a prototype for how to think and behave in the classroom. Those who use this style act as overseers and guides by showing how to do things.

4 In the *Facilitator style*, the faculty member emphasizes the personal nature of teaching-learning interactions. Those who use this style guide and direct learners by asking questions, exploring options, suggesting alternatives, and encouraging them to develop criteria to make informed choices.

5 In the *Delegator style*, the faculty member is concerned with developing learners' capacities to function autonomously. Those who use this style arrange for learners to work independently on projects or as part of project teams.

Grasha (1993) reports that the most frequently occurring clusters of teaching styles are:

• Expert/Formal Authority – used by 38 per cent of faculty. The teaching methods associated with this cluster of teaching styles include an emphasis on exams and grades, the use of lectures and mini-lectures, guest speakers, teacher-centred questioning and discussions, term papers, tutorials, and technology-based presentations.

• Personal Model/Expert/Formal Authority – used by 22 per cent of faculty. The teaching methods associated with this cluster of teaching styles include role modelling by illustration through discussing alternative approaches and sharing thought processes and personal experiences; role modelling by direct action through demonstrating ways of thinking/doing things and having learners emulate these strategies; and coaching and guiding students.

• Facilitator/Personal Model/Expert – used by 17 per cent of faculty. The teaching methods associated with this cluster of teaching styles include case studies, cognitive mapping, critical thinking, guided readings, laboratory projects, problem-based learning, role playing, simulations, and roundtable discussions.

• Delegator/Facilitator/Expert – used by 15 per cent of faculty. The teaching methods associated with this cluster of teaching styles include contract teaching, debate and symposium formats, independent study and research, co-operative learning, learning pairs, position papers, field-based activities, self-discovery activities, small work teams, and student journals.

LEARNING AND FACILITATING PRINCIPLES

Adults learn most productively when facilitating strategies match their needs and/or preferred learning behaviours and styles.

Adult learning behaviours tend to change as a result of increasing familiarity with a learning program or content. Facilitating strategies need to change in responsive ways at the same time.

There is no 'one best facilitating style' for use with adult learners. Each style is appropriate for some learners, in some settings, and for some content.

References

Abbey, D.S., Hunt, D.E., & Weiser, J.C. (1985). Variations on a theme by Kolb: A new perspective for understanding counseling and supervision. *The Counseling Psychologist, 13*, 477–501.

Adams, J.D. (1980). *Understanding and managing stress: A book of readings.* San Diego: University Associates.

Albright, M.J., & Graf, D.L. (Eds.). (1992). *Teaching in the information age: The role of educational technology.* New Directions in Teaching and Learning, no. 51. San Francisco: Jossey-Bass.

Angelo, T.A., & Cross, K.P. (1993). *Classroom assessment techniques: A handbook for college teachers* (2nd ed.). San Francisco: Jossey-Bass.

Arenberg, D. (1994). Aging and adult learning in the laboratory. In J.D. Sinnott (Ed.), *Interdisciplinary handbook of adult lifespan learning* (pp. 351–70). Westport, CN: Greenwood Press.

Argyris, C. (1991). Teaching smart people how to learn. *Harvard Business Review, May-June*, 99–109.

Argyris, C., & Schön, D.A. (1974). *Theory in practice: Increasing professional effectiveness.* San Francisco: Jossey-Bass.

Arlin, P.K. (1986). Problem-finding and young adult cognition. In R. Mines & K.S. Kitchener (Eds.), *Adult cognitive development: Methods and models* (pp. 22–32). New York: Praeger.

Astin, H. (1976). *Some action of her own: The adult woman and higher education.* Lexington, MA: D.C. Heath.

Atkins, H., Moore, D., Sharpe, S., & Hobbs, D. (2001). Learning style theory and computer mediated communication. Paper presented at the ED MEDIA, Tampere, Finland, 24–26 June. (accessed 29 March 2002 from oufcnt5.open.ac.uk/~Hilary_Atkins/edmedia.htm).

Baltes, P.B., Reese, H.W., & Lipsitt, L.P. (1980). Life-span developmental psychology. *Annual Review of Psychology, 31*, 65–110.

Barer-Stein, T. (2001). Cultural diversity and adult learners. In T. Barer-Stein & M.

Kompf (Eds.), *The craft of teaching adults* (3rd ed.) (pp. 183–98). Toronto: Irwin/ Culture Concepts.

Barker, J.A. (1993). *Paradigms: The business of discovering the future.* New York: Harper Collins.

Basseches, M. (1984). *Dialectical thinking and adult development.* Norwood, NJ: Albex.

Bateson, G. (1972). *Steps to an ecology of mind.* New York: Ballantine Books.

Baxter Magolda, M. (1992). *Knowing and reasoning in college: Gender-related patterns in students' intellectual development.* San Francisco: Jossey-Bass.

Beder, H. (1991). Purposes and philosophies in adult education. In S.B. Merriam & P.M. Cunningham (Eds.), *Handbook of adult and continuing education* (pp. 37–50). San Francisco: Jossey-Bass.

Belenky, M.F., Bond, L.A., & Weinstock, J.S. (1997). *A tradition that has no name: Nurturing the development of people, gender, and communities.* New York: Basic Books.

Belenky, M.F., Clinchy, B.M., Goldberger, N.R., & Tarule, J.M. (1986). *Women's ways of knowing: The development of self, voice and mind.* New York: Basic Books.

Belenky, M.F., & Stanton, A.V. (2000). Inequality, development and connected knowing. In J. Mezirow (Ed.), *Learning as transformation: Critical perspectives on a theory in progress* (pp. 71–102). San Francisco: Jossey-Bass.

Berg, C.A., Klaczynski, P.A., Calderone, K.S., & Strough, J. (1994). Adult age differences in cognitive strategies: Adaptive or deficient? In J.D. Sinnott (Ed.), *Interdisciplinary handbook of adult lifespan learning* (pp. 371–88). Westport, CN: Greenwood Press.

Berscheid, E. (1985). Interpersonal modes of knowing. In E. Eisner (Ed.), *Learning and teaching the ways of knowing.* 84th Yearbook of the National Society for the Study of Education (pp. 60–76). Chicago: University of Chicago Press.

Birren, J.E., & Bengtson, V.L. (Eds.). (1988). *Emergent theories of aging.* New York: Springer.

Birren, J.E., & Deutchman, D.E. (1991). *Guided autobiography groups for older adults.* Baltimore, MD: Johns Hopkins University Press.

Birren, J.E., Kenyon, G., Ruth, J.-E., Schroots, J., & Svensson, T. (1996). *Aging and biography: Explorations in adult development.* New York: Springer.

Birren, J.E., & Schaie, K.W. (Eds.). (1977). *Handbook of aging* (2nd ed.). New York: Van Nostrand Reinhold.

Blakemore, S.-J., & Frith, U. (2000). *The implications of recent developments in neuroscience for research on teaching and learning.* London: Institute of Cognitive Science.

Blunt, A. (2001). Workplace literacy: The contested terrains of policy and practice. In M. Taylor (Ed.), *Adult literacy NOW!* (pp. 89–107). Toronto: Irwin.

Bogen, J.E. (1977). Some educational aspects of hemispheric specialization. In M.C. Wittrock (Ed.), *The human brain* (pp. 133–52). Englewood Cliffs, NJ: Prentice-Hall.

Bonham, L.A. (1991). Guglielmino's Self-Directed Learning Readiness Scale: What does it measure? *Adult Education Quarterly, 41*(2), 92–9.

Bortner, R.W. (Ed.). (1974). *Adults as learners.* University Park, PA: Pennsylvania State

University, Institute for the Study of Human Development (ERIC Reproduction Document ED 106 462).

Borysenko, J. (1996). *A woman's book of life: The biology, psychology, and spirituality of the feminine life cycle*. New York: Riverhead Books.

Boshier, R. (1975). Behavior modification and contingency management in a graduate adult education program. *Adult Education, 26*(1), 16–31.

Boucouvalas, M. (1993). Consciousness and learning: New and renewed approaches. In S.B. Merriam (Ed.), *An update on adult learning theory.* New Directions for Adult and Continuing Education, no. 57 (pp. 57–68). San Francisco: Jossey-Bass.

Boud, D., Keough, R., & Walker, D. (Eds.) (1985). *Reflection: Turning experience into learning*. London: Kogan Page.

Boyd, E.M., & Fales, A.W. (1983). Reflective learning: Key to learning from experience. *Journal of Humanistic Psychology, 23*(2), 99–117.

Brammer, L.M., & Abrego, P.J. (1981). Intervention strategies for coping with transitions. *The Counseling Psychologist, 9*(2), 19–35.

Brandt, B.L., Farmer, J.A., & Buckmaster, A. (1993). Cognitive apprenticeship approach to helping adults learn. In D.D. Flannery (Ed.), *Applying cognitive learning theory to adult learning.* New Directions in Adult and Continuing Education, no. 59 (pp. 69–78). San Francisco: Jossey-Bass.

Brim, O.G., Jr., & Ryff, C.D. (1980). On the properties of life events. In P.B. Baltes & O.G. Brim, Jr. (Eds.), *Life-span development and behavior* (Vol. 3) (pp. 367–88). New York: Academic Press.

Brim, O.G., Jr., & Wheeler, S. (1966). *Socialization after childhood: Two essays*. New York: John Wiley & Sons.

Brookfield, S.D. (1987). *Developing critical thinkers: Challenging adults to explore alternative ways of thinking and acting*. San Francisco: Jossey-Bass.

———. (1990). *The skillful teacher: On technique, trust and responsiveness in the classroom*. San Francisco: Jossey-Bass.

Brown, B. (1980). *Supermind*. New York: Harper & Row.

Brown, J.S., Collins, A., & Duguid, A. (1989). Situated cognition and the culture of learning. *Educational Researcher, January–February,* 32–42.

Brundage, D., & MacKeracher, D. (1980). *Adult learning principles and their application to program planning*. Toronto: Ontario Ministry of Education.

Bruner, J. (1986). *Actual minds, possible worlds*. Cambridge, MA: Harvard University Press.

Burge, E.J. (2000). Synthesis: Learners and learning are the issues. In E.J. Burge (Ed.), *The strategic use of learning technologies.* New Directions for Adult and Continuing Education, no. 88 (pp. 88–95). San Francisco: Jossey-Bass.

Buzan, T., & Buzan, B. (1995). *The mind map book: Radiant thinking* (rev. ed.). London: BBC Books.

Caffarella, R.S. (1993). Self-directed learning. In S.B. Merriam (Ed.), *An update on adult learning theory.* New Directions for Adult and Continuing Education, no. 57 (pp. 25–35). San Francisco: Jossey-Bass.

Caffarella, R.S., & Merriam, S.B. (1999). Perspectives on adult learning: Framing our research. Paper presented at the 1999 Adult Education Research Conference, Northern Illinois University, DeKalb, IL, 21–3 May (accessed 5 November 2001 from www.edst.educ.ubc.ca/aerc/1999).

———. (2000). Linking the individual learner to the context of adult learning. In A.L. Wilson, & E.R. Hayes (Eds.), *Handbook of adult and continuing education* (pp. 55–70). San Francisco: Jossey-Bass.

Caffarella, R.S., & Olson, S.K. (1993). Psychosocial development of women: A critical review of the literature. *Adult Education Quarterly, 43*(3), 125–51.

Caine, R.N., & Caine, G. (1991). *Making connections: Teaching and the human brain.* Alexandria, VA: Association for Supervision and Curriculum Development.

Cajete, G. (1994). *Look to the mountain: An ecology of indigenous educators.* Durango, CO: Kivaki.

Candy, P.C. (1987). Evolution, revolution or devolution: Increasing learner control in the instructional setting. In D. Boud & V. Griffin (Eds.), *Appreciating adults learning: From the learners' perspective* (pp. 159–78). London: Kogan Page.

———. (1990). How people learn to learn. In R.H. Smith (Ed.), *Learning to learn across the life span* (pp. 30–68). San Francisco: Jossey-Bass.

———. (1991). *Self-direction for lifelong learning.* San Francisco: Jossey-Bass.

Cawley, R., Miller, S., & Milligan, J. (1976). Cognitive styles and the adult learner. *Adult Education, 26*(2), 101–16.

Charness, N., & Bieman-Copland, S. (1992). The learning perspective: Adulthood. In R.J. Sternberg & C.A. Berg (Eds.), *Intellectual development* (pp. 301–27). New York: Cambridge University Press.

Chickering, A.W., & Reisser, L. (1993). *Education and identity* (2nd ed.). San Francisco: Jossey-Bass.

Clandinin, D.J. (1993). *Learning to teach, teaching to learn: Stories of collaboration in teacher education.* New York: Teachers College Press.

Clark, M.C. (1993). Transformational learning. In S.B. Merriam (Ed.), *An update on adult learning theory.* New Directions for Adult and Continuing Education, no. 57 (pp. 47–56). San Francisco: Jossey-Bass.

———. (1999). Challenging the unitary self: Adult education, feminist theory, and nonunitary subjectivity. *Canadian Journal for the Study of Adult Education, 13*(2), 39–48.

Clinchy, B.M.. (1996). Separate and connected knowing. In N. Goldberger, J. Tarule, B. Clinchy, & M. Belenky (Eds.), *Knowledge, power and difference* (pp. 205–47). New York: Basic Books.

Clinchy, B., & Zimmerman, C. (1985). *Growing up intellectually: Issues for college women* (Work in Progress no. 19). Wellesley, MA: Wellesley College, The Stone Center.

Coleman, J.S. (1976). Differences between experiential and classroom learning. In M. Keeton (Ed.), *Experiential learning: Implications of cognitive style and creativity for human development* (pp. 49–61). San Francisco: Jossey-Bass.

Collett, D. (1990). Learning-to-learn needs for adult basic education. In R.M. Smith (Ed.), *Learning to learn across the life span* (pp. 247–66). San Francisco: Jossey-Bass.

Collins, A., Brown, J.S., & Newman, S.E. (1989). Cognitive apprenticeship: Teaching the crafts of reading, writing and mathematics. In L.B. Resnick (Ed.), *Knowing, learning and instruction: Essays in honor of Robert Glaser* (pp. 453–94). Hillsdale, NJ: Lawrence Erlbaum.

Combs, A.W. (1974). Humanistic approaches to learning in adults. In R.W. Bortner (Ed.), *Adults as learners* (pp. 51–62). University Park, PA: Pennsylvania State University, Institute for the Study of Human Development (ERIC Reproduction Document ED 106 462).

Connelly, F.M., & Clandinin, D.J. (1985). Personal practical knowledge and the modes of knowing: Relevance for teaching and learning. In E. Eisner (Ed.), *Learning and teaching the ways of knowing.* 84th Yearbook of the National Society for the Study of Education (pp. 174–98). Chicago: University of Chicago Press.

Cosmides, L., & Tooby, J. (1997). *Evolutionary psychology: A primer.* Santa Barbara, CA: University of California (accessed 18 February 2002 from www.psych.ucsb.edu/research/cep/).

Cranton, P. (1994). *Understanding and promoting transformative learning.* San Francisco: Jossey-Bass.

———. (1998). *No one way: Personal empowerment through type.* Sneedville, TN: Psychological Type Press.

———. (2000a). *Planning instruction for adult learners* (2nd ed.). Toronto: Wall & Emerson.

———. (2000b). Individual differences and transformative learning. In J. Mezirow (Ed.), *Learning as transformation: Critical perspectives on a theory in progress* (pp. 181–204). San Francisco: Jossey-Bass.

Cropley, A.J. (1977). *Lifelong education: A psychological analysis.* Toronto: Pergamon Press.

Cross, K.P. (1976). *Accent on learning: Improving instruction and reshaping the curriculum.* San Francisco: Jossey-Bass.

Csikszentmihalyi, M. (1990). *Flow: The psychology of optimal experience.* New York: Harper Perennial.

Curry, L. (1983). An organization of learning styles theory and constructs. In L. Curry (Ed.), *Learning style in continuing medical education* (pp. 115–23). Ottawa, ON: Canadian Medical Association. (ERIC Reproduction Document ED 235 185).

Darkenwald, G., & Merriam, S.B. (1982). *Adult education: Foundations of practice.* New York: Harper & Row.

Davis, B.G. (1993). *Tools for teaching.* San Francisco: Jossey-Bass.

Davis, J. (2002). *Notes on transpersonal experiences* (accessed 14 November 2003 from www.naropa.edu/faculty/johndavis/).

Debold, E., Tolman, D., & Brown, L.M. (1996). Embodying knowledge, knowing desire: Authority and split subjectivities in girls' epistemological development. In

N. Goldberger, J. Tarule, B. Clinchy, & M. Belenky (Eds.), *Knowledge, power and difference* (pp. 85–125) New York: Basic Books.

DeBono, E. (1990). *Lateral thinking for management: A handbook of creativity.* London: Penguin Books.

Delahaye, B.L., Limerick, D.C., & Hearn, G. (1994). The relationship between andragogical and pedagogical orientations and the implication for adult learning. *Adult Education Quarterly, 44*(4), 187–200.

Denis, M., & Richter, I. (1987) Learning about intuitive learning: Moose-hunting techniques. In D. Boud & V. Griffin (Eds.), *Appreciating adults learning: From the learners' perspective* (pp. 25–36). London: Kogan Page.

Deshler, D. (1990). Conceptual mapping: Drawing charts of the mind. In J. Mezirow (Ed.), *Fostering critical reflection in adulthood: A guide to transformative and emancipatory learning* (pp. 336–53). San Francisco: Jossey-Bass.

DeWinstanley, P.A., & Bjork, R.A. (2002). Successful lecturing: Presenting information in ways that engage effective processing. In D.F. Halpern & M.D. Hakel (Eds.), *Applying the science of learning to university teaching and beyond.* New Directions for Teaching and Learning, no. 89 (pp. 19–31). San Francisco: Jossey-Bass.

Dirkx, J.M. (1997). Nurturing soul in adult learning. In P. Cranton (Ed.), *Transformative learning in action.* New Directions for Adult and Continuing Education, no. 74 (pp. 79–88). San Francisco: Jossey-Bass.

———. (1998). Knowing the self through fantasy: Towards a mytho-poetic view of transformative learning. Paper presented at the 1998 Adult Education Research Conference, University of the Incarnate Word, San Antonio, TX, 15–16 May. (accessed 29 May 2000 from www.edst.educ.ubc.ca/aerc/1998).

DiVesta, F.J. (1974). Information processing in adult learners. In R.W. Bortner (Ed.), *Adults as learners* (pp. 81–104). University Park, PA: Pennsylvania State University, Institute for the Study of Human Development. (ERIC Reproduction Document ED 106 462).

Dombeck, M. (1991). *Dreams and professional personhood: The contexts of dream telling and dream interpretation among American psychotherapists.* Albany, NY: State University of New York Press.

Dowd, J.J. (1980). *Stratifications among the aged.* Monterey, CA: Brooks/Cole.

Draper, J.A. (2001). Philosophies embedded in adult education. In T. Barer-Stein & M. Kompf (Eds.), *The craft of teaching adults* (3rd ed.) (pp. 151–65). Toronto: Irwin/Culture Concepts.

Drath, W. (2001). *The deep blue sea: Rethinking the source of leadership.* San Francisco: Jossey-Bass.

Dunn, R., & Dunn, K. (1977). How to diagnose learning styles. *Instructor, 87*, 123–44.

———. (1978). *Teaching students through their individual learning styles.* Reston, VA: Reston Publishing.

Dunn, R.S., & Griggs, S.A. (Eds.) (2000). *Practical approaches to using learning style in higher education.* Westport, CN: Bergin & Garvey.

Edwards, B. (1979). *Drawing on the right side of the brain.* Los Angeles: J.P. Tarcher.

Eichler, M. (1988). *Non-sexist research methods: A practical guide.* Boston: Allen & Unwin.

Elbow, P. (1973). *Writing without teachers*. New York: Oxford University Press.

Elias, J.L., & Merriam, S.B. (1995). *Philosophical foundations of adult education* (2nd ed.). Malabar, FL: Krieger.

Engler, J. (1986). Therapeutic aims of psychotherapy and meditation: Developmental stages in the representation of self. In K. Wilber, J. Engler, & D.P. Brown, *Transformations of consciousness: Conventional and contemplative perspectives of development* (pp. 17–51). Boston: Shambhala.

English, L.M. (2000). Spiritual dimensions of informal learning. In L.M. English & M.A. Gillen (Eds.), *Addressing the spiritual dimensions of adult learning: What educators can do*. New Directions for Adult and Continuing Education, no. 85 (pp. 29–38). San Francisco: Jossey-Bass.

English, L.M., & Gillen, M.A. (2000). Editors' notes. In L.M. English & M.A. Gillen (Eds.), *Addressing the spiritual dimensions of adult learning: What educators can do*. New Directions for Adult and Continuing Education, no. 85 (pp. 1–5). San Francisco: Jossey-Bass.

Entwistle, N. (1981). *Styles of learning and teaching: An integrated outline of educational psychology*. Chichester, UK: John Wiley & Sons.

Erikson, E.H. (1968). *Identity, youth and crisis*. New York: W.W. Norton.

———. (1978). The life cycle of Dr. Borg. In E.H. Erikson (Ed.), *Adulthood* (pp. 1–31). New York: W.W. Norton.

Erikson, E.H., Erikson, J.M., & Kivnick, H.Q. (1986). *Vital involvement in old age*. New York: W.W. Norton.

Estes, C.P. (1992). *Women who run with the wolves: Myths and stories of the wild woman archetype*. New York: Ballantine Books.

Even, M.J. (1978). Overview of cognitive styles and hemispheres of the brain research. Paper presented at the 1978 Adult Education Research Conference, San Antonio, TX, 5–7 April. (ERIC Reproduction Document ED 152 992).

Feringer, R. (1978). The relation between learning problems of adults and general learning theory. Paper presented at the 1978 Adult Education Research Conference, San Antonio, TX, 5–7 April. (ERIC Reproduction Document ED 152 992).

Ferro, T.R. (1993). The influence of affective processing in education and training. In D.D. Flannery (Ed.), *Applying cognitive learning theory to adult learning*. New Directions for Adult and Continuing Education, no. 59 (pp. 25–34). San Francisco: Jossey-Bass.

Fisher, J., & Wolfe, M. (Eds.) (1998). *Using learning to meet the challenges of older adults*. New Directions for Adult and Continuing Education, no. 77. San Francisco: Jossey-Bass.

Fiske, M., & Chiriboga, D.A. (1990). *Change and continuity in adult life*. San Francisco: Jossey-Bass.

Flannery, D.D. (1993). Global and analytical ways of processing information. In D.D.Culture ConceptsFlannery (Ed.), *Applying cognitive learning theory to adult learning*. New Directions in Adult and Continuing Education, no. 59 (pp. 79–82). San Francisco: Jossey-Bass.

———. (1994). Changing dominant understanding of adults as learners. In E. Hayes

& S.A.J. Collins III (Eds.), *Confronting racism and sexism*. New Directions for Adult and Continuing Education, no. 61 (pp. 17–26). San Francisco: Jossey-Bass.

Freire, P. (1973). *Education for critical consciousness*. New York: Seabury.

Fry, R. (1978). Diagnosing professional learning environments: An observational scheme for matching learner style with situational complexity. Doctoral dissertation, Sloan School of Management, Massachusetts Institute of Technology, Cambridge, MA.

Fry, R., & Kolb, D.A. (1979). Experiential learning theory and learning experiences in liberal arts education. In S.E. Brooks & J. Althof (Eds.), *Enriching the liberal arts through experiential learning*. New Directions for Experiential Learning, no. 6 (pp. 79–92). San Francisco: Jossey-Bass.

Gallos, J.V., & Ramsey, V.J. (Eds.) (1997). *Teaching diversity*. San Francisco: Jossey-Bass.

Galotti, K.M., Clinchy, B.M., Ainsworth, K.H., Lavin, B., & Mansfield, A.F. (1999). A new way of assessing ways of knowing: The Attitudes Toward Thinking and Learning Survey (ATTLS). *Sex Roles: A Journal of Research, May* (accessed 15 May 2002 from www.findarticles.com/cf_0/m2294/mag.jhtml?issue=1).

Galotti, K.M., Drebus, D.W., & Reimer, R.L. (2001). Ways of knowing as learning styles: Learning MAGIC with a partner. *Sex Roles: A Journal of Research, April* (accessed 15 May 2002 from www.findarticles.com/cf_0/m2294/mag.jhtml?issue=1).

Gardner, H. (1983). *Frames of mind*. New York: Basic Books.

———. (1999). Are there additional intelligences? The case for naturalist, spiritual, and existential intelligences. In J. Kane (Ed.), *Education, information, and transformation: Essays on learning and thinking* (pp. 111–31). Upper Saddle River, NJ: Merrill.

Gardner, H. & Hatch, T. (1989). Multiple intelligences go to school: Educational implications of the theory of multiple intelligences. *Educational Researcher*, November, 4–10.

Gavin, J. (1992). *The exercise habit*. Champaign, IL: Leisure Press.

Gavin, J., & Taylor, M. (1990). Understanding athletic injuries: A process model with implications for rehabilitation. Paper presented at the American Psychological Association Convention, Boston, MA. Available from the authors, Department of Applied Human Sciences, Concordia University, Montreal.

Gergen, K.J. (1991). *The saturated self: Dilemmas of identity in contemporary life*. New York: Basic Books.

Gibb, J. (1964). A climate for trust formation. In L.P. Bradford, J.R., & K.D. Benne (Eds.), *T-group theory and laboratory method* (pp. 279–309). New York: John Wiley & Sons.

Gilligan, C. (1982). *In a different voice: Psychological theory and women's development*. Cambridge, MA: Harvard University Press.

Goldberger, N.R. (1996). Looking backward, looking forward. In N. Goldberger, J. Tarule, B. Clinchy, & M. Belenky (Eds.), *Knowledge, power and difference* (pp. 1–21). New York: Basic Books.

Goldberger, N., Tarule, J. Clinchy, B., & Belenky, M. (Eds.) (1996). *Knowledge, power and difference: Essays inspired by* Women's Ways of Knowing. New York: Basic Books.

Goleman, D. (1995). *Emotional intelligence.* New York: Bantam Books.

Goslin, D.A. (1969). *Handbook of socialization theory and research.* Chicago: Rand McNally.

Grasha, A.F. (1993). *Teaching with style.* Pittsburgh: Alliance.

Gregorc, A.G. (1982). *Inside style: Beyond the basics.* Maynard, MA: Gabriel Systems.

Griffin, V. (2001). Holistic learning. In T. Barer-Stein & M. Kompf (Eds.), *The craft of teaching adults* (3rd ed.) (pp. 107–36). Toronto: Irwin/Culture Concepts.

Grow, G.O. (1991). Teaching learners to be self-directed. *Adult Education Quarterly, 41*(3), 125–49.

Guglielmino, L.M. (1977). Development of the Self-Directed Learning Readiness Scale. *Dissertation Abstracts International, 38*(11A), 6467.

Hamilton, S.J. (1995). *My name's not Susie: A life transformed by literacy.* Portsmouth, NH: Boynton/Cook.

Hanna, R.W. (1987). Personal meaning: Its loss and rediscovery. In R. Tannebaum, N. Margulies, & F. Massarik (Eds.), *Human systems development* (pp. 42–66). San Francisco: Jossey-Bass.

Hansman, C.A. (1997). Examining borders and boundaries: Mentors and situated learning in academic culture. Paper presented to the International Standing Conference on University Teaching and Research in the Education of Adults (SCUTREA), University of London, Birbeck College, July. (accessed 3 February 2002 from www2.gasou.edu/ingear/profdev/hansman.html).

———. (2001). Context-based adult learning. In S.B. Merriam (Ed.), *The new update on adult learning theory.* New Directions for Adult and Continuing Education, no. 89 (pp. 43–51). San Francisco: Jossey-Bass.

Harding, S. (1996). Gendered ways of knowing and the 'epistemological crisis' of the West. In N. Goldberger, J. Tarule, B. Clinchy, & M. Belenky (Eds.), *Knowledge, power and difference* (pp. 431–54). New York: Basic Books.

Hart, L.A. (1975). *How the brain works: A new understanding of human learning, emotion, and thinking.* New York: Basic Books.

———. (1983). *Human brain, human learning.* New York: Longman.

Harvey, O.J., Hunt, D.E., & Schroder, H.M. (1961). *Conceptual systems and personality organization.* New York: John Wiley & Sons.

Hayes, E. (2000). Social contexts. In E. Hayes & D.D. Flannery (Eds.), *Women as learners: The significance of gender in adult learning* (pp. 23–52). San Francisco: Jossey-Bass.

Hebb, D.O. (1972). *Textbook of psychology* (3rd ed.). Toronto: W.B. Saunders

Heermann, A., Fox, R., & Boyd, A. (2000). Unintended effects in using learning technologies. In E.J. Burge (Ed.), *The strategic use of learning technologies.* New Directions for Adult and Continuing Education, no. 88 (pp. 39–48). San Francisco: Jossey-Bass.

Heermann, B. (1984). Computer-assisted adult learning and the community college response. In D.A. Dellow & L.A. Poole (Eds.), *Microcomputer applications in adminis-*

tration and instruction. New Directions for Community College, no. 47 (pp. 81–8). San Francisco: Jossey-Bass.

Heimlich, J.E., & Norland, E. (1994). *Developing teaching style in adult education.* San Francisco: Jossey-Bass.

Hersey, P., & Blanchard, K.H. (1982). *Management of organizational behavior: Utilizing human resources* (4th ed.). Englewood Cliffs, NJ: Prentice-Hall.

Hiemstra, R. (1988). Translating personal values and philosophy into practical action. In R.G. Brockett (Ed.), *Ethical issues in adult education* (pp. 178–94). New York: Columbia University, Teachers College.

Hiemstra, R., & Sisco, B. (1990). *Individualizing instruction.* San Francisco: Jossey-Bass.

Home, A.M. (1995). Predicting role conflict, overload and contagion in adult women university students with families and jobs. *Adult Education Quarterly, 48*(2), 85–97.

Home, A.M., Hinds, C., Malenfant, B., & Boisjoli, D. (1995). *Managing a job, a family and studies: A guide for educational institutions and the workplace.* Ottawa: University of Ottawa. (ERIC Reproduction Document ED 383 860).

hooks, b. (1994). *Teaching to transgress.* New York: Routledge.

Hopson, B., & Adams, J. (1976). Toward an understanding of transition: Defining some boundaries of transition dynamics. In J. Adams, J. Hayes, & B. Hopson, *Transition: Understanding and managing change* (pp. 3–25). London: Martin Robertson.

Horsman, J. (1999). *Too scared to learn: Women, violence and education.* Toronto: McGilligan Books.

Houle, C.O. (1961). *The inquiring mind: A study of the adult who continues to learn.* Madison, WI: University of Wisconsin Press.

———. (1972). *The design of education.* San Francisco: Jossey-Bass.

Hoyer, W.J. (1974). The adult learner: An operant perspective. In R.W. Bortner (Ed.), *Adults as learners.* University Park, PA: Pennsylvania State University, Institute for the Study of Human Development. (ERIC Reproduction Document ED 106 462).

Huber, K.L. (1993). Memory is not only about storage. In D.D. Flannery (Ed.), *Applying cognitive learning theory to adult learning.* New Directions for Adult and Continuing Education, no. 59 (pp. 35–46). San Francisco: Jossey-Bass.

Huberman, A.M. (1974). *Some models of adult learning and adult change: Studies on permanent education.* Strasbourg: Council of Europe, Committee for Out-of-School Education and Cultural Development. (ERIC Reproduction Document ED 105 177).

Huebner, D.E. (1985). Spirituality and knowing. In E. Eisner (Ed.), *Learning and teaching the ways of knowing.* 84th Yearbook of the National Society for the Study of Education (pp. 159–73). Chicago: University of Chicago Press.

Huff, P., Snider, R., & Stephenson, S. (1986). *Teaching and learning styles: Celebrating differences.* Toronto: Ontario Secondary School Teachers' Federation.

Hunt, D.E. (1971). *Matching models in education.* Monograph series 10. Toronto: Ontario Institute for Studies in Education.

———. (1987). *Beginning with ourselves: In practice, theory and human affairs.* Toronto: OISE Press.

Hunt, D.E., & Sullivan, E.V. (1974). *Between psychology and education*. Hinsdale, IL: Dryden Press.

Imara, M. (1975). Dying as a last stage of growth. In E. Kübler-Ross (Ed.), *Death: The final stage of growth* (pp. 147–63). Englewood Cliffs, NJ: Prentice-Hall.

Imel, S. (1998). Promoting intercultural understanding. *Trends and Issues Alert.* (ERIC Reproduction Document ED 424 451) (accessed 11 August 2002 from www.ericacve.org/).

Inglis, A. (1994). A new paradigm for the future. In M.S. Parer (Ed.), *Unlocking open learning*. Churchill, Australia: Monash University, Gippsland Campus, Distance Education Centre.

Jacobson, W. (1996). Learning, culture, and learning culture. *Adult Education Quarterly, 47*(1), 15–28.

Jarvis, P. (1987). *Adult learning and the social context*. London: Croom Helm.

Jonassen, D.H., & Grabowski, B.L. (1993). *Handbook of individual differences, learning and instruction*. Hillsdale, NJ: Lawrence Erlbaum Associates.

Jones, R.M. (1968). *Fantasy and feeling in education*. New York: Harper Colophon Books.

Josselson, R. (1992). *The space between us: Exploring the dimension of human relationships*. San Francisco: Jossey-Bass.

———. (1993). A narrative introduction. In R. Josselson & A. Lieblich (Eds.), *The narrative study of lives* (Vol. 1) (pp. ix–xv). Newbury Park, CA: Sage.

Joyce, B., & Weil, M. (1992). *Models of teaching* (4th ed.). Boston: Allyn & Bacon.

Jung, C.G. (1964). *Man and his symbols* (Ed. M.-L. von Franz). Garden City, NY: Doubleday & Company.

Kasl, E., & Elias, D. (2000). Creating new habits of mind in small groups. In J. Mezirow (Ed.), *Learning as transformation: Critical perspectives on a theory in progress* (pp. 229–52). San Francisco: Jossey-Bass.

Kasworm, C.E. (1983). Self-directed learning and lifespan development. *International Journal of Lifelong Education, 2*(1), 29–46.

Katz, D., & Kahn, R.L. (1970). Communication: The flow of information. In J.H. Campbell & H.W. Hepler (Eds.), *Dimensions in communication: Readings* (2nd ed.). Belmont, CA: Wadsworth.

Keefe, J.W. (1987). *Learning style theory and practice*. Reston, VA: National Association of Secondary School Principals.

Kegan, R. (1982). *The evolving self: Problem and process in human development*. Cambridge, MA: Harvard University Press.

———. (1994). *In over our heads: The mental demands of modern life*. Cambridge, MA: Harvard University Press.

Keirsey, D., & Bates, M. (1984). *Please understand me: Character and temperament types*. Delma, CA: Prometheus Nemesis Books.

Kelly, G.A. (1955). *The psychology of human constructs* (2 vols.). New York: W.W. Norton.

Kerka, S. (2000). Extending information literacy in electronic environments. In E.J.

Burge (Ed.), *The strategic use of learning technologies*. New Directions for Adult and Continuing Education, no. 88 (pp. 27–38). San Francisco: Jossey-Bass.

Kidd, J.R. (1960). The three R's — Relevance, relationships, responsibility. Speech to the Annual Spring Encaenia of the Thomas More Institute, Montreal, 16 May.

———. (1973). *How adults learn* (rev. ed.). New York: Association Press.

———. (1995). *Roby Kidd: Adult educator 1915–1982. Autobiography of a Canadian pioneer*. Toronto: OISE Press.

Kilgore, D.W. (2001). Critical and postmodern perspectives on adult learning. In S.B. Merriam (Ed.), *The new update on adult learning theory*. New Directions for Adult and Continuing Education, no. 89 (pp. 53–61). San Francisco: Jossey-Bass.

Klopf, G.J., Bowman, G.W., & Joy, A. (1969). *A learning team: Teacher and auxiliary*. Washington, DC: Office of Education. (ERIC Reproduction Document ED 031 438).

Knowles, M.S. (1970). *The modern practice of adult education: Andragogy versus pedagogy*. New York: Association Press.

———. (1980). *The modern practice of adult education: From pedagogy to andragogy* (rev. ed.). Chicago: Follett.

———. (1990). *The adult learner: A neglected species* (4th ed.). Houston, TX: Gulf.

Koberg, D., & Bagnall, J. (1981). *The revised all new universal traveler* (rev. ed.). Los Altos, CA: William Kaufmann.

Koestler, A. (1964). *The act of creation*. New York: Macmillan.

Kohlberg, L. (1973). Continuities of childhood and adult moral development. In P.B. Baltes & K.W. Schaie (Eds.), *Life-span developmental psychology: Personality and socialization* (pp. 179–204). New York: Academic Press.

Kolb, D.A. (1984). *Experiential learning: Experience as the source of learning and development*. Englewood Cliffs, NJ: Prentice-Hall.

———. (1985). *Learning style inventory*. Boston: McBer & Company.

Koplowitz, H. (1987). Post-logical thinking. In D.N. Perkins, J. Lockhead, & J.C. Bishop (Eds.), *Thinking: The second international conference*. Hillsdale, NJ: Lawrence Erlbaum Associates.

Kübler-Ross, E. (1970). *On death and dying*. New York: Macmillan.

Labouvie-Vief, G. (1992). A neo-Piagetian perspective on adult cognitive development. In R.J. Sternberg & C.A. Berg (Eds.), *Intellectual development* (pp. 197–228). New York: Cambridge University Press.

Lai, S. (1990). *Living with sensory loss: Hearing*. Writings in Gerontology, no. 8 (pp. 39–66). Ottawa: National Advisory Council on Aging.

Lam, Y.L.J. (1976). Transitional analysis of adult learners' needs. *Alberta Journal of Education Research, 22*(1), 59–70.

Lave, J., & Wenger, E. (1991). *Situated learning: Legitimate peripheral participation*. New York: Cambridge University Press.

Lawrence, P.R., & Nohria, N. (2001). *Drive: How human nature shapes our choices*. San Francisco: Jossey-Bass.

Levinson, D.J. (1976). *The seasons of a man's life*. New York: Alfred A. Knopf.

———. (1978). Growing up with the dream. *Psychology Today*, January, 20–31.

———. (1986). A conception of adult development. *American Psychologist, 41*(1), 3–13.

———. (1996). *The seasons of a woman's life.* New York: Random Press.

Lewin, K. (1936). *Principles of topological psychology.* New York: McGraw-Hill.

Loevinger, J. (1976). *Ego development: Conceptions and theories.* San Francisco: Jossey-Bass.

Lyons, N.P. (1987). Ways of knowing, learning and making moral choices. *Journal of Moral Education, 16*(3), 226–39.

———. (1988). Two perspectives: On self, relationships and morality. In C. Gilligan, J.V. Ward, & J.M. Taylor (Eds.), *Mapping the moral domain* (pp. 21–48). Cambridge, MA: Harvard University Press.

MacKeracher, D. (1993). Women as learners. In T. Barer-Stein & J. Draper (Eds.), *The craft of teaching adults* (rev. ed.) (pp. 69–86). Toronto: Culture Concepts.

MacLean, P.D. (1990). *The triune brain in evolution.* New York: Plenum.

Maher, F.A., & Tetreault, M.K.T. (2001). *The feminist classroom: Dynamics of gender, race and privilege* (expanded ed.). Lanham, MD: Rowman & Littlefield.

Malmstadt, S., & VonBargen, P.J. (1991). A guide for teaching seniors. *Adult & Continuing Education Today,* 25 February, 5.

Mama, A. (2002). Challenging subjects: Gender, power and identity in African contexts. *Research & Action Reports, 33*(2), 6–15. Wellesley, MA: Wellesley College, Centers for Women.

Marchese, T.J. (1997). The new conversations about learning: Insights from neuroscience and anthropology, cognitive science and work-place studies. In *Assessing impact: A collection of best speeches from the 1997 AAHE Conference on Assessment and Quality* (pp. 79–95). Washington, DC: American Association for Higher Education (accessed 8 March 2004 from www.aahe.org/pubs/TM-essay.htm).

Marshall, V.W. (1980). *Last chapters: A sociology of aging and dying.* Monterey, CA: Brooks/Cole.

Maslow, A. (1971). *The farther reaches of human nature.* New York: Viking Press.

Maudsley, D.B. (1979). A theory of metalearning and principles of facilitation. Doctoral dissertation, Ontario Institute for Studies in Education, University of Toronto, Toronto.

Mayer, R.E. (2002). Cognitive theory and the design of multimedia instruction: An example of the two-way street between cognition and instruction. In D.F. Halpern & M.D. Hakel (Eds.), *Applying the science of learning to university teaching and beyond.* New Directions for Teaching and Learning, no. 89 (pp. 55–71). San Francisco: Jossey-Bass.

McCarthy, B. (1985). *The 4MAT system: Teaching to learning styles with right/left mode techniques.* Barrington, IL: Excel.

———. (1986). *Hemispheric mode indicator: Right and left brain approaches to learning.* Barrington, IL: Excel.

McClusky, H.Y. (1970). An approach to a differential psychology of the adult potential. In S.M. Grabowski (Ed.), *Adult learning and instruction* (pp. 80–95). Syracuse, NY: ERIC Clearinghouse on Adult Education. (ERIC Reproduction Document ED 045 867).

McIntosh, P. (1989). *White privilege and male privilege: A personal account of coming to see correspondences through work in Women's Studies.* Working Paper no. 189. Wellesley, MA: Wellesley College, Center for Research on Women (excerpt entitled *White privilege: Unpacking the invisible knapsack* accessed 13 August 2002 from www.utoronto.ca/acc/events/peggy1.htm).

McKenzie, L. (1977). The issue of andragogy. *Adult Education, 27*(4), 225–9.

McLellan, H. (1996). Situated learning: Multiple perspectives. In H. McLellan (Ed.), *Situated learning perspectives* (pp. 5–17). Englewood Cliffs, NJ: Educational Technology Publications.

Melamed, L., & Devine, I. (1988). Women and learning style: An exploratory study. In P. Tancred-Sheriff (Ed.), *Feminist research: Prospect and retrospect* (pp. 69–79). Montreal: McGill-Queen's University Press.

Merriam, S.B. (2001). Andragogy and self-directed learning: Pillars of adult learning theory. In S.B. Merriam (Ed.), *The new update on adult learning theory. New Directions for Adult and Continuing Education,* no. 89 (pp. 3–13). San Francisco: Jossey-Bass.

Messick, S. (1976). Personality consistencies in cognition and creativity. In S. Messick (Ed.) *Individuality in learning: Implications of cognitive styles and creativity for human development* (pp. 310–26). San Francisco: Jossey-Bass.

Mezirow, J. (1991). *Transformative dimensions of adult learning.* San Francisco: Jossey-Bass.

———. (1995). Transformation theory of adult learning. In M.R. Welton (Ed.), *In defense of the lifeworld: Critical perspectives on adult learning* (pp. 39–70). Albany, NY: State University of New York Press.

———. (2000). Learning to think like an adult: Core concepts of transformative theory. In J. Mezirow (Ed.), *Learning as transformation: Critical perspectives on a theory in progress* (pp. 3–34). San Francisco: Jossey-Bass.

Mezirow, J., & Marsick, V. (1978). *Education for perspective transformation: Women's re-entry programs in community colleges.* New York: Columbia University, Teachers College. (ERIC Reproduction Document ED 166 367).

Michelson, E. (1996). Beyond Galileo's telescope: Situated knowledge and the assessment of experiential learning. *Adult Education Quarterly, 46*(4), 185–96.

Miller, A. (1991). *Personality styles: A modern synthesis.* Calgary: University of Calgary Press.

Miller, J.B. (1986). *Toward a new psychology of women* (2nd ed.). Boston: Beacon Press.

———. (1991). The development of women's sense of self. In J.V. Jordan, A.G. Kaplan, J.B. Miller, I.P. Stiver, & J.L. Surrey, *Women's growth in connection: Writings from the Stone Center* (pp. 11–26). New York: Guilford Press.

Miller, J.P. (1999). Education and the soul. In J. Kane (Ed.), *Education, information and transformation: Essays on learning and thinking* (pp. 207–21). Upper Saddle River, NJ: Merrill.

Moore, T. (1992). *Care of the soul: A guide for cultivating depth and sacredness in everyday life.* New York: Harper Collins.

————. (1994). *Soul mates: Honoring the mysteries of love and relationship.* New York: Harper Collins

————. (1995). The art and pleasure of caring for the soul. In A. Simpkinson, C. Simpkinson, & R. Solari (Eds.), *Nourishing the soul: Discovering the sacred in everyday life* (pp. 13–21). New York: Harper Collins.

More, W.S. (1974). *Emotions and adult learning.* Lexington, MA: Lexington Books.

Morrish, M., & Buchanan, N. (2001). Women's empowerment and adult education. In D.H. Poonwassie & A. Poonwassie (Eds.), *Fundamentals of adult education: Issues and practices for lifelong learning* (pp. 256–70). Toronto: Thompson.

Morstain, B.R., & Smart, J.C. (1977). A motivational typology of adult learners. *Journal of Higher Education, 48*(6), 665–79.

Myers, I. (1985). *Gifts differing* (7th ed.). Palo Alto, CA: Consulting Psychologists Press.

Naeyaert, K. (1990). *Living with sensory loss: Vision.* Writings in Gerontology, no. 8 (pp. 1–20). Ottawa: National Advisory Council on Aging.

Neugarten, B.L., & Datan, N. (1973). Sociological perspectives on the life cycle. In P.B. Baltes & K.W. Schaie (Eds.), *Life-span developmental psychology: Personality and socialization* (pp. 53–69). New York: Academic Press.

Noble, M.R. (2000). Learning to lead from the middle: An apprenticeship in diversity. *Adult Learning, 11*(1), 6–9.

Norman, D. (1973). *Cognitive organization and learning.* LaJolla, CA: Center for Human Information Processing. (ERIC Reproduction Document ED 083 543).

Novak, J., & Gowin, D. (1984). *Learning how to learn.* New York: Cambridge University Press.

Novak, M. (1993). *Aging and society: A Canadian perspective.* Scarborough, ON: Nelson Canada.

O'Connor, J., & Seymour, J. (1990). *Introducing neuro-linguistic programming: The new psychology of personal excellence.* London: Mandala.

Oddi, L.F. (1986). Development and validation of an instrument to identify self-directed continuing learners. *Adult Education Quarterly, 36*(2), 97–107.

Olgren, C.H. (2000). Learning strategies for learning technologies. In E.J. Burge (Ed.), *The strategic use of learning technologies.* New Directions for Adult and Continuing Education, no. 88 (pp. 7–16). San Francisco: Jossey-Bass.

Oltman, P.K., Raskin, E., & Witkin, H.A. (1970). *Group embedded figures test.* Palo Alto, CA: Consulting Psychologists Press.

Orenstein, M. (2001). *Smart but stuck: Emotional aspects of learning disabilities and imprisoned intelligence* (rev. ed.). New York: Haworth Press.

O'Rourke, J. (2000). Print. In E.J. Burge (Ed.), *The strategic use of learning technologies.* New Directions for Adult and Continuing Education, no. 88 (pp. 49–58). San Francisco: Jossey-Bass.

Perry, W.G. (1970). *Forms of intellectual and ethical development in the college years.* New York: Holt, Rinehart & Winston.

Peterson, D.A. (1983). *Facilitating education for older learners.* San Francisco: Jossey-Bass.

Pfeiffer, J., & Jones, J.E. (Various dates). *Handbook of structured experiences*. LaJolla, CA: University Associates.

Pine, G.J., & Boy, A.V. (1977). *Learner-centered teaching: A humanistic view*. Denver, CO: Love.

Pinker, S. (1997). *How the mind works*. New York: W.W. Norton.

Poonwassie, D.H. (2001). Adult education in First Nations communities: Issues and practices for lifelong learning. In D.H. Poonwassie & A. Poonwassie (Eds.), *Fundamentals of adult education: Issues and practices for lifelong learning* (pp. 271–85). Toronto: Thompson.

Pratt, D.D. (1979). Instructor behavior and psychological climate in adult learning. Paper presented at the 1979 Adult Education Research Conference, Ann Arbor, MI, 4–6 April.

———. (1988). Andragogy as a relational construct. *Adult Education Quarterly, 38*(3), 160–81.

———. (1999). *Five perspectives on teaching in adult education*. Malabar, FL: Krieger.

Pratt, D.D., & Collins, J.B. (2001). *Teaching perspectives inventory*. Vancouver: University of British Columbia (accessed 9 November 2001 from teachingperspectives.com/tpi_html).

Quigley, B.A. (1997). *Rethinking literacy education: The critical need for practice-based change*. San Francisco: Jossey-Bass.

Quigley, B.A., & Kuhne, G.W. (1997). *Creating practical knowledge through action: Posing problems, solving problems, and improving daily practice*. New Directions for Adult and Continuing Education, no. 73. San Francisco: Jossey-Bass.

Ramsey, S. (1996). Creating a context: Methodologies in intercultural teaching and training. In H.N. Seelye (Ed.), *Experiential activities for intercultural learning* (Vol. 1) (pp. 7–24). Yarmouth, ME: Intercultural Press.

Randall, W. (1995). *The stories we are: An essay on self-creation*. Toronto: University of Toronto Press.

Ray, R.E. (1999/2000). Social influences on the older woman's life story. *Generations, 23*(4), 56–62.

Reardon, M. (1999). The brain. Navigating the new reality: An exploration of brain-compatible learning. *Adult Learning, 10*(2), 10–17.

Renner, P. (1994). *The art of teaching adults*. Vancouver: Training Associates.

Riegel, K.W. (1973). Dialectical operations: The final period of cognitive development. *Human Development, 16*, 346–70.

Roberts, T.B., & Clark, F.V. (1975). *Transpersonal psychology in education*. Bloomington, IL: Phi Delta Kappa Educational Foundation.

Rogers, C.R., & Roethlisberger, F.J. (1991). Barriers and gateways to communication. *Harvard Business Review*, November–December, 105–11.

Rowe, C.J. (1975). *An outline of psychiatry* (6th ed.). Dubuque, IO: Wm. C. Brown.

Rubin, Z. (1981). Does personality change after 20? *Psychology Today*, May, 18–27.

Sagan, C. (1977). *The dragons of Eden*. New York: Random House.

Salovey, P., & Mayer, J.D. (1989–90). Emotional intelligence. *Imagination, Cognition and Personality, 9*(3), 185–211.

Schaie, K.W. (1977–8). Toward a stage theory of adult cognitive development. *Journal of Aging and Human Development, 8*(2), 129–38.

Schlossberg, N.K. (1987). Taking the mystery out of change. *Psychology Today*, May, 74–5.

Schön, D.A. (1971). *Beyond the stable state*. New York: Random House.

––––––. (1987). *Educating the reflective practitioner*. San Francisco: Jossey-Bass.

Scott, S.M. (1997). The grieving soul in the transformative process. In P. Cranton (Ed.), *Transformative learning in action: Insights from practice*. New Directions for Adult and Continuing Education, no. 74 (pp. 41–50). San Francisco: Jossey-Bass.

––––––. (1998). Philosophies in action. In S.M. Scott, B. Spenser, & A.M. Thomas (Eds.), *Learning for life: Canadian readings in adult education* (pp. 98–106). Toronto: Thompson.

Selman, M. (2001). Philosophical considerations. In D.H. Poonwassie & A. Poonwassie (Eds.), *Fundamentals of adult education: Issues and practices for lifelong learning* (pp. 44–62). Toronto: Thompson.

Selye, H. (1956). *The stress of life*. New York: McGraw-Hill.

Senge, P.M. (1990). *The fifth discipline: The art and practice of the learning organization*. New York: Doubleday/Currency.

Sheared, V. (1994). Giving voice: An inclusive model of instruction – A womanist perspective. In E. Hayes & S.A.J. Collins III (Eds.), *Confronting racism and sexism*. New Directions for Adult and Continuing Education, no. 61 (pp. 27–37). San Francisco: Jossey-Bass.

Sheehy, G. (1976). *Passages: Predictable crises of adult life*. New York: E.P. Dutton.

Shore, S. (1997). The white in the I: Constructions of difference and adult education. Paper presented to the International Standing Conference on University Teaching and Research in the Education of Adults (SCUTREA), University of London, Birbeck College, July (accessed 3 February 2002 from www.leeds.ac.uk/educol/documents/).

Simpson, E. (1979). *Reversals: A personal account of victory over dyslexia*. New York: Washington Square Press.

Sinnott, J.D. (1994). The relationship of postformal thought, adult learning and lifespan development. In J.D. Sinnott (Ed.), *Interdisciplinary handbook of adult lifespan learning* (pp. 105–19). Westport, CN: Greenwood Press.

Skinner, B.F. (1971). *Beyond freedom and dignity*. New York: Alfred A. Knopf.

Sloboda, J. (1993). What is skill and how is it acquired? In M. Thorpe, R. Edwards, & A. Hanson (Eds.), *Culture and processes of adult learning* (pp. 253–73). London: Routledge.

Smith, D.H. (1989). Situational instruction: A strategy for facilitating the learning process. *Lifelong Learning: An Omnibus of Practice and Research, 12*(6), 5–9.

Smith, R.M. (Ed.) (1990). *Learning to learn across the life span*. San Francisco: Jossey-Bass.

Sork, T.J. (2000). Planning educational programs. In A.L. Wilson & E.R. Hayes

(Eds.), *Handbook of adult and continuing education* (pp. 171–90). San Francisco: Jossey-Bass.

Spender, D., & Sarah, E. (Eds.). (1980). *Learning to lose: Sexism and education*. London: Women's Press.

Springer, S.P., & Deutsch, G. (1985). *Left brain, right brain*. New York: W.H. Freeman.

Squires, G. (1993). Education for adults. In M. Thorpe, R. Edwards, & A. Hanson (Eds.), *Culture and processes of adult learning* (pp. 87–108). London: Routledge.

Stein, D. (1998). Situated learning in adult education. *ERIC Digest No. 195* (accessed 14 November 2003 from www.ericacve.org). (ERIC Reproduction Document ED418 250).

Sternberg, R.J. (1988). *The triarchic mind: A new theory of human intelligence*. New York: Penguin Books.

———. (1997). *Thinking styles*. New York: Cambridge University Press.

Stone, S.D. (1992). Notes toward a unified diversity. In H. Stewart, B. Percival, & E.R. Epperly (Eds.), *The more we get together ...* (pp. 21–8). Ottawa: Canadian Research Institute for the Advancement of Women.

Stouch, C.A. (1993). What instructors need to know about learning how to learn. In D.D. Flannery (Ed.), *Applying cognitive learning theory to adult learning*. New Directions for Adult and Continuing Education, no. 59 (pp. 59–68). San Francisco: Jossey-Bass.

Suessmuth, P. (1985). A learning styles inventory. *Training Ideas, 44*, 2–20.

Surrey, J.L. (1991). The 'self-in-relation': A theory of women's development. In J.V. Jordan, A.G. Kaplan, J.B. Miller, I.P. Stiver, & J.L. Surrey, *Women's growth in connection: Writings from the Stone Center* (pp. 51–66). New York: Guilford Press.

Sutcliffe, J. (1990). *Adults with learning difficulties*. Leicester, UK: National Institute of Adult Continuing Education.

Tannen, D. (1990). *You just don't understand: Women and men in conversation*. New York: William Morrow and Company.

Taylor, E.W. (1994). Intercultural competency: A transformative learning process. *Adult Education Quarterly, 44*(3), 154–74.

———. (2000). Analyzing research on transformative learning theory. In J. Mezirow (Ed.), *Learning as transformation: Critical perspectives on a theory in progress* (pp. 285–328). San Francisco: Jossey-Bass.

Taylor, K., Marienau, C., & Fiddler, M. (2000). *Developing adult learners: Strategies for teachers and trainers*. San Francisco: Jossey-Bass.

Taylor, M. (1979). Adult learning in an emergent learning group: Toward a theory of learning from the learners' perspective. Doctoral dissertation, Ontario Institute for Studies in Education, University of Toronto, Toronto.

———. (1987). Self-directed learning: More than meets the observer's eye. In D. Boud & V. Griffin (Eds.), *Appreciating adults learning: From the learners' perspective* (pp. 179–96). London: Kogan Page.

———. (1990). Notes on empowerment for formal education. *Proceedings of the Cana-*

dian Association for the Study of Adult Education. Victoria, BC: University of Victoria, Division of Continuing Studies.

Thibodeau, J. (1979). Adult performance on Piagetian tasks: Implications for education. Paper presented at the 1979 Adult Education Research Conferences, Ann Arbor, MI, 4–6 April.

Thistle, M. (1968). Emotional barriers to communication. *Industrial Canada*, May.

Thomas, A.M. (1991). *Beyond education: A new perspective on society's management of learning*. San Francisco: Jossey-Bass.

Tisdell, E.J. (1999). The spiritual dimension of adult development. In S.B. Merriam (Ed.), *An update on adult development theory*. New Directions for Adult and Continuing Education, no. 84 (pp. 87–95). San Francisco: Jossey-Bass.

———. (2000). Feminist pedagogies. In E. Hayes & D.D. Flannery (Eds.), *Women as learners: The significance of gender in learning* (pp. 155–83). San Francisco: Jossey-Bass.

Toffler, A. (1970). *Future shock*. New York: Random House.

Tough, A.M. (1971). *The adults' learning projects*. Toronto: Ontario Institute for Studies in Education.

———. (1979). *The adults' learning projects: A fresh approach to theory and practice in adult learning*. Toronto: OISE Press.

Tulving, E. (1985). How many memory systems are there? *American Psychologist, 40*, 385–98.

Vaillant, G.E. (1977). *Adaptation to life*. Boston: Little, Brown.

Vanier, J. (1970). *Tears of silence*. Toronto: Griffin House.

Vella, J. (2000). A spirited epistemology: Honoring the adult learner as subject. In L.M. English & M.A. Gillen (Eds.), *Addressing the spiritual dimensions of adult learning: What educators can do*. New Directions for Adult and Continuing Education, no. 85 (pp. 7–16). San Francisco: Jossey-Bass.

Von Oech, R. (1983). *A whack on the side of the head*. New York: Warner Books.

———. (1986). *A kick in the seat of the pants*. New York: Harper & Row.

Walker, G.A. (1984). Written in invisible ink: Women in the adult education knowledge base. Unpublished manuscript, School of Social Work, Carleton University, Ottawa.

Watkins, K., & Marsick, V. (1993). *Sculpting the learning organization: Lessons in the art and science of systemic change*. San Francisco: Jossey-Bass.

Watzlawick, P., Weakland, J., & Fisch, R. (1974). *Change: Principles of problem formation and problem resolution*. New York: W.W. Norton.

Weibust, P.S., & Thomas, L.E. (1994). Learning and spirituality in adulthood. In J.D. Sinnott (Ed.), *Interdisciplinary handbook of adult lifespan learning* (pp. 120–34). Westport, CN: Greenwood Press.

Weiler, K. (1988). *Women teaching for change: Gender, class and power*. South Hadley, MA: Bergin & Garvey.

Welton, M.R. (Ed.). (1995). *In defense of the lifeworld: Critical perspectives on development*. Albany, NY: State University of New York Press.

West, C.K., Farmer, J.A., & Wolff, P.M. (1991). *Instructional design: Implications from cognitive science.* Englewood Cliffs, NJ: Prentice-Hall.

Wickett, R.E.Y. (2000). The learning covenant. In L.M. English & M.A. Gillen (Eds.), *Addressing the spiritual dimensions of adult learning: What educators can do.* New Directions for Adult and Continuing Education, no. 85 (pp. 39–47). San Francisco: Jossey-Bass.

Wilber, K. (1986). The spectrum of development. In K. Wilber, J. Engler, & D.P. Brown, *Transformations of consciousness: Conventional and contemplative perspectives on development* (pp. 65–105). Boston: Shambhala.

Williams, D. (1992). *Nobody, nowhere: The extraordinary autobiography of an autistic.* New York: Times Books.

Wilson, A.L. (1993). The promise of situated cognition. In S.B. Merriam (Ed.), *An update on adult learning theory.* New Directions for Adult and Continuing Education, no. 57 (pp. 71–9). San Francisco: Jossey-Bass.

Wingfield, L., & Haste, H. (1987). Connectedness and separateness: Cognitive style or moral orientation. *Journal of Moral Education, 16*(3), 214–25.

Wischnewski, M.M. (1983). *Humour: Why educators should take it seriously.* Toronto: Ontario Ministry of Education.

Witkin, H.A., & Goodenough, D. (1977). Field dependence and interpersonal behavior. *Psychological Bulletin, 84*, 661–89.

Wlodkowski, R.J. (1985). *Enhancing adult motivation to learn.* San Francisco: Jossey-Bass.

———. (1997). Motivation with a mission: Understanding motivation and culture in workshop design. In J.A. Fleming (Ed.), *New perspectives on designing and implementing effective workshops.* New Directions for Adult and Continuing Education, no. 76 (pp. 19–31). San Francisco: Jossey-Bass.

Wlodkowski, R.J., & Ginsberg, M.B. (1995). *Diversity and motivation: Culturally responsive teaching.* San Francisco: Jossey-Bass.

Wonder, J., & Donovan, P. (1984). *Whole-brain thinking: Working from both sides of the brain to achieve peak job performance.* New York: Ballantine Books.

Wong, A.T. (2001). Prior learning assessment: Looking back, looking forward. In D.H. Poonwassie & A. Poonwassie (Eds.), *Fundamentals of adult education: Issues and practices for lifelong learning* (pp. 159–70). Toronto: Thompson.

Yanoff, J.M. (1976). The functions of the mind in the learning process. In M.L. Silberman, J.S. Allender, & J.M. Yanoff (Eds.), *Real learning: A sourcebook for teachers* (pp. 77–84). Boston: Little, Brown.

Yorks, L., & Marsick, V.J. (2000). Organizational learning and transformations. In J. Mezirow (Ed.), *Learning as transformation: Critical perspectives on a theory in progress* (pp. 253–84). San Francisco: Jossey-Bass.

Ziegahn, L. (2001). Considering culture in the selection of teaching approaches for adults. *ERIC Digest, no. 231* (accessed 15 November 2003 from www.ericacve.org). (ERIC Reproduction Document ED 459 325).

Zinn, L. (1990). Identifying your philosophical orientation. In M.W. Galbraith (Ed.), *Adult learning methods: A guide to effective instruction* (pp. 39–56). Malabar, FL: Krieger.

———. (1999). *Philosophy of adult education inventory* (rev. ed.). Boulder, CO: Lifelong Learning Options.

Author Index

Subject Index